Origins of
Protective Labor Legislation
for Women, 1905-1925

SUNY Series on Women and Work
Joan Smith, Editor

Origins of Protective Labor Legislation For Women, 1905-1925

SUSAN LEHRER

State University of New York Press

Some of this material was originally published as a chapter in *Jobs and Gender:* Sex and Occupational Prestige, Christine Bose, Ed. (Praeger Publishers, N.Y., 1985). Copyright by Praeger Publishers. Used by permission.

Some material previously appeared in the *Review of Radical Political Economics.* Reprinted by permission of the Union for Radical Political Economics.

The cartoon on p. 2 is from the U.S. Women's Bureau Bulletin #18, "Health Problems of Women in Industry," 1921.

The cartoon on p. 140 is from the *American Federationist,* May 1923.

The Nina Allender cartoons on pp. 62, 94, 184, and 226 appeared in *Equal Rights,* 1923 and 1924. Used with permission of the National Woman's Party.

Photographs of some of the cartoons by Marion Ryan.

Published by
State University of New York Press, Albany

© *1987 State University of New York*

Library of Congress Cataloging in Publication Data

Lehrer, Susan, 1938 —
  Origins of protective labor legislation for
women, 1905-1925.

  (SUNY) series on women in work)
  Bibliography: p. 287
  Includes index.
    1. Women—Employment—Law and legislation—
United States—History. 2. Women—Employment—
United States—History. 3. Women—United States—
Social conditions. I. Title. II. Series.
KF3555.L44 1987   344.73'014   87-6485
ISBN 0-88706-506-6   347.30414
ISBN 0-88706-505-8 (pbk.)

Contents

PART TWO

Acknowledgments

In the course of this work, I benefited from the help, support, and suggestions of many people, and it is my pleasure to acknowledge them. First, my dissertation advisors, James Geschwender and Joan Smith at SUNY-Binghamton, provided the critical insight and personal support that is invaluable to a graduate student. The Women and Work Research Group, which has met faithfully twice a year in Boston and New York, has been an ongoing source of insights into the connections between women, family, and work, and our NYC bagels and Boston croissants have enriched my professional and personal life.

I want to thank friends and colleagues who offered their time and encouragement when I needed it most, and in numerous ways made my life easier while this project was progressing from research to book. They include Amy Kesselman, whose willingness to share her historical knowledge with a sociologist has been a constant comfort, Dorothy Jessup, Joel Greifinger, Cheryl Klausner, Carmen Sirianni, Andrea Walsh, Carole Turbin, Bill Miller. William Philliber and Susan Philliber offered their enthusiasm and editorial help. Steve Sconfienza provided encouragement and painstaking help with the references and index for which I am most appreciative. I am also grateful to Marilyn Glass for her adventurous approach and good sense in typing this manuscript on a word processor.

Vassar Library, which has been there since 1863, has had an interest in women and labor and has generously made its facilities available, as well as Tamiment Library and Cornell Law Library.

The particular bent which this work took—an interest in law combined with labor history—no doubt comes from my father, Gibby Needleman, whose reverent mention of Judge Learned Hand and Oliver Wendell Holmes to the child I was has no doubt made me feel at home with them now; my mother Edith's example and her confidence in me has accompanied me throughout my work. Bob Lehrer's caring support and his knowledge of the computer, and Ruth, Peter and Judy, have also been my important companions.

Part One

AMERICA WILL BE AS STRONG AS HER WOMEN.

Chapter One
Introduction

THE CONTROVERSY OVER EQUALITY

One of the bones of contention of the current movement for women's rights is whether the differences between men and women—their physical capacity to bear children, their social and economic status—should make a difference in their need for legal protection. In the early part of this century, during a period of intense social activism, the desire of social reformers to oppose the overwork and appalling industrial conditions of working women led to the passage of a number of state laws which limited or regulated the employment of women. These laws typically regulated the number of hours per day and per week that women could work, prohibited night work for women, prohibited women from working in certain occupations altogether (such as in mining or bartending), required special seating arrangements or restrooms, prohibited lifting of loads above a certain weight, and made other special provisions for women.

A broad spectrum of social reformers—suffragists, labor-oriented liberals and socialists, settlement house workers, and others—fought for passage of these protective labor laws for women from the turn of the century until after World War I, with very little doubt about the correctness of their cause. It was self-evident to them that women were among the worst-exploited and lowest-paid workers in industry, and that this injustice was directly related to the fact that they were women; it was all the more offensive because of women's roles as wives and mothers of the coming generation.

3

It was not until the early 1920s, after women had the vote nationally, that questions were raised about the wisdom and justice of these laws, and about whether placing women in a special legal category apart from men was an effective way to improve women's working conditions. A small group of militant feminists who supported an equal rights amendment argued that whatever protections existed for women ought to be extended to men if they were valuable, and removed if they were not. These feminists argued that most of the so-called protective laws for women served instead to discriminate against them and placed them at a disadvantage when competing with men for skilled jobs. Feminists also resented the patronizing assumption that women are weaker, inferior beings in need of special sheltering and protection.

These laws affecting working women were fought for and passed during the pre-World War I period in the United States. They are now presumptively invalid and counter to the 1972 guidelines of Title VII of the Civil Rights Act, which states that "the principle of non-discrimination requires that individuals be considered on the basis of individual capacities and not on the basis of any characteristics generally attributed to the group."[1] Title VII has been used to challenge many discriminatory practices which had previously been justified by appealing to women's need for special protections or restrictions in the workplace; it was also the first serious challenge to the idea behind these laws, that women should be considered primarily as the "mothers of the future generation" and only peripherally as wage earners.

In fact, the terms of the current debate have shifted in at least two significant directions: first, the demand for "equal pay for equal work" has broadened to include equal pay for work of *comparable* worth; second, the question has arisen whether women's childbearing functions— including fertility, pregnancy, and nursing—require "special treatment" in the workplace, or if "equal treatment" can be expanded from its present male-centered norm to include conditions which are specific to women. The failure of the Equal Rights Amendment to be ratified has not ended the controversy.

The proponents of "comparable worth" argue that it is not enough to ensure that *if* a women (or minority) does the same job that a (white) male does she should be paid equally. Although this is a necessary step, it is not sufficient to assure women equitable treatment in the labor force, because for typically "women's jobs" like secretary or nurse the whole job category itself is paid as "women's work," that is, poorly. Now, as in the beginning of the century, the root of the issue is, first, whether there is a "work-worth" of an employee which determines wage levels and, second, whether the wage bargain itself can or should be regulated by law or left to market forces. Proponents of these earlier minimum wage laws for women had argued that the low wages paid to women workers were attributable not to women's lower "work-worth" but to the employers' ability to exploit them more. They were paid less than men, regardless of the work performed, because they were women. In the earlier period, employers were quite candid about this discrimination; recently, in part because of sex discrimination suits under Title VII Affirmative Action guidelines, they are less open about it.

The aim of comparable worth is to make the existing wage structure gender neutral. This is a rather limited, liberal reform that need not challenge basic assumptions about wage inequalities, but it does have the potential for exposing gender-based wage differentials and the assumption that women will be paid less than men regardless of the skill involved. Pay scales for different job categories are less formalized in some areas than in others, but where classification systems are now used, like in civil service employment and large bureaucratic firms, jobs which have been traditionally female have routinely been assigned lower wages regardless of rating, and skills required in typically women's occupations go unrecognized.[2] By viewing the "wage bargain" in isolation from the social conditions which give rise to it, the opponents of comparable worth, like their predecessors in the minimum wage debate (see chapter 4), deny that employers have any responsibility to pay a living wage or that women workers are entitled to wages which would enable them to support a family.

During the Progressive Era under study here, when the majority of the protective laws for women workers were passed, social reformers did not challenge the sex-segregated labor market or the assumption on which it was justified—that is, that women's primary place was in the home anyway, certainly not as a permanent part of the industrial labor force. In the 1980s, this position has become increasingly untenable. A majority of women are in the work force regardless of whether they are also wives or mothers. Women constitute upwards of 40 percent of workers, and close to one-fifth of families with minor children are now headed by females.[3] With this dramatic increase of female-headed households, contemporary advocates of women's rights increasingly find support for policies which do not assume traditional patterns of work and family.[4] Yet the fact of women's increased work force participation has not meant economic betterment, because the jobs most women hold do not pay enough to keep a family out of poverty. According to Joan Smith, in 1979 almost half of all working women were in industries which paid wages below the poverty level for a family of four.[5] Now, as in the past period, the state is concerned about the number of families falling into "dependency" (the "welfare explosion"); this concern requires recognition (if not approval) of changes in family structure and *women's* low wage levels. In the time period which is the subject of study here, *men's* wages were considered the key problem.

In addition to the wage structure, the debate over the "protection" of working women's reproductive functions, especially pregnancy and reproductive hazards to women, has resurfaced in the contemporary period. Employers point out that a pregnant woman's exposure to toxic substances can damage the fetus, and have sought to exclude women from certain types of jobs that involve, for instance, exposure to toxic chemicals like vinyl chloride.[6] Others maintain that reproductive hazards affect men workers as well as women, and the point is to make conditions safe for all workers.[7]

The debate in the courts, as well as among women's rights advocates, is over how to apply the principle of equal treatment when pregnancy, childbearing, and nursing are unique to women. Although the terms of the current debate have shifted from the period under study here, the same kinds of questions come up. "Should Women be Treated Identically with Men by the Law?" was answered in the negative by Florence Kelley, who stated in 1923: "The inescapable facts are, however, that men do not bear the children, are free from the burdens of maternity and are not susceptible in the same measure as women, to the poisons characteristic of certain industries . . . The inherent differences are permanent. Women will always need many laws different from those needed by men. Mere identical treatment by the law is not enough."[8] By contrast, contemporary proponents of "equal treatment" argue that pregnancy is a basic condition affecting workplace participation, not a "special" need.[9] Court decisions have shifted several times, and the 1978 Pregnancy Discrimination Act now requires equal treatment of pregnant women (for example, they cannot be fired for pregnancy). However, the United States alone among all industrial countries lacks comprehensive medical care or a national policy for *parental* leave available to both fathers and mothers. Again, now as in the past, this problem leads advocates to push for reforms or "special treatment" for women workers, given the unlikely prospects for improving conditions for all workers in the near future.[10]

Protective labor legislation played an important part in the process of defining the position of working women in industrial capitalism. The pattern for this kind of legislation in the United States was established during the period from approximately 1905 to 1925. The legislative definition of the "proper" role of women in the work force which was developed during this critical period served in turn to define the subsequent status of women as workers. These kinds of laws, then, which are the focus of study here, must be seen as a limited response to a specific set of economic conditions and social forces.

The issue of protective labor legislation for women raises two critical theoretical problems. The first concerns the way in which women's position within the family, their responsibility for domestic work and reproduction of the labor force, is conceptually related to their situation as wage workers with a separate, lower wage structure than men workers. The family is the locus of reproducing and maintaining the labor force under capitalism and is one of the basic preconditions of capitalism's continued existence. Yet the capitalist mode of production, which is based on wage labor, uses labor as if there were no tomorrow and no need to insure continued reproduction of the work force. Protective labor legislation may be viewed as an accommodation between these two aspects of women's position. Therefore, the nature of the relation between these two aspects—the mode of production and the mode of reproduction, or, as it can also be referred to, between capitalism and patriarchy—will be considered first.

The second major theoretical issue centers on the state and how it is related to the economic sphere. In capitalist "free enterprise," the economy appears to be relatively autonomous and separate from the state. This study concerns the emergence of a body of legislation directly affecting economic relations between employers and employees. Therefore it bears directly upon the nature of the state's economic role and the implications of that role for understanding the political process and social reforms.

THE RELATION BETWEEN FAMILY AND WORKPLACE FOR WOMEN

The connection between family life and work has usually been viewed by contemporary researchers in terms that seek to understand it as men experience it. For example, the idea that a split between work and family developed with industrialization is more appropriate to men's lives than to women's. For women, the home was also the place of work; *women's work* means housework and childraising.[11]

Recent scholarship on women which seeks to understand this relationship has built upon analyses developed by Engels, Marx, and others and has extended their emphasis on class relationships as the primary source of oppressive relations to include a dynamic that is specific to gender. Conventional Marxists considered the position of women, especially under capitalism, to be analogous to that of the working class: exploitation and oppression of both these groups are a product of the oppressive relations of production. The solution for the working class is a revolution which will overturn private property in the means of production; the emancipation of women will follow in its wake.

According to Engels, in *Origin of the Family, Private Property and the State*, monogamy arose as the first form of the family to be based on economic interests, "on the victory of private property over primitive, natural communal property."[12] The development of the monogamous family as an economic unit also meant the "transformation of [women's] socially necessary labor into a private service" in the family household unit.[13] Engels argued that this change was a direct cause of women's subjection; therefore "the first condition for the liberation of the wife is to bring the whole female sex back into public industry, and this in turn demands that the characteristic of the monogamous family as the economic unit of society be abolished."[14]

Engels placed the family structure and the oppression of women as a sex in the context of a historically developed set of exploitive relations of private property, not a biologically determined condition arising out of childbearing or physical weakness. Engels's approach therefore provides the basis for further inquiry into the interplay between class structure and a gender hierarchy under capitalism. Recent feminist scholarship has begun to analyze this connection between capitalism and patriarchy, to understand the specific way in which women's position within the family is related to her secondary status in the workplace. For example, the anthropologist Eleanor Leacock argues that the monogamous family as an economic unit in a class society is the basic feature of women's oppression, *not* childbearing.[15] This distinction is important for understanding the nature of protective labor legislation for women, since the rationale for these laws was that women needed to be protected because of their natural, childbearing functions and their position as mothers of the future generation. Women were not defined primarily as workers but as mothers; even though women participated in the paid labor force, the gender hierarchy was maintained. Therefore, as Zillah Eisenstein points out, patriarchy is used by capitalism to provide "the sexual hierarchical ordering of society for political control and as a political system cannot be reduced to its economic structure."[16] But for the notion of "patriarchy" to be useful in pointing out the gains which men receive under capitalism, it must be defined within a historical context, not used as a transhistorical or universalistic force.[17] If the concept is used to analyze the form that gender hierarchy takes under capitalism, it must consider how class relations are reproduced and the way in which women's position within the family contributes to this reproduction. An earlier form of patriarchal family structure (in which the father controlled and administered the labor of women and children within it) was used and transformed under capitalism so that women's labor outside the home, which ought to have contributed toward the dissolution of women's dependence, was nevertheless maintained as a means of their subordination. One way in which this inequality was accomplished was through legislation restricting the conditions under which women could participate in the labor market.[18]

Heidi Hartmann contends that job segregation by sex "is the primary mechanism in capitalist society that maintains the superiority of men over women, because it enforces lower wages for women in the labor market"[19] Hartmann emphasizes the part played by male workers in excluding women and confining them to the least-skilled jobs, a response which was fostered by capitalists for their own reasons, since a divided work force with a highly segmented labor market works to their advantage. This subordinate status in the job market serves to reinforce women's dependence upon men, makes women anxious to marry for that reason, and also makes them willing to provide (unpaid) service in the home for men.

One way of expressing this relation, which emphasizes the primacy of women's position in the family, is as follows: "A wife's relation to capital is always a mediated one because of her primary responsibility to service the family: her relation to production is always mediated through her relation to her husband, precisely through the relation of human reproduction."[20] Thus, adult women are regarded in many senses (especially in the law) as dependents, despite the fact that they also have the means of earning an independent income. Protective labor laws reflected this ambivalence; some laws lumped women and children together as wards of the state, while court decisions sometimes struck down a protective measure for women on the grounds that they were *not* like children (See chapter 3.)

Although male unionists often did their best to reinforce the subordinate position of women in the labor force through outright exclusion and "protective" legislation, and defined women primarily in terms of their role in the family as wives and mothers, male workers did not create the conditions under which women worked—that is, wage labor. It is simplistic to blame the male worker for the oppression of women (as Heidi Hartmann sometimes appears to do), even though he was often a willing participant in that oppression. If men workers did not challenge that system but sought to shore it up with exclusionary policies toward women and demands for a "family wage" for men (a wage sufficient to support the family assumed to be dependent upon the male), they were no different from anyone else during the period. Neither women nor men of that period challenged the basis for that system. Suffragists and social-ists alike, with very few exceptions, were limited in the solutions they could propose by the social conditions of the time. What Ellen DuBois remarked about suffragists during the nineteenth century was still true for social reformers during the period under discussion here:

> Ultimately, it was the conditions of women's lives—specifically their dependence upon marriage and the sexual division of labor—that determined the shape of nineteenth-century suffragism. We should understand [their] inability . . . to develop solutions adequate to the oppression of women less as a failure of their political imagination or boldness than as a reflection of the state of historical development of capitalism and of male supremacy.[21]

The primacy of home and family for women was never seriously challenged during the period under study here; by contrast, the current women's movement attacks this specific aspect of women's subordina-tion, that is, the family structure and the position of women within it. The family structure, oppressive as it was to women, and beneficial (as it was in some ways) to men, is essential to the maintenance of a capitalist system of wage labor. Women's participation in the work force was con-ditioned by this factor, and measures like protective legislation were aimed at mediating the contradiction between women as workers in the paid work force and women as maintainers of domestic reproduction in the family.

Recent analyses of protective labor laws for women tend to view those laws as either sex discrimination pure and simple, inspired by capi-talists or male workers or both, or else as one of the beneficial reform measures of the Progressive Era. Those that view it as a typical example of bias against women question whether those laws ever were intended to protect women, and contend that from their inception they "were based on stereotypes about women's transient and secondary role in the labor market and their weak physical condition as well as on the desire of male workers to reduce competition for higher paying jobs."[22] Another com-mentator notes that while protective legislation may have served to "amel-iorate the worst features of the capitalist factory system in the United

States, we can now easily perceive the anti-feminist and reactionary legal and economic implications" of it. What appeared as a benefit, ended up as a "mixed blessing, at best."[23]

None of these analyses raises the question of what constitutes the nature of the connection at the societal level between women's work in the labor force and women's maintenance in the home of the class of workers, or the further question of why the state should take cognizance of this connection. They are unable to go beyond simply condemning the legislation for "stereotyping" women, on the one hand, or blessing it for reforming an industrial abuse.

The nature of women's participation in the work force grew out of the dynamic historical interplay between two aspects of women's lives, domestic and waged labor, which are sometimes described as women's dual roles, work and family. To refer to "role conflict," however, places the emphasis on the individual rather than on the societal level of analysis.[24] On the other hand, theories which look at the kinds of jobs women get by looking at characteristics of the labor market, not individuals, cannot answer the question of why it is that *women* are used for these jobs.

For example, dual labor market theory looks at the increasing division of jobs into two sectors, with women overwhelmingly confined to the secondary sector, that is, to dead-end, low-paid jobs with little security or benefits.[25] In this view, stability and career advancement possibilities are characteristics of the jobs, not the individuals who then find their way into the appropriate sector. As a description of the kinds of jobs that women (and minorities) get, this is accurate, but it does not consider why it is that women are thought to be "suitable" for secondary labor force jobs. It accepts as given what needs to be explained about women's jobs.[26]

WOMEN'S WORK AND INDUSTRIALIZATION IN THE UNITED STATES

Before the development of industry and the factory system in the United States, the home was a productive unit in which women worked producing the family's necessities, for instance, as spinners or weavers. With commercialization in the 1800s, women also worked at home for a manufacturer, for whom they received the materials and to whom they returned the finished products. The beginnings of the factory system meant little more than that women began first to work on commission in the home for small cloth-making establishments, and then, when looms were installed by some businessman under one roof, to follow them into the "factory."

Work of this sort was not considered detrimental for women. On the contrary, especially in the case of otherwise dependent women and children, it exemplified the puritan view of hard work and protected women from the sins of idleness and sloth. Male labor was scarce and expensive in this early period, and agriculture was still mens' main source of employment. The textile mills provided "the means of employment to thousands of poor women and children [with] no [other] opportunities for earning a livelihood."[27] When the first power loom was set up in the United States in Waltham, Massachusetts, in 1814, all of the weavers were women.[28]

The mill girls of the early nineteenth century were almost entirely young and single, and saw their jobs as a temporary interlude before marriage. This view did not make them less militant as workers, and they were active in protesting the worsening working conditions with walkouts and strikes as early as 1824.[29]

In textiles, in the boot and shoe industry in New England, and in other industries as well, women participated in the industrial work force right from the beginning. From the beginning they were also paid less than a man would work for, and were confined to certain types of jobs and excluded from others (see chapter 2). Protective legislation for women did not create these sex-based divisions, but it built upon them and reinforced the subordinate position of women in the work force. The state acted to maintain women's unpaid contribution within the family while "protecting" their subordinate position within the paid labor force. The next major theoretical issue to consider, then, is the state's role in economic relations in a capitalist economy.

THE STATE AND CAPITALISM

As various theoretical analysts have noted, with the end of feudalism, and the rise of industrial capitalism a relative separation of the political sphere from economic relations emerged. However, this separation does not make the state independent of the economically dominant class or mean that the state exists as an institution to serve "society as a whole" for the purpose of mediating conflicts within it. I contend that this view, that the state is a neutral mediator of conflicting interest groups, is not a reasonable explanation of the role of the state, although it does appear to have a surface validity, particularly regarding the kind of issue under examination here, that is, the passage of a particular kind of legislation. This kind of pluralist view sees government policy as a kind of prize which can be won, temporarily, by one or another group or coalition, depending upon the issue or the relative strength of the interest group in that area.

One task of this study will be to explore differing social groups and their efforts to gain acceptance for certain legislative policies, but that by itself provides an inadequate understanding of the social and economic processes at work. Without a clearer understanding of the nature of the state, this study would remain a discussion of simple interest-group politicking.[30] This study will explore the processes by which protective labor legislation for women emerged during the period it did, including the arguments advanced by advocates and opponents in the course of legislative debates, government investigating committees, and court challenges. However, this evidence must first be placed in a broader context, both in terms of historical processes and in terms of theoretical understanding.[31]

The state is an institution capable of using force to maintain both itself and the existing set of property relations; this is another way of saying that it serves, in particular, to protect capitalist private property and is "the assurance of social domination to owners over non-owners."[32] As Paul Sweezy points out, it is only when existing class relations are taken as given that it is possible to view the state as neutral. The next question to raise here becomes the following: if the state is an institution to reproduce class relations but in relative, apparent separation from them, how does the *subordinate* group's influence act in the political arena, particularly when the "democratic process" provides them with a forum within the state's processes?[33]

The state is neither devoid of class bias nor a simple reflection of the interests of the "ruling class." It is not my intention to set forth a comprehensive theory of the state, but rather to draw upon various formulations which present a useful picture of class relationships and political power. Nicos Poulantzas describes the situation as follows:

> The establishment of the State's policy must be seen as the result of the class contradictions inscribed in the very structure of the state . . . Class contradictions are the very stuff of the State: they are present in its material framework and pattern its organization; while the State's policy is the result of their functioning within the State.[34]

According to this view, class interests of the subordinate classes *are* represented within the state, and struggles that take place outside the political realm, like strikes, also can have long-term influence within the state. But the way in which the subordinate classes affect and influence the state is qualitatively different from the way the dominant classes influence it: "The dominated classes exist in the State not by means of apparatuses concentrating *a power of their own,* but essentially in the form of centres of opposition to the power of the dominant classes."[35] During the Progressive Era under study here, new forms of that relationship were emerging. The gradual acceptance of labor legislation is one example.

SOCIAL REFORMS AND THE STATE

Many historical analyses of the Progressive Era view it as a reform period, and labor legislation, antitrust laws, etc., are interpreted as proof that government policy is responsive to pressure from interest groups. Protective legislation for women workers is viewed as part of this "social justice" movement, which "sought governmental means to lessen the impact of industrialism on the less fortunate members of society."[36]

A more critical view, by James Weinstein, is that these reforms were "the product, consciously created, of the leaders of the giant corporations and financial institutions that emerged" during the period.[37] That these reforms did in fact ultimately reinforce the strength of the capitalists is considered the logical outcome by Poulantzas, and also by Ralph Miliband. Miliband cites one writer who contended that although these laws were proposed by men sympathetic to labor and were "designed to protect the workers and directed against their exploitation by employers," they would ultimately be "useful to the latter by inducing them to make a greater effort to rationalise or mechanise the productive process."[38] This analysis suggests that all reforms are doomed in advance to be swallowed up by the state in the interest of maintaining the dominant class in power.

A more complex view of this process, however, considers popular movements as part of "an unstable equilibrium of compromises between the dominant classes and the dominated."[39] E.O. Wright describes the process of capital accumulation as beset by a variety of constraints which must be overcome for capitalist production to continue. As one impediment is overcome, the "solution" becomes the next problem.[40]

Reforms can result in real, material improvements for the subordinate classes, but they also serve an ideological function: to legitimate the state in the eyes of the lower classes. One problem that arises (illustrating the continuing contradictions in the role of the state), is that while these reforms and state services are intended to "coopt potential sources of popular discontent by [e.g.] attempting to transform political demands into economic demands," the legitimating aspect of each reform tends to decline. Once a social service (such as social security) is provided, it tends to be viewed as a right, so that keeping it does not shore up the legitimacy of the state, but any cutbacks undermine it.[41] This was considered a potential problem with the passage of labor legislation. Employers feared that once a condition became established as a basic standard, further demands would whittle away the normal workday from ten hours to eight hours to four hours, with no end to the trend except a life of leisure and paychecks for their workers.

In the wisdom of hindsight, these protective labor laws are shown here to have had a variety of effects, many of which contributed to rationalizing and stabilizing existing power relations in the society, both between workers and capitalists, and also with regard to women's subordinate position in the family and in the work force. The task is to show how these effects took place and which different groups supported and opposed these kinds of laws, without assuming that the legislation was inevitable just because it was potentially useful for at least a portion of the dominant class.

In this study I will assume that the state is a *capitalist* state which nevertheless contains class contradictions within it. This approach avoids the pitfall of assuming that every action undertaken by the state is done either for the direct benefit or at the behest of the dominant class; at the same time, it takes into account the way in which reforms are capable of being used by capitalists, or regulations are evaded.[42]

This point raises the next issue: if the state represents the interests of the dominant classes in general, how does this take place, and how does the relative autonomy of the state from the economic sphere assist this process? The state acts to preserve the long-run interests of capitalists, even though it may run counter to their immediate demands.[43] In England, the Factory Acts had to be forced upon employers because without legal limitations the capitalist would have destroyed the health of the working class and its ability to reproduce itself as a class. At each step along the way, employers claimed that it would be utterly impossible to operate within the confines of the act in question and to maintain profits, but as each limitation of their abuse of the workers was enacted, their fears did not materialize. In fact, the acts worked to their benefit in a variety of ways.[44] The same thing was true in this country, when employers in the National Association of Manufacturers objected to any kind of labor legislation and then lived with it after it was finally put through. The state, then, does for capitalists what they are unable to do for themselves individually. Those employers who did support some kind of protective labor legislation recognized its potential long-range benefit to them, as will be discussed here.

A second and related role of the state is to represent within it different conflicting interests within the dominant class. There are competing interests among capitalists and among different parts of the dominant group, for example, regarding monopoly or nonmonopoly capital, or whether or not they employed women in their industry. These interests "exist as contradictory relations enmeshed within the state."[45] This interpretation allows for the possibility of alliances between sections of otherwise opposing classes.

Protective labor laws in the United States during the period under study here also emerged out of a broad range of often conflicting class interests, with each class supporting or opposing the legislation in question for its own purposes. Although the dominant classes agree on the necessity of maintaining the existing power relations in the long run, they are not necessarily in agreement about the tactics or political strategy to pursue. At any given period, the contradiction between one sector of capital and the working class might be subordinated to their opposition to another sector. For example, the conservative trade unionism which developed during the period studied here allied itself with a sector of big business on certain types of labor legislation, while both opposed the socialists in the unions and also the smaller manufacturing interests. However, the fundamental similarities between two sectors of business (represented by the National Civic Federation and the National Association of Manufacturers) remain.

Thus, support for and opposition to protective labor legislation for women did not follow class lines, just as its benefits did not accrue exclusively to one side or the other. Protective labor legislation is a result not of the unmediated, direct power of labor, but of some other constellation of forces which affected and influenced state policy.

OUTLINE OF THE STUDY

This study will explore the social forces which led to the emergence of protective labor legislation for women. These laws were developed during a specific period in the course of industrial capitalist development, and were the result of constraints and priorities in many spheres. The study is divided into two parts. The first considers economic and legal aspects, while the second looks at the different groups which supported or opposed the passage of these laws.

Chapter 2 analyzes economic changes in industrial conditions, including the increasing rationalization of the work process, the role of scientific management in promoting a specifically capitalist form of efficiency, and technological changes affecting women's position in the work force which had direct material bearing on the emergence of these laws.

In addition to being affected by work relations and economic conditions, the legal system shapes and influences the nature of the legislation which is developed, allowing it to develop along certain lines while hindering it in others. In the period under study, Supreme Court decisions, as well as other states' decisions on labor laws, affected legislatures' willingness to undertake certain kinds of labor legislation. The constitutionality of all labor legislation was problematic throughout this period, and this uncertainty affected the type of laws proposed, as well as their durability. Chapter 3 discusses legal ideologies and Supreme Court decisions. Chapter 4 considers minimum wage legislation for women; because these laws affect the wage bargain directly, they reveal the legal structure and its relation to social and economic conditions. Minimum wage laws clearly demonstrate the way legal doctrine and societal assumptions about women's position in the family are connected.

But legislation does not get passed in mechanical response to either economic conditions or legal precedent. It must be proposed, and lobbied for or against, by specific groups. Part 2 of this study examines the groups that were involved in the debate over labor legislation affecting women. Support for, and opposition to, these laws was not divided neatly along either class or sex lines. The most important of the groups involved here were of three types: social reform organizations, labor unions, and employers' organizations.

Chapters 5 through 8 considers these groups. Chapter 5 discusses the role of women suffragists; while the labor laws became a divisive issue after women gained the vote in 1920, they had also been a concern of these women before the vote. Suffragists provided the key vocal "feminist" opposition to these laws in the postwar period, and their arguments are therefore particularly important. Chapter 6 discusses a labor-oriented social reform group, the Women's Trade Union League, and chapter 7 looks at the position of organized labor, including the American Federation of Labor and the male-dominated unions within it, and the International Ladies' Garment Workers Union. Chapter 8 discusses the employers' position regarding labor legislation in general, and legislation affecting women workers specifically. This chapter considers two types of employers' organizations, the National Association of Manufacturers, which generally represented smaller manufacturing and commercial interests, and the National Civic Federation, which was representative of larger corporate firms.

The conclusion in chapter 9 provides an explanation for the development of protective labor legislation for women, taking account of the economic and legal forces which were at work and the specific groups which were actively involved pro and con. It is my position that these laws represented an accommodation between two aspects of women's position: as providers of domestic services within the family (maintaining and reproducing the labor force), and also as (low) wage labor under capitalist relations of production. It is necessary to recognize both these aspects to understand why these laws were developed when they were, and also why they are no longer a possible accommodation under present conditions. The concluding chapter also discusses the process by which these social reforms were developed and by which potentially disruptive civil protests were channeled into formalized legislative hearings. The analysis takes account of the influence of labor both within the arena of the state and outside it, as well as the long-term interests of capitalists in maintaining and reproducing existing power relations in the society. It will also indicate the means by which women's subordinate position in the work force itself was created and maintained, and by which a separate, lower wage structure was perpetuated with the active help and support of male unionists as well as of employers and social reformers.

Chapter Two
The Work Process: Scientific Management, Efficiency, and Labor Legislation for Women

Protective labor legislation was one facet of a general trend toward the rationalization of the labor process. The trend included increasing the efficiency of labor through changes in technology; substituting less skilled (lower-paid) labor for more skilled labor; and increasing the specialization of tasks, which contributed to the segmentation of the labor force. Technological changes in the labor process affect the type of jobs women do, since a change in the kind of machinery used may result in the substitution of women for men (or vice versa). This occurred in, for example, the printing trades. In this chapter, the close connection between the efficiency movement of management and the rationale for protective labor legislation will be demonstrated to reveal the ways in which both these forces contributed to shaping the work process under capitalism.

Protective labor legislation was seen by the social reformers of the time as one means of limiting the intense exploitation and overwork of women workers. However, these laws also contributed toward increasing the productivity of labor, by making employers use labor more "effectively." This result was considered a benefit by its middle-class proponents, who wished to shorten the hours of women's working day but without questioning the capitalist priorities which had given rise to it. During this period, the increasing concentration of capital (the rise of "big business"), along with worker militancy and radicalism, led to increasing concern on the part of employers to develop more effective strategies of control over workers.[1]

The most explicit statement of the employer's need to gain control of the work process by systematically transferring the worker's knowledge into the hands of management was Taylorism, or *scientific management*. It was strongly opposed by workers and labor-oriented observers, as well as by the U.S. Commission on Industrial Relations in a controversial report by the commission's head. This chapter will discuss the role which scientific management was expected to play in achieving "industrial peace," and the social reformers' reasons for supporting it.

The connection between employer-oriented strategies like scientific management and the push for protective labor legislation for women during this period is made explicit in the work of one reformer, Josephine Goldmark. Goldmark wrote the brief for the landmark Supreme Court decision in Muller v. Oregon by arguing that overwork and fatigue could be scientifically determined; hence shorter hours for women workers were justified by the greater efficiency of the workers on the job, in addition to the preservation of their health. This chapter will conclude with a comparison of Goldmark's proposal for a method to "scientifically" determine the length of the working day with Marx's analysis of the forces which determine the working day under capitalism.

DISCIPLINING THE WORK FORCE UNDER CAPITALISM

Changes in the work process with industrialization mean the development of a free labor force, that is, labor as a commodity, in the historically specific conditions of industrial capitalism. However, this process was influenced by specific factors of past development, including "custom" and culture, and can be described only superficially if abstracted from concrete conditions in a particular time and place.

The dissolution of feudal relations and the rise of a class of "free laborers" (workers not tied to a manorial lord and owning nothing but their ability to labor) developed in England through the seventeenth century. This transformation, in turn, created the need to discipline these newly created wage laborers. Industrialization cannot be discussed apart from the development of capitalism, and attempts to conceive of this process in terms of "modernization" which usually implies technological change without reference to a specific set of relations of production) will miss one of the chief determinants of the direction and forms that this process has taken.

Technical "efficiency," that is, increased output per cost, has often been assumed by Marxists and non-Marxists alike to be the main force behind technological changes. Recent works also look at hierarchical relations in the capitalist firm and the direction that technology has taken as a consequence of the need to control and discipline a work force.

Sidney Pollard's analysis of these processes in England assumes that it was because of the machinery (that is, the interdependence of different aspects of production) that the employer needed to enforce discipline upon a restless work force that regularly took off work in observance of "St. Monday," feast days, and other holidays, some of which were celebrated by the employers as well.[2] This new discipline was achieved by a variety of means, including the introduction of formalized work rules; dismissals (abolishing the apprentice system made this new policy possible); beatings, especially for children, whose work in factories meant they were no longer under direct control of their parents as in the earlier work patterns; shaming of the worker for infractions; and laws against workers' combinations (unions) and breach of contract. Sometimes prizes were given to the most industrious workers.

Prohibitions against Saturday and Sunday leisure, drunkenness, and other aspects of the traditional village culture, then, have meaning in light of the larger emphasis on instilling factory discipline and developing a tractable work force. This was seen as a reflection of the individual employer's character and ability, not a matter for scientific analysis, as in the later emphasis on scientific management. The entrepreneurs' belief in their own superior virtues implied a corresponding lack of these virtues in their subordinate wageworkers, and in order to make the worker receptive to the idea that work in itself was a good thing, the employer needed to instill in him the "bourgeois values which he lacked."[3]

One assumption by the employers in this period was that no worker would work any longer than he needed to maintain his subsistence. Therefore, higher wages would not result in any greater output or take-home pay for the worker, but in greater absenteeism (that is, lack of discipline), and the time spent in idleness would contribute to drunkenness and immorality. Subsistence wages were justified as being in the workers' and owners' best interests. The wage structure itself was affected by the preindustrial wage level, as Eric Hobsbawm points out. The unskilled laborer generally received a subsistence wage (however it was defined at the time), while skilled workers received several times that much. Hobsbawm concludes: "The wage structure of a developed capitalist economy was not formed in a void. It began as a modification or distortion of the pre-industrial wage hierarchy and only gradually came to approximate the new pattern."[4]

These analyses do not consider the way in which work discipline specifically affected women workers. The emphasis on morality would have had the additional impact on women of reinforcing the traditional, male-dominated sexual hierarchy and extending it from the family to the workplace. Women's wages were also considerably lower than men's in this period.

THE ROLE OF TECHNOLOGY

Employers' objectives of taking control of the productive process away from the workers and also of meeting competition and raising production to increase profits are so intertwined that any attempt to determine their relative importance must consider the specific conditions in a given industry at a given period in its development. David Gordon's model deals with these objectives as two aspects of the same process: "efficiency" is both *qualitative* (having control over the work force to reproduce the class relations of domination) and *quantitative* (technologically cost reducing—the most output from a given input). Under conditions where competition between capitalist firms is paramount, the quantitative aspect will assume greater importance. When the class struggle appears to threaten these gains, concern for qualitative efficiency will take precedence (hence the concern to "break the unions" before the turn of the century;[5] the open shop drive was concerned with just this aspect of productive relations.) Calling these "qualitative" and "quantitative" aspects of one factor, efficiency, amounts to redefining the concept of efficiency to emphasize nontechnological aspects of production.

Technology developed in heavy industry, for example, in making steel, in the 1890s and after; it eliminated much of the arduous physical labor by introducing overhead cranes, electric trolleys, and other machines. Changes in production and technology which dramatically increased labor productivity made possible the reduction of hours in a number of industries, including steel, in the period around World War I. Under the existing relations of production, these changes in technology were dangerous for the working class and served to further limit its control over the productive process—control which was essential for it to maintain its position regarding wages and conditions. The technology which was developed thus had a dual aspect: it was conducive to limited improvement in working conditions, especially for unskilled labor, and to increase in output, but it also led to loss of craft skills (and hence loss of control).

TECHNOLOGICAL CHANGE AND WOMEN WORKERS

In addition to changing the kind of skill required, changes in technology in a trade may also result in the substitution of women for men, or vice versa. The printing industry presents an interesting case in point. According to the U.S. census of 1910, after the clothing trades, the leading industry in New York City was printing and publishing. Some 2,883 establishments employed 48,322 wage earners.[6] The printing trades are relevant here because one kind of protective labor law, prohibiting night work for women, had the effect of eliminating a group of women printers from their jobs. These women formed a small but vocal and organized opposition to these laws.

The number of women employed in the printing trades was increasing rapidly at the turn of the century. Printing is one of the older craft skills and has always employed large numbers of women. Although women had been hand compositors and typesetters for a long time, they constituted only about 5 percent of the new linotype machine operators by 1904.[7] The proportion of women employed in printing trades showed a small, steady increase between 1880 and 1905; for example, in book and job printing it rose from 12 to 23 percent.[8] The proportion of women employed in binderies, however, was much higher, and by about 1910 the industry employed roughly equal numbers of men and women, up from about 30 percent female representation in 1870. Mary Van Kleeck noted that this was not a simple displacement of men by women. Changes in the processes and type of work done, as well as introduction of machinery, sometimes caused a process to undergo a sex change.[9] Women were displaced by folding machines when the job of point folding was transformed by a wire-stitching and gathering machine using automatic feeding devices tended by men. As Van Kleeck noted, this change was "not a displacement of women by men; it [was] rather the substitution of rubber fingers ... for women's hands, and as a result a reorganization of the force."[10]

There was a tremendous variety of kinds of shops within the trade, and there was also a difference in the kind of binderies employing women. Only a few women worked in job and art binding, which required artistic skill and also business skill. Since there was a long apprenticeship for this craft, women also had to have some means of support during the apprentice period. According to Van Kleeck, these women had more in common with professional women than the majority of bindery women, and she did not think it was likely to be an area which would employ increasing numbers of women in the future.[11]

During the period under study by Van Kleeck, the printing and bindery trade was undergoing changes in processes which resulted in unemployment, but there was also an increase in the binderies doing the more routine work, away from hand binderies where men predominated. Van Kleeck noted that "without any shifting of the line between men's work and women's work, the proportion of women steadily increased between 1870 and 1900."[12] She also noted that there was no apparent friction in the trade between men and women over competition for the same jobs, but that there had been some transfer of women's work to men or boys, rather than the reverse.

The trade was characterized by irregularity of work. Slack times alternated with periods of intense overwork or "long days." Sometimes as many as 21¼, 22½, and even 24½ hours in one shift once or twice a week were reported. Without the night work prohibition, New York's nine-hour law, which had just gone into effect, would have been virtually unenforceable, since a woman legally could be required to work two nine-hour shifts back to back from midnight in the absence of a prohibition against night work. H. Seager noted that this situation indicated the need for reforms, adding, "None seem to stand out more clearly than an effective prohibition on the employment of girls from 14 to 18."[13]

The introduction of machinery which combined several processes might render a woman's skill at one process obsolete. Van Kleeck stated: "The machine is the great fact which looms large before the eyes of bindery women when they describe changes in their trade."[14] One bindery stated that the machines had cut the work force in half (from sixty to seventy girls to about thirty). The larger establishments were more likely to introduce machinery than the smaller ones, since, as one employer put it, they couldn't "risk the capital for a machine which might change soon again."[15] Smaller businesses might not have the workroom space for the larger machinery, the smaller jobs which they received probably would have meant resetting the machines too often to make the machines practical, and they might not have enough work to keep the machines busy all day. All of these factors put pressure on the smaller shops as the larger ones mechanized their processes.

Not surprisingly, the wages paid to women bindery workers were much lower than the wages paid to men. The 1905 census for New York State indicated average weekly earnings for women in the trade at $6.13 per week and those for men at $12.09 per week, while the average for women in all manufacturing industries was $6.54. According to the Van Kleeck study, which was confined to Manhattan binderies, over half the women workers received less than $8.00 per week. Moreover, the irregularity of work showed in their yearly income; the average for all women surveyed was $308.00, whereas if they had been employed all year at the average rate per week of $7.22, they would have earned $375.00. Despite the fact that they worked at other occupations during slow periods in bindery work, they still showed a relative loss of over $50.00. On this income, the vast majority of the women surveyed (193 out of 199) lived at home. In only 55 percent of the families was the father the head, however.[16] Information about these men indicated that only one of them was earning the $900.00 per year that one standard budget study by Robert Coit Chapin indicated was a sufficient income to support a family in 1907.

Thus the printing industry was in flux during the period under study here. The craft skills (which had been the basis for the International Typographical Union, an old established union in printing) were giving way to new processes which in many cases increased production while reducing the need for workers. Bindery work required some skills but was generally very low paid and had long hours. Restrictions on hours, brought about as part of protective legislation, would then help provide an impeus for further changes in technology in the industry, since it had traditionally depended upon spurts of long days alternating with periods of no work. If such schedules were no longer possible, the introduction of machinery might seem like a more attractive alternative.

Cigar making is another trade in which the interplay between changing technologies and changes in sex composition can be seen. "Cigar making is one of the few industries in which men and women compete directly, and for this reason the difference in their wages is extremely interesting," Edith Abbott noted.[17] In some processes men worked more hours per week than women, and in others the wage differential was not as great as where there was a difference in hours. In this as in other industries, however, women's wages were much lower than men's, even though women competed directly with men. This situation raised important questions about women workers for Abbott: "Why is their labor 'cheaper' than that of men? And are there reasons other than this to explain why, in coming into an industry, they drive out the men instead of working side by side with them? Does their monopoly of a trade mean a permanent lowering of the standard of living of the workers employed in it?"[18]

This trade illustrates the way in which changes in the work process reveal capitalist priorities of increasing technical efficiency. Cigar factories mass-produced cheap cigars under the newer "team" organization and also used molds. At the same time, however, women's inferior status in the work force was perpetuated and continued. In this industry, the growth of the tobacco trust went hand in hand with the increased use of female and child labor. Their labor was "cheaper" than the men's, to use Abbott's term, not because they were less productive, "efficient" workers, but because they were women workers, and this fact formed part of the impetus to change over to technologies which could be used to turn a process into women's work.

THE FATE OF SKILLED LABOR

The preceding discussion indicates that part of the process of industrial development which was accelerating during the beginning of this century in the United States included the substitution of machine processes for handcraft and of less skilled labor for more skilled. This general trend has been obscured by the effect of machine production on certain kinds of hard physical labor, however. For example, an early article in *International Socialist Review*, certainly not inclined to be favorably disposed to the motives of capitalists, nonetheless described the mechanization of a coke plant in generally positive terms, and concluded that in this case backbreaking physical labor had been replaced by mechanical effort, and

> "Men required to run a machine coke plant will be of a higher economic and intellectual status than those that furnish the labor at an old-style plant."

The writer also noted that skilled molders had *lost* status in this shift, and concluded: "The levelling goes on . . . which will soon make industrial organization as easy as craft organization is now."[19] But the writer made no mention of potential unemployment as a result of this shift.

The decline of skill in a variety of different trades and the growing importance of unskilled labor were also noted by William Walling, who used 1900 census data to classify a number of different occupations according to the proportion of unskilled labor. He defined "unskilled" by *wage* rates, and found 90 percent in cotton (mills) and 91 percent in clothing, down to 41 percent in printing.[20] The percentage of unskilled relative to skilled workers increased between 1890 and 1900 in most of the major industries he analyzed. Walling ascribed this increase to several tendencies:

> First—Unskilled operations have been taken away from the artisan, and placed in the hands of the unskilled.

Second—Skilled operations have been subdivided and specialized and the new work largely taken away from the skilled and distributed among unskilled workmen. At the same time the work remaining to skilled men is simplified and the degree of skill required is lessened. To this double tendency is due the increasing uniformity of rates of wages of the skilled and unskilled.[21]

Thus the line between skilled and unskilled labor was becoming less distinct, and the divisions among trades within an industry was also breaking down as groups of processes developed which were common to a number of different industries (such as packing and transportation). Walling also contended that the wages of unskilled labor between 1890 and 1900 either decreased or remained about the same, while only eight out of the twenty-five industries examined showed an increase, and this during a time when per capita wealth showed a large increase. Later studies of wage rates found this period to be relatively favorable for workers when compared with the period following 1900.

Walling argued that these tendencies were going to be accompanied by a "new unionism" which would include unskilled workers with skilled, and would organize on an industrywide basis rather than attempt to restrict the supply of skilled labor and exclude unskilled workers entirely. Although several of the industries he analyzed (such as cotton mills and clothing manufacture) had large numbers of women workers and the printing trades had growing numbers of women, Walling did not consider this factor relevant to his analysis. He included women workers categorically in his enumeration of unskilled *tasks* in these industries.[22]

Subdivision of work processes and degradation of skills were also occurring in traditionally women's jobs. A study by Louise Odencrantz of Italian women's work noted that although many of the women had learned fine hand sewing and embroidery in the schools and convents of Italy, they learned that "cheap and fast" was in more demand in the United States: "They do only cheap work in this country. Everything must be done in a hurry. In Italy it would take six months to do a pillow and here it must be done in three or four hours." "Cheap work!" was one woman's comment.[23] Of sixty-five women who had done sewing or dressmaking in Italy, only four were working as custom dressmakers here. The rest "were struggling with the piece-work system, extreme specialization of processes, the operation of the power machine, with the emphasis on speed and output rather than on quality."[24] While Odencrantz emphasized that the work process itself was forcing this specialization on the women, another less astute observer felt that they could learn different skills despite the subdivision of labor; she said, "Most of the workers . . . do not care to acquire this general skill, being satisfied, apparently, to learn their special tasks."[25]

Changing technology and subdivision of tasks in the needle trades was used by Josephine Goldmark as an example of "the new strain in industry." She did not attribute this limitation to lack of ambition on the part of the worker to learn new skills, however. For instance, in the textile industry, where there was "increasing strain upon the workers, due to improved equipment," one woman who formerly would have tended two slowly running looms was now expected to tend twelve or sixteen new looms. Moreover, workers could no longer vary their work by stopping to clean and oil their own machines or do other tasks. Goldmark commented: "In all trades, operations tend to become more and more machine-like in regularity and sameness. Labor tends to become more and more subdivided, each worker performing steadily one operation, or part of one operation.[26] This kind of subdivision made for "speed and perfection of output" and was "part of the new efficiency," but, according to Goldmark, was also accompanied by increased strain and monotony.

SCIENTIFIC MANAGEMENT

Although division of labor and specialization of jobs are generally thought to flow from the nature of modern technology, the principles of how to manage the new industry were most clearly and systematically developed with little attention to technological innovation. Taylorism, or scientific management, was concerned mainly with developing a means by which management could take control over the work process, especially the pace of work, by taking it out of the workers' hands and putting it into the employers', while at the same time eliminating "waste" movements and thereby attaining maximum "efficiency" out of the work force.

What Taylor called "development of a science to replace rule of thumb"[27] was the concentration in the hands of management of the knowledge and control of the work process that had formerly enabled the workers to set limits to tasks. The contribution of Taylorism was its explicit statement of the objective of furthering the capitalist's control over the work force as a weapon in the conflict between two opposing interests.[28] It was, as Harry Braverman put it, "the explicit verbalization of the capitalist mode of production."[29] It was intended to mark the end of "past custom" about matters of work load and manner of execution, and to replace that with a workday determined purely by capitalist rationality, that is, by maximum output for minimum increase in wages. Subdividing work processes into their simplest constituent elements wherever possible enabled the employer to use unskilled labor for a large part of the process which had formerly been considered part of the task of a more skilled (and better-paid) worker.

Despite Taylor's claim to the contrary, the introduction of scientific management in plants did cause strikes, most notably in the Watertown Arsenal in 1911, where attempts to introduce rates determined by a stop-watch among the iron molders appear to have precipitated a walkout. In this plant, the rates set by the time study man were clearly arbitrary, and the workers learned that they could be opposed. It was not the "discipline of impersonal scientific law," but a (dishonest) man with a stopwatch making guesses.[30] Time study was subsequently forbidden by law in certain classes of federal employment, including the arsenal.

Most labor-oriented observers were very skeptical of scientific management's claim that it benefited labor. Helen Marot, a member of the Women's Trade Union League and a union member herself, noted: "Scientific Management is advocated by representatives of capital. It proposes to increase industrial output by managing labor scientifically"; but labor wanted to manage itself.[31] Marot continued: "Every strike, every difference between organized labor and capital, is an attempt of the former to wrest management . . . from the latter."[32] She then went on to criticize Taylorism for being a tool of management:

> Scientific management logically follows and completes the factory process . . . [by] deliberately gather[ing] in all the rule of thumb knowledge of all workmen and transferring this knowledge to the management. That is exactly what machinery did and is still doing to craft workers. It usurped the knowledge of the worker and transferred that knowledge to the management.[33]

Marot stated that labor viewed scientific management as a scheme to squeeze more work out of them, and the supposedly scientific determination of rest and fatigue was especially suspect. Motions which were "waste" from the point of view of efficiency management were really "nature's attempt to rest the strained and tired muscles," and a skilled workman had a grace and flourish that were essential for him.[34]

Marot was also skeptical of the bonus system. According to the efficiency engineers, the bonus was never supposed to be cut, but workers knew that it always was. Even if the employer promised to maintain the higher rate, he would not be able to do so if his competitors did not.

Scientific management required certain "ethical standards" of industry, which Taylor called a "'complete change in mental attitude' on both sides." Marot sarcastically commented, "Labor would agree with Mr. Taylor, and add that it would require as well a mental revolution in Wall Street."[35] Marot here makes the same basic analysis of Taylorism that Braverman makes: it deskills, removes control of the work process from the worker to management, and also pretends to a scientific neutrality while its standards are really those of management.

The report of the U.S. Commission on Industrial Relations was also unimpressed with the value to labor of scientific management. The commission was established in the aftermath of the bombing of the *Los Angeles Times* in 1911 and was to investigate the causes for industrial violence and unrest. A study by the commission of shops under scientific management was generally critical of the method for a variety of reasons. The report stated the following:

> [There is a] lack of scientific accuracy, uniformity and justice in time study and task setting. Far from being the invariable and purely objective matters that they are pictured, the methods and results of time study and task setting are in practice the special sport of individual judgment and opinion, subject to all the possibilities of diversity, inaccuracy and injustice that arise from human ignorance and prejudice.[36]

Although the system purported to pay workers in accordance with their efficiency, the report found that rates for women in scientific management shops were not based on productivity but on sex (that is, they were lower). The report quoted one manager as follows: "There is to be no nonsense about scientific management. If by better organization and administration, what is now regarded as man's work can be done by women, women will be employed and women's wages will be paid."[37] Thus the system of differential wage rates for men and women went unchallenged. Instead, the potential for substituting women as a lower-paid category of workers for higher-priced male labor was incorporated into scientific management.

The commission also found a general tendency toward rate cutting which seemed "to be almost of necessity an essential part of its very nature."[38] It also found a "failure to protect the workers from overexertion and exhaustion,"[39] which, of course, was one of the method's major claims. In fact, cases of overspeeding were found particularly in the case of girls and women.[40] The commission was also skeptical of the assertion that scientific management develops a common interest between workers and employers:

> Scientific management in practice generally tends to weaken the competitive power of the individual worker, and thwarts the formation of shop groups and weakens group solidarity; moreover, generally scientific management is lacking in the arrangements and machinery necessary for the actual voicing of the workers' ideas and complaints."[41]

It maintained that scientific management "inevitably tend[ed] to the constant breakdown of the established crafts and craftsmanship and the constant elimination of skill," and it described the logical conclusion of this process: "Any man who walks the street would be a practical competitor for almost any workman's job. Such a situation would inevitably break down the basis of present-day unionism and render collective bargaining impossible."[42] It would also lead to a leveling of wages as the differential between skilled and unskilled worker would break down. The report concluded: "It is certain that scientific management is a constant menace to industrial peace."[43]

In contrast to this almost unequivocal condemnation of the purpose, method, and effect of scientific management, Louis Brandeis testified before the commission that there was "nothing in scientific management itself which [was] inimical to the interests of the workingmen," and that the stopwatch could be "the greatest protection for labor."[44] Unions would still have a role to play "as long as there [was] a wage system," he stated, and under scientific management unions would still be necessary to bargain for wages, hours, and conditions.[45] Brandeis, who was the lawyer for shippers opposing Eastern Railroad's request to the Interstate Commerce Commission for a rate hike, claimed that scientific management could save the railroad a million dollars a day. The railroads had claimed that the increase was necessary because of a wage increase they had just granted. The unions, together with the railroads, opposed Brandeis. The rate increase was denied.[46]

Scientific management appealed to a number of liberal social reformers, who hailed it as a means of preventing exploitation, especially of women workers, because it relied on "science," not on unionization or even primarily legislation. Sue Ainslie Clark and Edith Wyatt devoted an entire chapter of their budget study, *Making Both Ends Meet: The Income and Outlay of New York Working Girls*, to an assessment of scientific management. At a cloth-finishing factory employing large numbers of women, they concluded that scientific management had increased wages and shortened hours, although the effect on "health and fatigue" was less clear. In one part of the factory, "when the general vague impression that the new system was more exhausting than the other was sifted down, the grist of fact remaining was small."[47]

Goldmark also was cautiously optimistic about the potential of scientific management to improve working conditions and eliminate fatigue.[48] "Scientific" speed was not like ordinary speedup, but she noted that unless it was carefully applied, the stopwatch could be used to increase exploitation, not overcome it. Under scientific management, poor working conditions (lighting, poor ventilation, and so forth) became signs of inefficiency, and their elimination was not merely "welfare work,"[49] but a matter of the employer's self-interest as well as the workers'. Goldmark did not openly take a management perspective, however, as her work in support of protective labor legislation for women shows. Her support for protective legislation complements rather than undermines management's interest in efficiency; in her views, both these tendencies coalesced. Because she was so influential in getting protective legislation for women legitimated in the courts, her views of the working day are clearly formulated, and the contrast with Marx's attack on the wage system shows what the social reformers hoped would result from industrial reform measures.

The principles of scientific management contributed to the process of rationalizing the labor process and also sought to invest it with an aura of scientific objectivity that Taylor fervently hoped would remove the issue from the arena of class struggle and union-management battles. If "a fair day's work" could be determined by time-and-motion studies with scientific accuracy, then both the worker and the employer could agree that their mutual interests lay in increased productivity.

Both Taylorism and protective labor legislation for women contributed to segmenting the work force and furthering the process of deskilling and degrading conditions of work for the work force as a whole (even though "protective" legislation might appear to do exactly the opposite). Each contributed in different ways to the same end during this, the Progressive Era. Goldmark, who, as noted, was an ardent supporter of protective labor legislation for women and instrumental in compiling the evidence of overwork and fatigue, that was used in Louis Brandeis's briefs (especially *Muller v. Oregon*), was seeking to establish a "scientific" basis for determining conditions of work and "a fair day's work." The ideological purpose of this effort can now be shown by a comparison of Goldmark's view with Marx's analysis of "the working day" under capitalism.

THE WORKING DAY: MARX AND GOLDMARK

What is a working day? What are the factors that must be considered in this determination? These are the questions that both Karl Marx, writing in the midnineteenth century, and Josephine Goldmark, at the beginning of the twentieth, sought to answer. The contrast between their approaches to the problem of determining the length of the working day reveals something about the impetus for social legislation which was developed here in the early twentieth century.

Marx stated that the creation of surplus value, or profit, for the employer hinges on the peculiar nature of labor as a commodity. Labor as a commodity is paid for at its exchange value, which is (more or less) what it takes for labor to reproduce itself. Labor power as used by the capitalist, however, has the unique property, as a commodity, of being able to create more value than it itself is worth. But how?

One answer employers gave was that all the "profit" of the employer was made during the last hours of work during each day, and that therefore to cut the day (for example, from twelve to ten hours) would be to cut out all the profit in the enterprise. This explanation was considered and rejected by both Marx and Goldmark, but for very different reasons.

It is true that *prolonging* the working day will result in the production of more surplus value for the employer. The importance of this fact was noted by Marx and was also the basis for the employers' concerted opposition to the English Factory Acts of the 1830s and 1840s. The problem of determining the length of the working day for Marx, then, became the question of fixing the amount of time necessary for the replacement of the worker's labor power, plus the amount of surplus labor, or that amount which is over and above the time required for labor to reproduce its own value. The capitalist, Marx pointed out, is only asking of his laborers what he has paid a fair exchange rate for: a working day. He pays the going rate for labor power. The determination of the working day, then, becomes a struggle between the "just" claims of the capitalist for the labor power he has bought, and the equally "just" claims of the worker for a day of "normal" length.

For Marx, the question of the "normal" length of the working day could not be answered outside the context of the specific historical relations between capital and labor, and it was determined by the social context and the nature of the class struggle at the time. Marx also noted that it was somewhat in the interests of the capitalist class to prevent the working day from exceeding some extreme limits. The English Factory Acts, which "curb[ed] the passion of capital for a limitless draining of labor power," were necessary both to undercut organized opposition by workers and also to permit the working class to regenerate itself physically.[50] What follows, then, in his chapter on the working day in *Capital*, is a detailed presentation of evidence of the extremities of exploitation and abuses in industry after industry in England, much of it from testimony before various government commissions on factory conditions. Even such minimal amenities as providing for meal times within the period of a ten-hour day were fought tooth and nail by the employers of the 1840s.

These same conditions, which resulted in the Factory Acts in England, did not become issues for government regulation in this country until the period under examination here. The significance of this legislation for women workers, which was generally ignored by Marx, lies in the assumptions about women that were made in the course of defending it. This legislation helped shape the participation of women in the work force by reinforcing their secondary status in the labor force and their primary function in the home.

Josephine Goldmark was one of the most articulate supporters of restrictive legislation for women. She, with Louis Brandeis, compiled the evidence and arguments submitted before the U.S. Supreme Court in the case of Muller v. Oregon (1907). The document (known as the "Brandeis Brief," discussed in chapter 3) demonstrated the inherent health hazards of overwork, the detrimental effect of this overwork on women in particular (as mothers of the future generation), and women's special need of protection. By considering working women as primarily mothers, this legislation was therefore helping to insure the reproduction of the *working* class specifically.

The Brandeis Brief was only one aspect of Goldmark's work on labor legislation. The assumptions of the inequality of women and their innate dependence on men (which appear, in fairness to Goldmark, not in the original brief, but in the decision by Justice Brewer in the case), were side issues to the main argument that Goldmark used to justify the need for legislation to regulate conditions of work in modern industry. This purpose appears quite clearly in her work, *Fatigue and Efficiency*. She wrote: "The aim of this book is to present, as a new basis for labor legislation, the results of the modern study of fatigue." It thereby hoped to provide a "scientific basis of legislation" which was lacking, and to use modern work on physiology "for aid in the practical problem of reducing the long working day in industry."[51]

Goldmark argued that the common physiological phenomenon of fatigue would provide an objective standard for the regulation of human labor. She presented a detailed description of cellular metabolism and the production of chemical wastes and impurities in the blood resulting in fatigue. Overexertion could result in exhaustion and even death—not from failure of any particular organ (such as the heart), "but from sheer chemical poisoning due to the unexpelled toxins of fatigue."[52]

Goldmark then examined the results of this process for the contraction of muscle tissue in experiments done on animals. Equipment was devised to test the curve of fatigue for specific muscle groupings in man and to compare individuals. Goldmark demonstrated that making a fatigued muscle work requires more nervous energy and requires proportionately more time to recover than when shorter periods of work and rest alternate. Even though nervous fatigue is sometimes accompanied by temporary increase in work (what is called "nervous energy"), this increase merely hides the coming fatigue and may lead the worker to the point of exhaustion without his or her really being aware of it. Goldmark then concluded:

> At this point the scientific interpretation of industrial problems advocated at the outset of this study becomes obvious enough. A flood of light is thrown upon the intricate injuries of speed, overtime, piecework, and the like industrial requirements. For if fatigue be due to demonstrated chemical action, removable only by proper intervals of rest; if overfatigue or exhaustion results ... then the need for the short workday rests upon a scientific basis. Science makes out its case for the short day in industry.[53]

Thus, from the worker's point of view, Goldmark stated that the length of the working day should depend on clearly measurable standards that take into account the "average" worker's limits of fatigue. But this was only half of the story, because although the worker might desire legislation which would limit his opportunities to reach utter exhaustion at work, the employer could still maintain that it was necessary in order to remain in business for more than *his* health. To counter this objection, Goldmark again relied upon the "methods of the laboratory," which take into account "the human element," that is, the " 'spoiled work' which had to be thrown away, or done over again the next day" during the last hours of a twelve-hour day.[54]

Goldmark then cited industrial studies done in various countries and for different occupations, all of which indicated that output could be maintained even though hours of work were shortened. This was particularly true for piecework, where the average weekly earnings remained about the same under the shorter work week of forty-eight hours as they had with fifty-four hours.[55] Goldmark attributed this fact to the increased vigor of the workers in their generally rested condition; the notion that some sort of speedup might also be involved was never considered.

Thus Goldmark was telling the capitalists that they could, in effect, have their cake and eat it too. They could shorten the hours of work for labor and still increase profits through intensified productivity, and all this without harm to the workers' health. This argument was based upon objective scientific criteria of fatigue. The contrast between Goldmark and Marx now becomes clear. For Marx, "the creation of a normal working day [was] . . . the product of a protracted civil war, more or less dissembled, between the capitalist class and the working class."[56] Goldmark claimed that the matter could be settled without reference to the relative strengths of opposing classes or to any basic conflict of interest between labor and capital. Marx contended that the length of the working day was an index of the level of exploitation of the worker by the capitalist. For Goldmark, work in itself was not exploitation, but "the essence of life"; it was only "overwork" that was detrimental.

For Marx, the length of the working day was determined by social forces. Goldmark took the entire question out of the realm of social and historical conditions under capitalism and sought to determine the length of the working day by an appeal to scientific findings concerning the physiology of fatigue. This working day was then shown to be completely compatible with increased profits for the capitalist, who could, by heeding the "physiological laws of fatigue," get more work for less pay out of the worker without the worker even noticing it. The similarity of this theory with the aims of scientific management is striking. Goldmark was very consciously attempting here to mediate between the militant demands of labor for a shorter workday and better working conditions, and the counterdemands of capital for maintaining profits and insuring control over the workers.

Some of the implications of this argument did not go unquestioned at the time, however, even among the group of reformers to whom it was addressed. An article on overwork agreed with the Brandeis-Goldmark defense of an Illinois ten-hour law for women, noted that overwork was especially dangerous to women because "it interfere[d] with their ability to bear children,"[57] yet nonetheless questioned whether the presence of toxins of fatigue ought to be used to determine the working day:

> Suppose the scientists succeeded in producing an anti-toxin for fatigue. What effect will it have on our labor legislation? Would we abolish

all prohibitions on overtime and all maximum limits ... Or would we work as hard for short hours as we should do now but put the emphasis on the positive arguments of the value of leisure rather than on the negative arguments of the dangers of overwork?[58]

Fatigue and Efficiency, written in 1912, takes the very modern line of turning social questions into technical problems with scientific solutions. It is in their approach to scientific management that the attitude of reformers to the relation between labor and capital is revealed most clearly, and with it, their reasons for favoring protective labor legislation for women.

IMPLICATIONS: MOTHERS OF THE FUTURE GENERATION

Goldmark and Brandeis were key influences in shaping the rationale used to defend labor legislation for women. The case they made for labor laws for women regarding hours limitations and night work prohibition argued first that the long hours women worked were detrimental to health and motherhood, and then that reducing hours did not result in financial loss to the entrepreneur because well-rested workers were more efficient. The explicit connections among the protection of the future generation of workers, "efficiency," and protective labor legislation can now be shown. Women are first and foremost responsible for the future generation, and their participation in the work force must be limited so that it does not interfere with this responsibility. As one study concluded:

The prime function of woman in society is not "speeding up" on a machine; it is not turning out so many dozen gross of buttons or cans in a day ... The prime function of woman must ever be the perpetuation of the race. If these other activities render her physically or morally unfit for the discharge of this larger social duty, then woe to the generations that not only permit but encourage such wanton prostitution of function. The woman is worth more to society in dollars and cents as the mother of healthy children than as the swiftest labeler of cans. Yet our present industrial practice would indicate a preponderance of value in the latter. Five years of factory work may, and frequently do, render a girl of twenty-one nearly or quite a physical wreck, so far as normal functioning is concerned.[59]

Florence Kelley put it more succinctly: "Family life in the home is sapped in its foundations when the mothers of young children work for wages."[60]
This position was reiterated throughout social reformers' pleas for

protective labor laws for women.[61] It was also accepted by the United States Women's Bureau. For example, in a bulletin discussing "health problems of women in industry," a picture of a woman holding up a small child appears above the caption "America will be as strong as her women."[62] Although many of the health recommendations contained in the bureau's report were said to "apply fully as strongly to men as to women," they applied "*especially* to women," since they especially affected *women's* health. The report continued: "Long hours in the factory are not as serious for the man, who is through work when he leaves his job at night, as they are for the woman who has often several hours of house-work to do after she gets home . . . and her health will suffer if hours of work are not limited."[63]

Although these laws affected the working population directly, reformers were constrained to point out that this purpose did not make the laws "class legislation" (which would be unconstitutional); on the contrary, they said that "raising the standard of industrial life [was] . . . the concern of the whole community," since "to the community a worn-out worker is an economic loss."[64] The meaning of this for women workers was that an exhausted woman was "unfit to be a wife and mother." Van Kleeck concluded here: "If we believe in laws to protect children who toil, we must believe in laws to protect them in their birthright of health and strength" by caring for the generation before them.[65]

The no-night-work laws were linked with the hours limitation; otherwise there would be no way of telling how long a woman had been working that day. But the justification was that night work was detrimental to the "health and morals" of women. The Brandeis Brief submitted in the successful defense of the law in New York (*People v. Schweinler Press*) drew on a wide range of official and unofficial sources throughout the world to demonstrate the need for the legislation. For example, a German factory inspectors' report from 1884 stated: "Above all else, however, the physical well-being of the worker demands the strictest possible avoidance of night work . . . The worker shortens her time of rest in order to attend the family duties and her health suffers gradual injury."[66] A Chicago study cited in the brief concluded that it was almost impossible to estimate the amount of sleep a woman could get during the day upon her return from a ten-hour night's work. She could not sleep when she returned home at 6:00 A.M. "if there were a husband who demanded his breakfast at 6:30, since his daily tasks begin at seven," or if there were babies and schoolchildren who got up at the same time.[67] Forty-two of the forty-six women studied, who worked in the packing house at night, had children under school age. The New York Factory Investigation Commission noted that married women working at night averaged about four-and-a-half hours of sleep during the day.[68]

The generally inferior quality of sleep during daytime was stressed by both American and European reports mentioned in the brief. Although night work was unhealthy for men, it was considered especially detrimental for women, both because women had household responsibilities in addition to their wage labor, and because women's physiological makeup differed from men's and rendered them more susceptible to injury. A British report quoted by the brief mentioned these physical differences and added: "Account must be taken ... also of those contributions which women alone can make to the welfare of the State. Upon the womanhood of the country most largely rests the privileges of creating and maintaining a wholesome family life and of developing the higher influences of social life."[69]

Although this legislation was sought for the protection of the race, it was stressed that it would work no economic hardship on business either. On the contrary, the experience of countries with no-night-work laws for women showed the following:

> Commercial prosperity is not hampered by such regulation ... the increased efficiency of workers, due to regular rest at night, has reacted so favorably upon output that commercial prosperity has profited instead of being injured by the prohibition of women's night work."[70]

Evidence from international experience was also used to demonstrate that the output of night work was inferior to that of day work, both in quality and quantity.[71] Employers throughout the world had been able to abolish night work for women and still maintain their output by "increasing their day force, by enlarging their establishments, by improving machinery and processes of manufacture." Except for the first, these changes which took place as a consequence of the legislation constitute an important component of the rationalization of production.

CONCLUSION

The changes in the nature of work, including mechanization and specialization of labor, and their detrimental effect on workers were becoming increasingly evident to observers during this period. Protective labor legislation was seen as one means of relieving the worst effects of this "efficiency" on the workers' lives and health. Scientific management, although itself a contributing factor to the subdivision of tasks, monotony, and loss of control over the pace and manner of work, appeared to many reformers as the solution to these problems. It would guarantee productivity while also taking into account the "human element," that is, the worker's limits of endurance, and without causing an increase in the level of conflict between employer and employee. Only middle-class reformers could take this position, however; workers remained unconvinced. The arbitrary nature of the tasks determined by stopwatch and the underlying assumptions about the nature of work and craft skills were obvious to labor.

Protective labor legislation, by contrast, appeared to be a worker-oriented response to these problems, and often did result in material improvements for workers' lives. But protective labor legislation for women also contributed, as did scientific management, to the development of a fragmented work force characterized by internal divisions by sex, skill, and other factors. Scientific management took the sex-based division of labor for granted, and included a lower wage scale for women in its calculus of a "fair day's pay."

However, protective labor legislation appeared to be against the interests of employers, and the laws were often challenged by them on constitutional grounds. The legal issues involved in the gradual legitimation of these laws will be considered in the next chapter.

Chapter Three
Legal Ideologies and Social Change: Protective Labor Legislation for Women

Case law resembles a patch-work quilt; . . . to see the pattern you must have distance.

Charles M. Hough

INTRODUCTION

This section will examine how a legal doctrine developed which first hindered all legislation interfering with the wage contract, and then changed to permit a basis for that legislation. Wage labor was increasingly held by the courts to come under the same type of law that property rights did; the few restrictions which were upheld with regard to property were usually held *not* to apply to wage labor. However, as it became increasingly evident that industrial conditions were threatening both the health and safety of workers and the public peace as well, the impetus for the shift and the process by which these laws became legitimated can be seen.

As long as the law is analyzed as an internally consistent, autonomous sphere which exists above and beyond the influence of economic relations, the impetus for these shifts in legal doctrines is hard to see. It then appears that some legal principle like freedom of contract was the primary restraint hindering passage of these laws. However, as will be shown in the course of this chapter, what is upheld by the courts as constitutional can do a complete about-face in response to changed conditions. The previous chapter considered the shifts in the work process, working conditions, and the position of women workers during the period in which labor legislation began to be passed and legitimated. This chapter will consider the legal means by which this legislation was achieved.

By the turn of this century, the "wage bargain" was considered a contract undertaken by two formally equal parties, the employer and the worker, and laws which attempted to regulate that relation were frequently struck down as an infringement of the right of contract. This right then appeared to be a legal constraint operating outside of economic influence; as will be shown, however, this doctrine itself was developed only in the 1880s, and, along with natural law principles, became the legal means by which employers pushed the full commoditization of labor. Both the changing uses of natural law doctrines, and their corollary, "freedom of contract," illustrate the way in which ideologies developed out of one set of social and economic relationships can be used under changed conditions or used to uphold a state of affairs completely alien to its original purposes. Unless the social bases of its advocates are examined, the changed use of its principles will be obscured.[1]

Social legislation in the late nineteenth century was struck down as an unconstitutional infringement on workers' basic right to freedom of contract, although this "right," and the laissez-faire economic principles from which it drew its justification, were very recent developments. But when legislation was struck down, and as opinions accumulated, it was increasingly assumed that the Constitution itself guaranteed this freedom. The shape which legislation then took and the kinds of laws which were passed were influenced by what legislators believed would be upheld as constitutional. Therefore, since it could be argued that women workers were not formally equal bargaining agents with respect to the wage contract, legislation for women workers was proposed with an eye to differentiating their need for protection from that of men workers: women's bargaining power was weaker, and their "physical and maternal functions," in particular, placed them at a disadvantage. Legislators attempted to make their laws conform with those from other states which had been successfully defended in the courts; legislation which was struck down, whether in the U.S. Supreme Court or, to a lesser extent, by the state supreme courts, was less likely to be replicated by other states.

But to see protective labor legislation for women solely as a result of this legal issue would ignore the underlying conditions of women's participation in the work force. Women were not only wage workers, but were also responsible for the maintenance and reproduction of the working class through their domestic labor in the home. These laws, therefore, emerged to protect that function by defending women's primary importance to "society" as the *reproducers* of the labor force, while allowing their continued but circumscribed participation in the wage labor force.

LAW AND SOCIETY

Although the relation between law and society is primarily a socio-logical question, theories of jurisprudence have not viewed it as such. During the eighteenth and nineteenth centuries especially, legal philoso-phies tended to view law in isolation, as a formal system divorced from any consideration of the way social and economic considerations might affect legal doctrine. This kind of analytical perspective reinforces the appearance of the neutrality and impartiality of law.

This view of law developed in opposition to a philosophy which argued for the "rights of man" which existed above and prior to any man-made (that is, positive, or statutory) law. These "natural rights," or higher ethical principles which even the sovereign must respect, became a force for measuring the existing system of law and justice and (during revolutionary periods) for finding it wanting. This force was attacked from several directions. For the formalists, to declare that the state was the sovereign, absolute authority was to deny the critical import of natu-ral law doctrine. (For example, John Austin defined law as whatever the sovereign says it is.) This reinforces the appearance of impartiality of the law by stressing its formally logical properties; questions concerning "jus-tice" then become extraneous and are relegated to the domain of morality not law. Natural law theories were also attacked by the historical, or cultural, school of jurisprudence. This interpretation found the deriva-tion of law in past customs and history of the people, as an expression of the "spirit" of the people or nation which the positive law reflected. Law must not be used as an agent of social change. This view provides no clue as to what specific social interests might be responsible for the emergence of a given kind of law.

With "sociological" theories of law, the emphasis on what the law actually does becomes paramount. Oliver Wendell Holmes stated that the law is what the courts in fact do (the "law in action"); the opinions which Justice Holmes handed down, as well as his insistence that judges must know the "facts" which gave rise to a specific law, reflect this perspective of "legal realism."

A more satisfactory analysis views the relation between society and law as a process by which different forces in the society develop legal definitions which become accepted into the law. If the legal institutions of the society operate for the long-term preservation of the given economic system as a whole, they still achieve relative independence from specific capitalists. The law also responds in a limited fashion to demands of the underclass as well, and can be the result of alliances between otherwise opposing forces. Throughout this period, seen with the clarity of hindsight, the trend of social legislation was to expand in many different spheres, including workmen's compensation, child labor laws, extension of compulsory education, and health and safety regulations in industry.

A further question might be the extent to which legal ideology expresses the inspirations of a group that eventually overthrows an existing set of social relations. Legal principles that develop during a period when a social class (such as the bourgeoisie in the eighteenth century) is struggling for power can then be used to defend the interests of that class after they have achieved power. Or these same principles can return to haunt them and be used in turn by a newly insurgent group. Principles embodied in the American constitution reveal both possibilities.

NATURAL LAW AND JUDICIAL REVIEW

Natural law philosophy, which can be traced to ancient Greece, took root in this country in a form which emphasized natural rights—"qualities inherent in man which it was the duty of the state to protect."[2] These laws were thought to exist over and above any given body of existing law and became, in the hands of French Enlightenment thinkers, a normative standard by which positive (that is, statutory) law could be judged, and which was prior and superior to it. Doctrines of natural law or inalienable rights can therefore have a revolutionary import because they deny the validity or "justness" of existing law unless it accords with the principles of "reason." In England, common law tradition acted to minimize the overt influence of natural law doctrines, although even there that influence was not completely lacking.

American colonists relied upon European ideas, interpreting them in ways that emphasized individual rights. This reliance can be seen in the American Declaration of Independence, which states that men "are endowed by their Creator with certain inalienable rights, that among these are Life, Liberty and the pursuit of Happiness. That to secure these rights governments are instituted among men . . . ." The rights, in other words, precede the charter, which must embody these rights to be a legitimate statement of powers. During this early period, an appeal to natural rights constituted a justification for revolution, both in this country and in France.

Natural law philosophy was incorporated into the American system of checks and balances. By the end of the eighteenth century these ideas were used to justify the power of the courts to pass judgment on the validity of the acts of the legislature. Fears that state legislatures might interfere with the rights of property were responsible for placing final review of legislation in the hands of the judiciary, which could then, in effect, act as a check upon popular will. This policy was justified in a very early court decision by referring to a law higher than legislatures: "I cannot subscribe to the omnipotence of a state legislature, or that it is absolute and without control . . . . An act of the legislature (for I cannot call it a law) contrary to the great first principles of the social compact, cannot be considered a rightful exercise of legislative authority."[3] Through the middle of the nineteenth century, the use of natural law doctrines waxed and waned; they were used, alternately, to defend the protection of vested rights (rights by law to do or possess certain things), and again to attack slavery.

From the outset, then, how the courts will rule and the principles that it uses to judge the law become an important and explicitly articulated part of legal ideology, which carries the force of fundamental principles that appear to be above and beyond specific material interests. The Constitution is the written source of the principles to be applied to each situation. Certain issues are relatively easily to decide—for example, ex post facto laws are unconstitutional. But other kinds of statutes, such as social legislation, do not simply apply mechanical legal techniques but invoke standards of reasonableness and fairness, as in new applications of police power, liberty of contract, and due process of law. These questions cannot be decided in a legal vacuum. The interpretation of these principles then becomes the point at which legal doctrine and social standards must meet.

Attempts to discredit legislation seek to establish legal constructions of these concepts which go back to immutable first principles—to God, or, lacking His authority, to English common law. Thus "Due process of law became the weapon for the application of a class reason and a class justice," in other words, to insure that "certain classes of property rights" remained undisturbed.[4] Those favoring the extension of social legislation emphasized the disparity between social conditions—the actual effect of the law—and the principle which it was supposed to embody, for example, equality under the law.

DUE PROCESS

The Fifth Amendment of the Constitution states that no person shall be deprived of life, liberty, or property without "due process of law." In

1868 that guarantee was extendeed by the Fourteenth Amendment to include protection from infringement by states. The phrase can be traced back to the Magna Charta, which is considered to be the keystone of English liberties. "By the law of the land" meant to secure a *procedure* which would justify an infringement on personal liberty, property, etc.[5]

This usage of "the law of the land" was carried over into the American states' constitutions. It was a statement of procedural limitations, rather than a limitation on the powers of the legislatures. It was extended in the early nineteenth century along lines that specified the *process*—for example, that the law must in general be equally applied in order not to violate "the first principles of civil liberty and natural justice."[6] Limitations on "natural and inalienable rights" thus were prohibited by the protection of "due process of law." It was not until the mid- to end of the nineteenth century that this phrase—this time through the Fourteenth Amendment—was used principally as a limitation on legislatures. (In 1849, it was used in New York to invalidate a law for the protection of married women's property rights.) But the chief importance of the clause toward the end of the nineteenth century became its gradual extension to include not just procedural fairness but also substantive limits on what the legislature could interfere with. It became the means of reversing the traditional presumption in favor of a law's constitutionality unless clearly proven otherwise, if that legislation concerned social issues.

LAISSEZ-FAIRE

The constitutional "restraints" under which labor legislation developed can be said to have emerged as the legislation itself developed; the Constitution itself makes no reference to labor laws (as it does, for example, to laws regulating religious practice). The growing corporate sector which sought to have labor laws invalidated, then, made use of certain aspects of the Constitution which it sought to have interpreted according to its own definitions. The original issue of the treatment of freed slaves receded; "a new set of problems—those namely arising from the growth of capital and the development of corporate industry—confronted government and particularly the state legislatures," and the court then "began a reinterpretation of the Fourteenth Amendment in the light of the principles of Lockian individualism and of Spencerian Laissez Faire."[7]

Both clauses of the Fourteenth Amendment—"due process" and "equal protection"—became "an ideology for individualism"[8] and the vehicles for writing into the Constitution the current economic principles of laissez-faire. The Fourteenth Amendment became a kind of judicial substitute for natural law principles in limiting the power of legislatures. First, the Fourteenth Amendment was extended to include individuals other than the freed Negroes it was designed to protect; then corporations were defined as individuals entitled to its protection. Hugh Evander Willis argued that because the *content* of due process is undefined, "the real origin of the doctrine is in the U.S. Supreme Court itself. It did not find the law, it made it."[9] The court is thereby destroying the separation of powers at the behest of corporations, which would rather rely on the court than the legislatures or the people to define what is properly legislative activity.

Economic doctrines of laissez-faire and social Darwinism were upheld by successive arguments, first in dissents and then in majority opinions of the court. In 1873, the court denied that the Fourteenth Amendment was to be applied to any interest except freed slaves: "We doubt very much whether any action of a State not directed by way of discrimination against the negroes as a class or on account of their race will ever be held to come within the preview of this provision."[10]

The dissent by Justice Field in the Slaughterhouse cases, however, laid the groundwork for the growing acceptance of laissez-faire. In these cases, corporate interests were trying to strike down a Louisiana law which gave, in effect, a state monopoly to one specific business concern. Although the law was upheld, the arguments by counsel contained the basic element which was to become the dominant court opinion in future attacks on labor legislation—the right of the *individual* to engage in economic activity without state interference. It was also the first time that the Fourteenth Amendment was used to justify laissez-faire.[11]

How was this economic doctrine of laissez-faire incorporated into court decisions? Benjamin Twiss argues that "the link is to be found in the role of leading lawyers who, by propagating and defending laissez-faire before the courts . . . secured its adoption into the law of the land. They did this in the interest both of clients in cases and of protecting a philosophy and a way of life which they shared with their clients."[12] Twiss contended that corporation lawyers were the "liaison between businessmen and judges"[13] and "natural allies of the propertied classes," since they were the elite end of the American bar, disposed both by their own social origins and the class interests of their clients to defend principles of individualism and property rights. It should be noted that these arguments were not necessarily intended to justify the growing power of monopoly capital by either lawyers or judges. Nonetheless, the protections of the Fourteenth Amendment were extended to include the corporation.[14]

The 1880s were also a time of agrarian, Populist opposition to the growing power of railroad and grain trusts, and farmers' push for state regulation of railroad rates. The railroad lawyers argued against regulation by redefining the concepts of liberty and property in accordance with laissez-faire principles, extending the "due process" protection to the *use* of property; regulation of rates would arbitrarily deprive the railroad owners of a portion of its value. The railroads lost the battle here but won the war, since the court maintained the right to regulate but granted the extended definition of "property," which included property in one's labor and the right to follow a calling.[15]

In 1885, the upper-class patrician lawyer William M. Evarts successfully argued that a law which made it criminal to employ cigar makers in a tenement with four or more families deprived individuals of their freedom of labor. One's "property in labor" was just as important to the poor as the other rights inhering in "property" were to the rich. To deprive a man of what he required in "the unceasing struggle for success and existence," then, "arbitrarily deprives him of his property and of some portion of his personal liberty."[16] Although under the police power, regulations for health or welfare of society is acceptable, there was judged no such hazard to the *public* from tenement house manufacture of cigars. The language of this decision used both Spencerian concepts (survival of the fittest) and the newfound interpretation of laissez-faire. This view of property and economic freedom, designed to operate where small, independent producers vied in an open, competitive market, was to gain judicial acceptance at precisely the time when monopoly capitalism was rapidly growing. The irony of this turn of events was not lost on contemporary proponents of social legislation. Thus, over time, the legal rationale for laissez-faire became translated into constitutional language through the "freedom of contract" interpretation of the Fourteenth Amendment.[17]

FREEDOM OF CONTRACT

Throughout the period in which protective labor legislation developed, the most frequently used objection was the claim that this legislation violated the constitutionally guaranteed right of both the laborer and the employer to set the wage bargain upon such terms as they might mutually see fit. Any interference with this "contract" was vigorously protested by employers under the prevailing interpretation of laissez-faire. "Freedom of contract" came to be included in the "inalienable rights" arising out of law and guaranteed by the founding fathers in the Constitution.

In fact, the first judicial mention at all of the right of "freedom of contract" appeared in a Pennsylvania Supreme Court decision in 1886.[18] The law in question aimed at prohibiting the payment of wages in scrip redeemable at the company store by requiring wages to be paid in money each month. The court's decision declared the law unconstitutional on the ground that the legislature had done "what, in this country, cannot be done; that is, prevent persons who are sui juris from making their own contracts." The decision continued:

> The act is an infringement alike of the right of the employer and employee; more than this it is an insulting attempt to put the laborer under a legislative tutelage which is not only degrading to his manhood, but subversive of his rights as a citizen of the U.S. He may sell his labor for what he thinks best, whether money or goods, just as his employer may sell his iron or coal, and any or every law that proposes to prevent him from so doing is an infringement of his constitutional privileges, and consequently vicious and void.[19]

The question of fact, whether there existed any incapacity of one of the bargaining parties, was not raised in this case. It was referred to and dismissed in a similar case the same year.[20] The court thus asserted a kind of "natural capacity to contract" which could not be abridged; the legislation was attacked as "class" legislation and hence impermissible since all persons are entitled to equal protection of the law.

However, the law does allow for differential treatment where some specific kinds of "incapacities" exist. This tenet goes back to common law tradition, where laws prohibiting usury recognized the helplessness of the borrower; his "necessities deprive him of freedom in contracting and place him at the mercy of the lender."[21] But the justice in this instance mentioned the usury laws only to show that the principle did not apply to the case at hand (an Illinois law prohibiting wages to be paid to company stores). Since usury laws had existed prior to the Constitution, he claimed that they were not to be considered an abridgement of rights guaranteed under the Constitution.[22] But laws directed at regulating the wage bargain had no such honorable lineage; they were therefore abridging a fundamental liberty as well as a property right, and violated the principles of laissez-faire as well. As one decision stated:

> The property which every man has in his own labor, as it is the original foundation of all other property, so it is the most sacred and inviolable. The patrimony of the poor man lies in the strength and dexterity of his own hands; and to hinder him from employing these in what manner he may think proper . . . is a plain violation of this most sacred property.[23]

The court went on to state that the "right to labor" ultimately derived from God's injunction to man when He drove him from the Garden of Eden: "He invested him with an inalienable right to labor in order that he might again eat and live."[24]

According to the tenets of laissez-faire and social Darwinism, economic inequalities did not constitute a basis for legislative action; they were rather in the nature of things. One Supreme Court justice stated before the Bar Association that legislation was powerless to affect the laws of supply and demand in relation to wages—that if the American worker did not succeed in owning his own home that was due to his own "improvidence," "idleness," or other personal defect.[25] During the 1890s, the bar was also interested in defending the community against anarchism, socialism, and other threats like the 1892 Homestead steel strike. Through the bar associations, especially the New York and national bars, ideologies of laissez-faire and social Darwinism were articulated and translated into legal terminology by the most influential corporate lawyers and judges. The American Bar Association became a "juristic sewing circle for . . . the gospel of Laissez-Faire."[26]

This discussion has centered on the process by which an ideology denying the validity of labor legislation was developed and accepted by the courts. As has been shown, the key concept in the argument was the notion of freedom of contract. It was vested with all the legitimacy and sacred qualities of both natural rights philosophy and of laissez-faire political theory. By 1905 it could be asserted to be an "inalienable right." Yet this "right" was first avowed only in 1886. No mention of it is made in natural law theories of the eighteenth century, nor is it referred to in the U.S. Constitution itself. It is rather an example of a principle that has been erected to serve a very specific end—in this case, as "a practical means of maintaining freedom to take maximum profits."[27]

REASONABLENESS

From the foregoing discussion of the development of the concepts of 'equality' and 'contract', it is clear that, as one jurist put it, "the root fallacies of such reasoning lie in the assumption that economic relations do not affect political and moral relations."[28] This assumption might be true if both parties had equal power in setting the bargain or contract; where one party is at the mercy of the other, however, the formal "equality" serves the stronger and also legitimates its power. Some instances of this "substantive" inequality recognized by common law are usury regulations, as indicated, and also laws regulating payment of sailors' wages.

The German sociologist Max Weber noted that western law generally conforms to "formal rationality"—that is, its principles are in form applicable to all parties alike; are general, not particular, in form; and are based on "rational" principles rather than, for example, revealed truth. Such a system of law is eminently suitable to a system of developing capitalism, which requires calculable, rational forms of law in order to flourish. It also, as Weber pointed out, serves to legitimate the substantive (economic or real) inequality that exists. The interests of an economic underclass are not served by principles of formal equality before the law; rather, formal equality serves to hinder their attempts to achieve "substantive" equality, which can only be achieved by formally "unequal" treatment of the two groups. Therefore, disadvantaged groups will seek *substantive* equality rather than a "formal" equality which serves to legitimate and maintain their inferior position.[29]

Even the most abstract juristic principles must have some relation to the real world, however, and the link between the legal form and substantive reality is achieved through the legal principle of "reasonableness." This principle recognizes that certain limitations on one's "freedom" are permissible, for instance, under the police power of the state, which grants authority to pass laws for protection of public order, health, morals, or safety.[30] Such restrictions must be "reasonable"—that is, not "arbitrary"; they must have a "reasonable relation to a purpose which it is competent for government to effect"[31] and must not violate "due process" of law. Thus, the court must judge, first, whether the purpose of the law is legitimate, and, second, whether the law is a proper means of achieving that purpose.[32]

The earliest protective labor laws, those limiting hours of work in mines, were upheld as a legitimate exercise of the police power because it was "reasonable" to consider mines dangerous, unhealthy places to work; hence legislation limiting the time a laborer had to spend underground seemed "reasonable." The appeal to the "police power," then, is just as vague as the appeal to "due process" in deciding what is "reasonable."[33] John Commons stated: "Reasonableness, in law, means simply that *all of the facts* must be investigated and *due weight* must be given to each."[34]

But what, then, are "the facts"? Moreover, how is a judge to take them into account, particularly when that judge sits on the Supreme Court, which is supposed to be limited to the consideration of arguments presented before it?

One way of including social and economic data was to have the court take "judicial notice" of some existing condition. This phrase meant that the court, in effect, was relying on "common knowledge" or some other idiosyncratic sources of the judges themselves.[35] There was "no formal test by which the courts [could] judge the fairness of [legislation]."[36] The criteria used by the court to decide these issues were "unarticulated," as Holmes put it.[37] Sometimes the court responded to a case which required an adjudication of fact in order to determine if the law was constitutional by taking notice of conditions which were not specifically raised in argument but which the court felt warranted mention. In other cases, it specifically decided to ignore conditions which it knew existed, but did not use this knowledge in its decision.[38]

During the period under study here (from about 1905 to 1925), the court came increasingly to refer to factors outside the formal legal structure to justify its rulings. In the period just before the turn of the century, the court upheld labor legislation, when it was explicitly defended as a public health or safety measure, according to criteria which seemed "reasonable" to the justices. Then this purpose was expanded to include more diffuse ends like promoting the "public good" or "public welfare," although, as Judge Learned Hand pointed out, all laws are supposed to do this. The Court therefore decided that it did have the power to examine the expediency and suitability of the means proposed by the legislation to the end desired, and this position meant that each case was unique, with little value as a precedent. As early as 1908, Judge Hand asserted, "It is too late for the adherents of a strict laisser-faire to condemn any law for the sole reason that it interferes with the freedom of contract."[39]

In such a climate, it became imperative that judges recognize the existence of industrial conditions that "justified" protective labor legislation if that legislation were not to be struck down as illegitimate in either its purpose or the means it used to achieve that purpose. In the tenement house case mentioned previously (*In re* Jacobs), the law was struck down because it did not appear "reasonable" to the majority of the justices that cigar making in tenements could be construed as a danger to the health of the community. A law in Colorado which limited hours of work in smelters to eight per day was declared unconstitutional by the state's supreme court because it infringed upon "the right of both the employer and the employee in making contracts relating to a purely private business, in which no possible injury to the public [could] result."[40]

In another case, the court questioned both the legitimacy of purpose of a law (that is, whether an individual could be protected) and its suitability (Ritchie v. People, 1895, Illinois). The court struck down this law, which limited the work of women in factories to eight hours a day, and stated:

> There is no reasonable ground—at least none which has been made manifest to us in the arguments of counsel—for fixing eight hours in one day as the limit which woman can work without injury to her physique, and beyond which if she works, injury will necessarily follow . . . [I]t is questionable whether [the police power] can be exercised to prevent injury to the individual engaged in a particular calling.[41]

Whether or not a specific trade was unhealthy and therefore could be a legitimate subject for legislation regulating it was again decided in the negative in a New York court in 1905. In Lochner v. New York, a ten-hour law for bakers was not considered "reasonable":

> We think the limit of the police power has been reached and passed in this case. There is, in our judgement, no reasonable foundation for holding this to be necessary . . . as a health law to safeguard the public health, or the health of the individuals who are . . . baker[s] . . . To the common understanding the trade of a baker has never been regarded as an unhealthy one.[42]

The decision went on to state that all occupations might in some way affect one's health, and "not only the hours of employees, but the hours of employers could be regulated, and doctors, lawyers, scientists . . . could be forbidden to fatigue their brain and body by prolonged hours." In response to this decision, Edward Corwin commented:

> This method of proceeding by the reduction *ad absurdum* is scarcely convincing, since the whole question at issue is whether the statute under consideration is reasonable or unreasonable; and to the query, whether all trades are to be at the mercy of legislative majorities, inquiry may be returned, whether they are to be at the mercy of judicial majorities.[43]

In opposition to this trend, Justice Holmes stated the following in his dissent in the Lochner case:

This case is decided upon an economic theory which a large part of the country does not entertain. If it were a question whether I agree with that theory, I should desire to study it further and long before making up my mind. But . . . my agreement or disagreement has nothing to do with the right of a majority to embody their opinions into law . . . The Fourteenth Amendment does not enact Mr. Herbert Spencer's Social Statics . . . A constitution is not intended to embody a particular economic theory, whether of paternalism and the organic relation of the citizen to the State or of laissez-faire. It is made for people of fundamentally differing views.[44]

The conflicting decisions of courts made it difficult to know which legislation was going to be upheld and which struck down. Holden v. Hardy upheld an hours limit for miners in 1895; in New York the Lochner decision struck down a ten-hour law for bakers in 1905, and in 1907 a law prohibiting night work was also stricken (People v. Williams, 189 New York 131). An eight-hour law for women was struck down in Illinois in 1895, while a Nebraska law was upheld. No clear pattern had yet emerged regarding labor legislation either for men in certain trades or for women workers. Decisions of state courts thus could set the tone for other states to follow, or they could be ignored, as the Colorado court ignored legislation which was upheld in other states regulating working conditions in mines.

In each of the above negative decisions, no attempt had been made to demonstrate to the court that a factual situation existed which would reasonably warrant legislation. Under the umbrella of "freedom of contract," the usual presumption that the legislature knows its business and therefore laws are constitutional unless in clear violation of the Constitution had been, in effect, reversed.[45]

THE BRANDEIS BRIEF

It was in this legal context that Louis Brandeis and Josephine Goldmark set about to document the conditions of industrial work, the evils of overwork, the existence of a definable state of "fatigue," and the special susceptibility of women workers to these evils. They argued in favor of the legitimacy of an Oregon law limiting the hours of work for women in factories to ten per day and sixty per week. The Brandeis Brief is a legal argument that presents a body of substantive, economic evidence documenting specific conditions which are used to establish the "reasonableness" of a law and to show that it bears some legitimate legislative purpose.

The innovation of this approach was recognized by the Court in its opinion. Although Brandeis did not use more than a small number of cases as precedent, he explicitly referred to an adverse decision (Lochner, striking down a ten-hour law for bakers) in which the Court's opinion did grant that freedom of the wage contract could conceivably be limited if it could be proven to be "reasonable." But, in addition to the sparse precedents, the brief included the "world's experience upon which the legislation [was] based," and also the large variety of both domestic and foreign experience with such laws.[46]

The purpose of this extralegal data was to show that it was *reasonable* to hold that the legislature acted rationally in believing that the public welfare was served by the law. This kind of evidence was used successfully in several cases following Muller, including laws affecting women's working conditions, for example, a minimum wage (Stettler v. O'Hara, 1917), and also laws that applied to men and women and which limited the hours of work to ten per day (Bunting v. Oregon, 1917). Sitting as a judge on the Supreme Court, Brandeis later commented:

> Unless we know the facts on which the legislators may have acted, we cannot properly decide whether they were . . . unreasonable, arbitrary, or capricious. Knowledge is essential to understanding; and understanding should precede judging. Sometimes, if we would guide by the light of reason, we must let our minds be bold.[47]

The Brandeis Brief presented a body of material consisting of the presentation of facts which were used to show the reasonableness of the law in question. In other words, it was used to reinforce the presumption of constitutionality that the court ought to have assumed to begin with.

LABOR LEGISLATION FOR WOMEN

It was through the Brandeis Brief that substantive economic conditions were first presented to the court in a systematic, comprehensive fashion in order to establish the need for labor legislation: the state could intervene on behalf of one of the parties to a contract because one party was demonstrably weaker than the other. That workers in certain respects are not the equal of employers in their bargaining power had been recognized in some previous court decisions. In Holden v. Hardy, the Court had stated: "Proprietors of these establishments [i.e., mines] and their operatives do not stand upon an equality, and their interests are, to a certain extent, conflicting . . . [T]he proprietors lay down the rules and the laborers are practically constrained to obey them."[48] The court also commented on the fact that the law was being contested by the employer, but it added:

> His defense is not so much that his right to contract has been infringed upon, but that the act works a peculiar hardship to his employees, whose right to labor as long as they please is alleged to be thereby violated. The argument would certainly come with better grace and greater cogency from the latter class.[49]

In this and other decisions, the court did uphold labor legislation for men workers, but only where the occupation presented some special, patently obvious dangers or abuses. Mining, smelters, and other such situations were regulated by law relatively early, especially regarding hours and payment of wages. But other laws, such as those concerning tenement house cigar makers, bakers, and printers, were struck down.

It was *not* the pattern to uphold legislation when it applied to women workers while striking it down if it applied to men. But there was additional ammunition available when the legislation affected women only, and it should be remembered that the problem was to prove that the law was *reasonable*. To reasonable men, legislation for women might be upheld where similar legislation affecting men would not. The nature of the evidence in a Brandeis Brief can never be conclusive but always requires a judgment about social and economic circumstances. Therefore, prevailing notions about women's frailty, and the general view that, although women might work out of necessity, it was never a desirable state of affairs, entered the process as another kind of "unarticulated premise," whether or not it was also explicitly stated.

In some cases, legislation regarding women's work was struck down. In 1895, the Illinois Supreme Court held that there were no such reasonable grounds for a law limiting women workers in factories to eight hours a day. Since woman was to be considered a "citizen" and a "person" under the Constitution, her right to acquire and possess property, and her right to a livelihood, must not be limited: "Before the law, her right to a choice of vocations cannot be said to be denied or abridged on account of sex."[50] Some occupations were forbidden altogether to women, but the court specifically did not comment on this issue, since the act in question did not claim that the occupations being restricted were improper for women. It then stated that just because an occupation was considered dangerous for a man, like working in the manufacture of white lead or in some iron-smelting jobs which "materially shortened" the lives of the men involved, was no ground for prohibiting men from working at those jobs. No such prohibition against women would be constitutional either.

In 1907, a New York court also struck down a no-night-work law for women on the grounds that it was "certainly, discriminative against female citizens, in denying to them equal rights with men in the same pursuits."[51] The night work prohibition was not defended as a health measure, and the court noted that this was the first time that the state had attempted to "restrict [women's] liberty of person, or their freedom of contract, in the pursuit of a vocation."[52] It added, "An adult female is not to be regarded as a ward of the state, or in any other light than the man is regarded, when the question relates to the business pursuit or calling."[53] However, just a few years later, in 1910, the Illinois court upheld a law which limited women's hours of work to ten. It ignored the argument that the law was still designed only to protect individuals (not "the community health or welfare") and decided that a ten-hour limit could be considered "reasonable" and might also have been upheld in the earlier case if that law had been a ten-hour law instead of eight.

Where the law was struck down, the court held that, with respect to the limitation imposed, women were to be treated equally with men, and since no such limit was (or possibly could be) imposed on men also, the law was invalid. But when the law was upheld, it was frequently based on assumptions about women's greater need for protection. For example, a Nebraska law which limited women's working hours to ten per day and also forbade night work for them was upheld as early as 1902 on the grounds that "women and children [had] always, to a certain extent, been wards of the state."[54] The court went on to state that women are unable, by reason of their physical

> limitations, to endure the same hours of exhaustive work as may be endured by adult males. Certain kinds of work which may be performed by men without injury to their health would wreck the constitutions and destroy the health of women, and render them incapable of bearing their share of the burdens of the family and the home.[55]

The court added that laws which would interfere with the right of adult males in this fashion would be unconstitutional, since "the employer and the laborer [were] practically on an equal footing, but these observations [did] not apply to women and children." It went on to state that "of the many vocations in this country, comparatively few [were] open to women," and that the competition for these jobs resulted in an unfair advantage for the employer.[56]

The physical frailty of women was also used to uphold a law limiting the hours of work in a Washington decision in 1902, which stated for the first time, according to George Groat, what was to become a leading justification for protective labor laws for women after Muller. The judge concluded:

> It is a matter of universal knowledge with all reasonably intelligent people of the present age that continuous standing on the feet by women for a great many consecutive hours is deleterious to their health. It must logically follow that that which would deleteriously affect any great number of women who are the mother of succeeding generations must necessarily affect the public welfare and the public morals.[57]

He also commented that law is "a progressive science" and ought to respond to changing conditions. Rights of employment which in the past were considered inalienable were now, due to the "necessity of changed conditions," subject to legislative control. This time, the court stated the following:

> It is known to all men (and what we know as men we cannot profess to be ignorant of as judges) that women's physical structure and the performance of maternal functions place her at a great disadvantage in the battle of life . . . It would therefore seem obvious that legislation which limits the [hours to ten per day] would tend to preserve the health of women and insure the production of vigorous offspring by them, and would directly conduce to the health, morals and general welfare of the public, and that such legislation would fall clearly within the police power of the state.[58]

As Groat noted, the two principles, that women are, and are not, different from men in ways that justify treatment by law, stand in direct contrast to each other, lending credence to the view that the courts are in fact free to choose their premises. When presented with two conflicting patterns of precedent, the court can rely on whichever one it wishes, and either ignore or explicitly disavow the other. It is here, then, that the "systematic" nature of the law visibly comes apart at the seams and reveals the ways in which the law is dependent upon, or a response to, changing social conditions.

The question, then, is in whose interests these protective labor laws were being passed, and how the different groups defined their interests over time. Although social reform legislation of all kinds was attacked for its "socialistic" tendencies, proponents of such laws usually saw them as anything but revolutionary. On the contrary, one rationale for this kind of legislation was that it would tend to reduce class strife.

A representative example of the opposition to these laws is that of Rome Brown, who filed the brief in Stettler v. O'Hara (minimum wage law in Oregon). Brown made the following statement:

> This sort of legislation is a new expression of the paternalistic and socialistic tendencies of the day. It savors of the division of property between those who have and those who have not, and the leveling of fortunes by division under governmental supervision. It is consistent with the orthodox socialist creed, but it is not consistent with the principles of our government which are based upon the protection of individual rights.[59]

This attitude was also expressed on the other side of the bar by Justice Brewer in an address before the New York Bar Association (1893), an address which also illustrates the connections among corporate lawyers, the bar, and the bench. Before this group, among friends, the justice, who was later to hand down the decision in Lochner (striking down a ten-hour law for bakers), proclaimed the need to strengthen the judiciary by insulating judges from popular pressure in order to defend the "ten thousand millions of dollars invested in railroad property." Faced with the frequent necessity of going "before the people for re-election," he said that judges need support to buck popular sentiment and

> to stay the wave of popular feeling, to restrain the greedy hand of the many filching from the few . . . The black flag of anarchism flaunting destruction to property, and therefore relapse of society to barbarism; the red flag of socialism inviting a re-distribution of property, which in order to secure the vaunted equality, must be repeated again and again, at constantly decreasing intervals . . . against these schemes . . . the eager and earnest cry and protest of the Anglo Saxon is for individual freedom and absolute protection of all his rights of person and property.[60]

Against this view (which was also reiterated in the business journals of the National Association of Manufacturers almost until World War I) was the view of social reformers. Since legislation could be upheld under the police power if it tended to promote the public welfare, they argued that these laws did precisely that, if for no other reason than that they tended to limit industrial strife. R. Pound contended that the court decision which struck down a Colorado law regulating payment of wages to miners in that state was a bad mistake: "The assumption that the public had no interest in the way in which miners' wages were paid, which dictated the decision, was speedily refuted by the ensuing wrangles, strikes and disorders, due to attempts to secure by force what could not be had by law."[61] Seager also connected the Colorado Supreme Court's decision with labor unrest, saying that whatever connection the "embittered struggle to secure the eight-hour day may have had with the sanguinary labor troubles, from which Colorado [had] recently suffered," could best be judged by those there to see.[62] If the issue is really social well-being and not just an individualistic freedom of contract, certain questions then become social and economic issues, rather than narrow legalistic ones: for example, "whether it is unreasonable and oppressive to secure industrial peace by compelling employer and employee to arbitrate . . . [or] . . . to alleviate the poverty of the servant by requiring that the master increase her wages."[63]

Promoting industrial peace was also explicitly mentioned by the court as a reason for upholding a Tennessee truck act as early as 1899. After noting the (substantive) inequality between the laborer and his employer in the matter of wages, which the act in question tended (however "slight it may be") to correct, the court continued:

> The passage of the act was a legitimate exercise of the police power . . . Besides the amelioration of the employee's condition, the act was intended and is well calculated to promote the public peace and good order and to lessen the growing tendency to strife, violence and even bloodshed in certain departments of important trade and business.[64]

Perhaps it is in this context that the contention that these laws were in the best interests of the community may be understood.

CONCLUSION

In this chapter, I have examined the way in which legal principles created the climate in which protective labor laws were developed, and also how those laws responded to changes in economic and social conditions in the society. In the United States, judicial review, that is, the Supreme Court's power to declare state laws unconstitutional, had a strong influence. European countries like England did not have to worry that the Factory Acts or minimum wage rates would be struck down by the judiciary. American reformers felt this difference keenly when minimum wage legislation for women was declared unconstitutional in 1923.

Court decisions are couched in language that makes the law appear to rest on principles like freedom of contract and due process. But, as legal scholars of the period pointed out, a court which is free to choose its principles and selectively use precedent need not fear the rules of logic. Around the turn of the century, state legislatures passed labor laws which limited employers' power over their workers, both male and female. They used their right to legislate under the police power to protect the "health and welfare" of the community, and also the real control employers exerted over the "wage bargain," which made it coercive, not freely contracted. The courts sometimes upheld these laws, and sometimes struck them down as unwarranted legislative meddling.

State legislatures, then, passed labor laws which seemed "reasonable" (a legal term of imprecise meaning in practise), that is, which drew on the prevailing custom and culture of the time. Judges and legislatures both took for granted that women's position as wives and mothers was their foremost consideration. Women's employment, given the prevailing family structure and wage structure, was subordinated to that position. Therefore, laws which limited or circumscribed women's employment did not seem "unreasonable." This stance was balanced by the employers' opposition to any legislation interfering in the way they dealt with "their" workers.

During this period, employers gradually came to accept the fact of labor legislation for both men and women workers, even though they sought to overturn it in the courts (and evade it in their factories). However, there was one kind of legislation which was *not* accepted throughout this period, and that was minimum wage regulation for women. The rationale for this type of law was qualitatively different than that for other kinds of labor legislation. Even though it was not proposed in this country until other types of limitations (like hours laws) were fairly common, it was not accepted by the court. The next chapter will discuss the special issues surrounding the passage of minimum wage legislation; the discussion will attempt to clarify the reason for its failure despite the growing acceptance of protective labor legislation.

Drawn by Nina E. Allender

THE PARTING OF THE WAYS

Chapter Four
Minimum Wage Legislation: Legal and Economic Aspects

INTRODUCTION

The economic changes just described and the characteristics of developing capitalism created changes in workers' lives and their relation to their work as the production process under capitalism developed along certain lines and foreclosed others. Opposition by workers to the naked exploitation of long hours, low pay, and life-threatening working conditions was expressed in the strikes, "unrest," and violence which periodically erupted during this period. There was also nuisance value, if not threat, from socialist and anarchist groups, including the Industrial Workers of the World (IWW). But the majority of organized labor tended to define its role rather narrowly: they were concerned with craft protection rather than class interest. Their actions speak louder than their words here: they excluded women and blacks, they opposed immigration, and they had a general tendency to write off unskilled labor completely, all of which speaks of a very limited kind of opposition to capital.

The American Federation of Labor (AFL) did not favor legislation as a means of improving working conditions, fearing that doing so might undermine the impulse to organize unions, although in England and other places it had had precisely the opposite effect. In England, unions supported the Factory Acts, minimum wage rates, and other measures for all workers, not just for women and children. But in the United States, the unions' position tended to reinforce the limited legislation which emerged, since unions supported it, finally, for women but not generally for men.

And the wage scales which were adopted under these laws reflected the accepted differential between men's and women's wages.

The type of labor legislation in which economic issues were most sharply defined was minimum wage legislation, because wage rates cannot be determined solely by legalistic arguments but must refer to existing, substantive conditions of life among wage earners. In this country, minimum wage legislation was among the last kind of protective labor legislation to be accepted as constitutional. After laws regulating hours of work, night work, seating, and rest periods were accepted as legitimate, minimum wage regulations for women were still being struck down by the courts. Minimum wage laws at this time were generally written only for women workers (and sometimes for children), not for men workers. It was not until the New Deal that they were finally upheld as constitutional, this time for both men and women.

Economic and social changes in the society during this period can be seen through the different arguments used in defense of, and in opposition to, these laws. Some employers who finally conceded the right of workers to unionize remained adamantly opposed to minimum wage legislation as an unwarranted interference in the way they ran their businesses. Moreover, this kind of legislation appeared to employers to have the most direct effect on profits, much more so than, for example, laws prohibiting night work for women. Possibly for this reason, this legislation was strongly opposed first by employers, and later, but for different reasons, by women's groups. This chapter will examine the legal ideologies with which these laws were debated and will then look at the specific economic conditions and living standards of women workers and families during the period.

HISTORY OF MINIMUM WAGE LAWS

During the fourteenth century and after, wage fixing existed in the context of mercantile or feudal economic relations. It was not a minimum but a fixed wage, and by the seventeenth and eighteenth centuries in England these local systems of wage determination disappeared as capitalist relations of wage labor and capital began to emerge. This kind of wage fixing is therefore not comparable to modern minimum wage rates, although attempts to discredit it sometimes noted the similarity.

The first capitalist wage regulation was in 1894 in New Zealand, where conciliation boards were established to set minimum wage rates as a means to end "sweated" labor. Wage regulation was also introduced in

Victoria in six specific trades in 1896, over bitter opposition from employers.[1] Rates were extended to cover every major trade (except agricultural occupations) in a matter of a few years. Although this legislation was opposed by many employers, the government claimed that it also had support for wage rates from employers who had asked that their businesses be covered. By 1904 wage boards were considered a part of industrial life in Victoria. In England a system of wage regulation developed a few years later, but by 1912 it was extended there too, to cover coal miners after a strike occurred in 1912 which paralyzed the industry.[2]

As late as 1911 in the United States, an extensive discussion of labor legislation, *Attitude of American Courts in Labor Cases*, by George Groat contained no reference whatever to minimum wage regulation. Some regulation of wage rates in public employment developed after the turn of the century, but not in private enterprise. By 1912, the first state to pass minimum wage legislation, Massachusetts, had established a commission to study industrial conditions and to set wage rates. Minimum wage boards were set up in several states from 1912 on, but although there was a court case which challenged the constitutionality of minimum wage legislation in 1917, the court did not actually rule on it but let stand lower courts' approval of the law. Therefore, in 1923, when a Washington, D.C., minimum wage law for women was declared unconstitutional, it evoked special indignation, the more so for being unexpected on the basis of recent decisions upholding other protective labor laws.

During the period covered here, during which monopoly capitalism emerged, a corresponding shift in the role of the state was also being negotiated. The increase in government regulation (and hence, determination) of spheres of private business activity such as transport meant that business interests became inseparable from government activity; thus business interests administered government policy in areas that affected those interests.

In the late nineteenth century, court decisions providing the legal environment within which businesses could flourish established the legitimacy of government regulation in businesses that were "affected with a public interest." Although the ideology of laissez-faire was intended to prevent this intervention from doing harm to "business and commerce," social and economic changes in the country were leading to new relations between the state and civil society. Arguments for and against the minimum wage reveal these tensions. Investigations by government and unofficial social reform agencies like the National Consumers' League were carried on to show the prevailing conditions and wage rates in various industries in differing locales.

As noted, minimum wage legislation was not even considered seriously in the United States until labor legislation affecting the hours of work (usually ten per day and fifty-four or sixty per week) and no-night-work laws for women were being accepted both by courts and by employers. The shift in the courts' attitudes towards hours laws is clear from two sets of court decisions, one in Illinois regulating hours per day for women (the two Ritchie cases, one in 1895 striking down an eight-hour law, and one in 1910 upholding a ten-hour law), and the other in New York prohibiting night work for women (in 1907 in People v. Williams this law was struck down, and in People v. Schweinler Press in 1915 it was upheld). The two night work cases in New York are interesting legally because in the first case no attempt was made to justify the law by using substantive evidence that night work is dangerous to health or safety, while the second made extensive use of such evidence in a Brandeis Brief type of argument and was upheld.

Unlimited "right to contract" arguments were losing their effectiveness (although they were far from dead), and employers were realizing that labor regulations might not only be in the workers' interests but might also benefit some employers. The industrial studies of fatigue and worker efficiency and the growing demand for worker's compensation had made this clear. But regulating wages was another matter entirely.

THE WAGE BARGAIN: LAISSEZ-FAIRE IDEOLOGY IN THE LAW

What determines the price of labor? That is the basic question behind minimum wage arguments. Not all employers opposed a minimum wage from the start, and not all workers favored it (at least in the United States). But both sides recognized that it could have potentially profound effects not just on wages but on the processes of production.

The primary objection of employers to the minimum wage law was based in part on the same arguments used against other labor legislation in the past—that it was an infringement on the right to contract the conditions of labor, and that it was class legislation, that is, favoring one group at the expense of another; for these reasons it violated "due process" and "equal protection" clauses of the Constitution. Legal arguments did not distinguish between men and women workers on this point. Speaking against the wage regulation, Rome Brown (counsel for the employers in the Oregon minimum wage cases) in 1917 argued that the law:

1) fixes a wage based solely upon the individual needs of the employee, measured not by anything which has relation to the fact of employment or to the particular occupation in question, but measured solely by the individual needs of the person employed . . .

2) it puts the burden on the employer to supply these individual needs to the extent that the money required therefore is in excess of what the employee earns, or can earn, or is worth . . .[3]

The Oregon law, in Brown's opinion, went even further than the Massachusetts law in violating the Constitution because it was "directly compulsory and penal."[4] The Massachusetts law was "non-compulsory" because the only penalty for violation was that the name of the employers who refused to pay the minimum would be published in the newspapers. Brown commented, "Such a statute holds over every employer the threat of an official, public blacklist and boycott, more severe and more damaging that any private boycott ever established."[5] But the most significant objection was that the board fixed different wages for different occupations, as well as different kinds of jobs within a given occupation. Brown asked:

As the wage is fixed irrespective of the earning capacity of the employee and is theoretically based upon the individual cost of living, then why has one worker a right to a living wage greater than that of another? . . . Moreover, each wage, when fixed, is only a stepping-stone to a higher wage. Each class of emploļyees is constantly seeking an increase . . . regardless of the worth of the employee to the employer.[6]

Here he is expressing the employers' fear, as E.O. Wright pointed out, that once a benefit or social reform is accepted as a right, the result is to make that the new standard, and any cutbacks become delegitimating.

Since the courts had upheld other laws restricting the employment contract, it was necessary to show that this law was different if it were to be struck down. An Oregon maximum hours statute had been upheld by the court because it was considered a legitimate use of the police power in the interests of public health and welfare. But the minimum wage law was different from the state's power to regulate both hours and wages in *public* employment; it was also different from workmen's compensation acts, which protected the worker from job-related hazards. The court had decided that these statutes did have "real, substantial relation" to the employment itself. The state could also regulate *rates* of public services because these businesses were "quasi-public," or "affected with a public interest," factors which justified the regulation in the court's eyes. But *wage* regulation between private parties was a different matter, counsel contended:

> The need to any person of a "living" is an *individual* need. It exists before employment, and during employment, and after employment. Such need is, indeed, diminished, or supplied, during employment to the extent of the wage actually paid. Hazards and dangers that arise from this individual need are less with employment than they are without employment. The need itself is one which is a natural or purely individual need and has no origin in the fact of employment.[7]

The problem with minimum wage laws, counsel stated, is that they assume that every individual has a "generic right" to receive not just mere subsistence, but the "full means of living in health and comfort, including reasonable expenditures for pleasure and diversion." And if the individual cannot earn this living, the law then demands that it be paid "by the one who happens to have that individual on his pay-roll," even if it has to come out of his profits, or if that is not possible, then out of his capital. If the owner canot support this need, then he will have to go out of business and will also be charged with being a "parasite" because he cannot pay this "forced contribution."[8]

The other possible precedent for justifying the minimum wage for women, (aside from the police power to regulate areas of public health or welfare), was that inequalities in the bargaining power of employer and employee warranted state intervention. But this justification, counsel argued, was refuted by the reasoning used in another case:

> And, since it is self-evident that, unless all things are held in common, some persons must have more property than others, it is from the nature of things impossible to uphold freedom of contract and the right of private property without at the same time recognizing as legitimate those inequalities of fortune that are the necessary result of the exercise of those rights.[9]

The argument which was carried before the Supreme Court also followed this line of legal reasoning. In the brief before the court in Stettler v. O'Hara on behalf of the plaintiffs (employers), counsel argued that the minimum wage statute for women was in principle no different from the statute applying to men: "One right which nature has conferred equally on men and women is the right to work for a living at such wages as he or she shall deem satisfactory, and at such employment as he or she shall choose if it be not harmful to others or to himself or herself."[10] That right is unquestioned regarding men, and, he argued, there is no reason in this instance to distinguish men from women in their need for protection. Although Muller and other cases had established the need for women to be protected from long hours because of their "physical structure and powers of endurance," and although that need had been established in some occupations for men as well, counsel argued (in a somewhat irrelevant aside, since hours laws were based on supposed physical limitations) that the "control" which men had established over women was now a thing of the past. Women had the vote in Oregon and most of the Pacific states, as well as the right to hold office. The legal and social position of women was approaching equality with men:

> Their influence in public affairs is equally as potent as is that of the men. They are in all states largely entering the professions and are competing on equal terms with their brothers in every industry and line of employment to which their physical strength is adapted. In truth, from many lines of employment they are, because of their superior qualifications, excluding men.[11]

Counsel further stated that hours legislation was based on the public's interest in "the preservation of a vigorous race and in preventing citizens from becoming dependents on public charity" through ill health. Since "women are more delicately organized than men, and hence a woman's health may be injured when and where a man's would not," such laws could legitimately go further in regulating women's work than in regulating men's.[12] But a minimum wage involved different principles entirely: it concerned the value of a commodity, labor, which depends, like other commodities, on the laws of supply and demand. Unlimited price fixing by the legislature would be preposterous.

If the law would require that work be paid in excess of its market price, for the "public benefit," then the logical response of the employer would be, "If the public requires this, the public should pay the difference." [13] Employers argued that these laws could not be justified on the grounds that they protected public health or the morals of women, because the same might be said of men. Moreover: "the wage does not in anywise affect the physical or moral well-being of the employee. It may not be sufficient of itself to support him in health and comfort, but *it aids him in so doing*. So far as it goes, it contributes to the well-being of the employee."[14]The workers' wage is not part of the problem but part of the solution: "The wages paid, however inadequate to support, inflict no injury.

They may not be sufficient to supply every comfort, but so far as they go, they contribute to the comfort and welfare of the earner."[15]

In the Stettler case, the lower court's decision prevailed because of a split court, since one justice did not participate. (Brandeis had just been appointed to the court, but was involved in preparing the brief for counsel.) In other states also, such legislation was upheld initially. Courts made plain that they were not passing on the wisdom of such laws, which would only become clear with time, but solely on the issue of whether it was "reasonable" to think that detrimental conditions existed and might be remedied by the laws passed by the legislature.

Although the Oregon minimum wage law applied only to women, that state also passed an hours law which applied to both men and women. The law set a limit of ten hours of work per day, but provided that time-and-a-half overtime must be paid between ten and thirteen hours per day. This law was challenged in Bunting v. Oregon for being a wage law, not a health law; for arbitrarily defining the class of employments which it affected (that is, mills, factories, and manufacturing establishments); and for taking property without due process. The wage provision for overtime was intended to aid in the enforcement of the law, but this intention was disputed by lawyers for the employer (the owner of a flour mill), and the attack on the law was directed mainly at the wage provision:

> Insufficiency of wage does not justify legislative regulation . . . It can scarcely be seriously contended that the amount of money one receives for his labor has any bearing upon his health. If the amount of money received as a wage is not sufficient to support a laborer in that one of the numerous modes of living which he selects as the proper one for himself, is society to demand of the employer an arbitrary increase in wages regardless of the ability of the business to support such increase?[16]

Although a substantive ("Brandeis") brief of over one thousand pages was prepared in defense of the law, the opposition argued that the court must confine itself to the situation before it, and that "not a single page [was] devoted to the health dangers inherent in work in a flour mill." They conceded that work in flour mills used to be unhealthy, but argued that with changed technology and improved milling methods, it was no longer so. In reply to the charges that mortality figures demonstrated that the occupation was unhealthy, counsel for Bunting contended that mortality figures could not be used to judge health hazards in a given employment. Age of death, cause, and other factors cited from a U.S. Bureau of

Labor source suggested that working in a flour mill was "favorable to life *and health.*"[17]

This case, which upheld an hours law for *men* in nonhazardous industries, was argued by presenting voluminous evidence of the effects of overwork on the physical and moral health of *all* workers, male and female. However, what seemed scientific and "reasonable," legally speaking, to the Supreme Court in 1917 was declared "indiscriminative legislative and judicial jugglery . . . whereby property rights [were] being curtailed," in the court's opinion in 1922.[18]

In summary, employers argued against minimum wage legislation by claiming that the wage bargain was a private matter to be decided by individual employers and employees, and that any interference with this bargain was an infringement on their rights of freedom of contract. Since wages represented the "worth" of the worker, the employer was under no obligation to provide full support to the worker. Women were considered the equal of men in this respect. Employers contended that wage labor was a commodity with a price like any other, and that minimum wage laws were a kind of price fixing. They denied that any circumstances differentiated women workers from men in this respect.

DEFEAT OF THE MINIMUM WAGE AND THE
EMERGENCE OF FEMINIST OPPOSITION

In the 1923 decision in Adkins v. Children's Hospital, which centered on a minimum wage regulation for women in the District of Columbia (and was therefore under congressional rather than state jurisdiction), the Supreme Court again came up on the side of freedom of contract and in opposition to regulation of the wage bargain. However, times had changed since the last significant decision regarding wages in 1917. Women had the vote nationally. In addition, a principled feminist position had begun to express opposition to all special provisions for women if they did not also apply to men (see chapter 5). Employers could therefore expand their usual arguments regarding contract and property rights to include the "new position" of women.

In 1922 Justice Van Orsdel, speaking for the lower court (and cited by the brief opposing the law before the Supreme Court), contended that to say that an employer had to pay a wage sufficient "to protect the morals" of women, as the law stated, was "a reflection upon their intelligence."[19] The dire implications of the law and the direction such government regulation was taking were explicitly spelled out by counsel:

"Price fixing means the control of all industry by the state, and the control of all industry means government ownership, and government ownership means the leveling of all men and women to an industrial army working for the state—and then production ends. This was the experience of Russia."[20] In this respect, counsel Ellis was elaborating on a point, made by the lower court, which deplored "the tendency of the times to socialize property rights under the subterfuge of police regulation." He said further, "Of the three fundamental principles which underlie government, and for which government exists—the protection of life, liberty and property—the chief of these is property."[21]

However, in addition to playing on antisocialist sentiment, employers also could invoke women's rights: "Can it be that the women of this country favor such laws, and especially for them alone? . . . All over the country today thoughtful and progressive women are contending for industrial equality which follows as a natural and logical sequence to political equality."[22] Ellis cited National Woman's Party opposition to labor laws for women only (see chapter 5) and other women's groups, including the Equal Rights Association, Carrie Chapman Catt of the National Women's Suffrage Association, and the Federation of Business and Professional Women's Clubs, all of which were on record against minimum wage laws and other labor legislation that applied only to women. With the possible exception of the Equal Rights Association, all of these groups held feminist views concerning women's equality with men and also considered these laws to be "protecting women out of their jobs."[23]

Counsel for the employers argued that the harmful effects of the bill could be seen in the fate of Willie Lyons (plaintiff), who worked as an elevator operator in a hotel, for which she was paid $35.00 per month and two meals per day. The Wage Board allowed $18.00 per month as the value of the meals (which actually, counsel argued, was much greater).

> But, at any rate, she was satisfied with the terms of her employment—contented in her work, and she wanted to keep her job. But the Minimum Wage Board said this woman needed special police protection. They ordained that she must get $71.50 per month, without regard to meals. And so she lost her job.[24]

Ellis dismissed the idea that she might have been coerced or otherwise induced to act against her own best interest, saying that perhaps those who believe in such laws would also deny her the right to sue on the grounds that she can't decide what is in her own interest. Dissociating himself from this patronizing attitude, he stated:

The women of this country are entitled to a little more respect than that. They want, and they deserve, equal rights with men. They believe in self-reliance, independence and character. And they believe that the right to make their own bargains will result ultimately in better pay, a finer sense of self-respect and a higher quality of citizenship.[25]

One senator from Missouri (quoted at length in the legal argument before the Supreme Court), speaking in opposition to the bill, asked:

Do women need protection? Are women unable to take care of themselves? . . . In one breath you are standing here telling us they are capable of performing all the duties of citizenship; . . . and that they are entitled to these privileges because of their intellectual equality if not their mental superiority over men, and in the next breath you say they are children and they need guardians and commissions to look after their wage. Where now are the knightly ladies whose flaunting banners have recently been borne back and forth in front of the White House and who have demanded with militant processes militant rights? . . . to repudiate and denounce this ignominious classification with infants.[26]

In 1923 the Court struck down the District of Columbia minimum wage law, much to the surprise of both sides. Choosing its precedents carefully, the Court made no mention of the previous minimum wage law in Oregon which it had let stand in 1917, but instead invoked Lochner v. New York (the 1905 decision which struck down a ten-hour law for bakers, and had been allowed to lie fallow throughout the upsurge of protective labor legislation in the interim). Chief Justive Taft's dissent said that he had always thought that the Lochner decision had been "overruled sub silentio."

In the majority opinion, delivered by Justice Sutherland, laissez-faire, individualist principles, and the new position of women were all used to strike down the law. The extensive two-volume "Brandeis" brief (this time prepared by Felix Frankfurter with Mary W. Dewson of the National Consumers' League) was dismissed by Justice Sutherland as "interesting but only mildly persuasive."[27] He stated that the function of such substantive evidence [was] to establish the desirability of the legislation, but could not decide upon its "validity," and that "the elucidation of that question [could not] be aided by counting heads."[28]

In saying this, Sutherland was, in effect, denying the legitimate function of substantive evidence in court, since it is not designed to "prove" the facts it sets forth, but rather to demonstrate that a body of evidence exists which makes it "reasonable" for the legislature to accept it. Instead, he stated the laissez-faire position that "freedom of contract is ... the general rule and restraint the exception; and the exercise of legislative authority to abridge it can be justified only by the existence of exceptional circumstances."[29]

In addition, Justice Sutherland accepted the view of the "wage bargain" that laissez-faire opponents of minimum wage had used in the brief against the law:

> To the extent that the sum fixed exceeds the fair value of the services rendered, it amounts to a compulsory exaction from the employer for the support of a partially indigent person, for whose condition there rests upon him no particular responsibility, and therefore, in effect, arbitrarily shifts to his shoulders a burden which, if it belongs to anybody, belongs to society as a whole.[30]

He stated that the law in question was "simply and exclusively a price-fixing law, confined to adult women ... who [were] legally as capable of contracting for themselves as men."[31] He disputed the claim that there was any connection between wages and women's morals, and said that, in any event, if women needed a minimum wage "to preserve their morals, men require[d] it to preserve their honesty."[32]

The aspect of Justice Sutherland's decision which invoked the most indignation was his argument that since women now had political equality with men (the vote), such a distinction between men and women was unwarranted. However, feminist opponents were pleased. The decision was quoted at length in the National Woman's Party Journal, *Equal Rights*, which was delighted with the "advance by the Supreme Court over its attitude toward women" since the Muller case in 1908. They approved of the reasoning in the decision (including the defense of liberty contract regarding women), and noted:

> The courts are among the last places to express changes in popular opinion. When one finds the Supreme Court of the U.S. beginning to realize ... that women should be "accorded emancipation from the old doctrine that she must be given special protection ..." one can feel that at last the world is beginning to realize that women are adult human beings.[33]

By contrast, the dissenting opinion of Justice Holmes stated, "It will need more than the 19th Amendment to convince me that there are no differences between men and women, or that legislation cannot take those differences into account."[34] He also denied that a distinction could be made between the legislature's right to regulate one side of the contract (hours) and not the other (wages). Justice Taft concurred that "the 19th Amendment did not change the physical strength or limitations of women upon which ... Muller v. Oregon rests."[35] Commentaries attacking the decision picked up on this point, arguing that minimum wage legislation was not directed at political or civil inequalities of women, but "upon evils to society resulting from the exploitation of women in industry, who *as a class labor under a tremendous economic handicap*." The problem was said to be one of "economic fact, not of political, contractual or civil status."[36]

Thus, legal arguments surrounding the passage and constitutionality of minimum wage laws during the period before and after World War I used the same legal justifications that other kinds of protective labor laws did, but because of the success of the women's suffrage movement following the war and the first equal rights amendment agitation, new kinds of issues arose. Truly "feminist" arguments were articulated, especially by the National Woman's Party, which opposed all special protections, privileges, or limitations for women. When an employer argued for his "girls'" right to freely contract with him for twelve and fourteen hours a day at starvation wages, it is doubtful at best to think he was really subscribing to the principle of equal rights for women—not even the right to be equally exploited with men—since he in fact was exploiting them *more* by paying them *less* (on principle). But when, after a period of several years' deliberation, some suffragists decided to support an equal rights amendment and an end to sex-based legislation in all spheres, in full cognizance of the difficulties which this legislation would cause, a qualitatively new kind of opposition had appeared. They recognized the economic hardships which women were subjected to as women and determined that this kind of inequality must also be overcome, but they denied that special legislation for women could achieve that aim. On the contrary, they contended that these laws were having precisely the opposite effect of what was intended— they hampered women in competing effectively with men for better-paid, skilled jobs and consigned women to second-class status economically.

MINIMUM WAGE: ECONOMIC AND SOCIAL ASPECTS

Opposition to the laissez-faire view of the "wage bargain" described above centered on the question of what determines a wage. As shown, employers contended that there is a "value" of labor which is determined by the same market conditions that determine the value of other commodities; a minimum wage would in effect be a forced donation to the worker who was not "earning" the minimum, and would have disastrous economic repercussions. They were assuming that low-wage labor is also "low-value" labor, and that if an employer were forced to pay more than a worker was "worth" to him, either he would discharge the worker, or else lower the pay of those who were actually more efficient workers and worth "more" to him. The "minimum" would then tend to become the maximum, and benefit nobody.

This position was disputed by proponents of the legislation, who argued that "competition leads to a wage; but it does not necessarily follow that it leads to an 'economic' wage or to a 'fair' wage."[37] The "wage bargain" is affected by the relative powerlessness of one party, and therefore the going wage bears no necessary relation either to its worth or to the employer's ability to pay. One critic of the decision against minimum wage laws asked:

> And would the learned Justice [Sutherland] furnish the scale for ascertaining and measuring what this "worth" [of the labor performed] might be! The range of opinion swings all the way from that of the Marxian socialist who maintains that the whole product and nothing less is the "worth"—the true equivalent of the laborer's toil ... to that of the most hard-fisted of employers, who maintains that in hard times they are worth nothing and in good as little as he can possibly pay.[38]

This view, that the "wage bargain" must not be seen in isolation from the social conditions which give rise to it, also entails the proposition that the employer bears some responsibility for the reproduction of the labor force. This is not "paternalistic" or a compulsory redistribution of property, it was argued; the statute simply says to the employer: "If you choose to seek profit from the labor of a woman, you must pay what it costs to keep her in condition to furnish that labor. If it is not to your advantage to pay for labor what it costs to produce it, you need not employ that labor."[39] The statute does not compel any employer to make a wage contract that they would not profit by, but states that if they do choose to so employ a woman (or child), there is a minimum below which the wage cannot fall. It is a law that is prohibitory rather than compulsory in nature; as Brandeis had commented: "How potent [are] the forces of conservatism that could have prevented our learning that like animals, men and women must be properly fed and properly housed, if they are to be useful workers and survive."[40]

Supporters of a minimum wage rate argued that if an employer pays less than it takes to support the labor he uses, then he is in effect a parasite on the community, since the differences must be made up from other sources. A legal minimum is necessary because wages are below the necessary cost of living. When starvation wages are paid, for example, to young girls in unskilled jobs when there is an oversupply of available labor, the difference is made up either by her family or by charity (including subsidized boarding houses and lunchrooms, which were common during the period). Or, as Henry Seager pointed out, they also die of undernutrition and sickness, or turn to prostitution. The minimum wage, then, "does commit organized society to a more responsible attitude toward the whole labor problem."[41] Since wages are not fixed by the "worth" of labor, but rather by the desperation of the "marginal" female worker, competition from other employers will force even the "fair" employer to squeeze wages down. Lack of regulation places the progressive employer at a disadvantage, one reformer argued. An example of this could be seen in Friday night laundry work. The practice of bringing in laundry to be done at the last minute worked great hardship on the women workers, who were forced to work long hours to meet the customers' expectations. Any individual laundry owner who attempted to close early would be at a disadvantage, but if all had to close, he would not fear loss of business. Similarly, Paul Kellogg pointed out, the protocol agreement in the garment industry was enforced by the employers as well as the workers in order to prevent unfair competition.[42]

Another, more long-range aspect to the question of "community interest" was expressed by Marx regarding the early Factory Acts in England: "Apart from the working-class movement that daily grew more threatening, the limiting of factory labour was dictated by the same necessity which spread guano over the English fields. The same blind eagerness for plunder that in one case exhausted the soil, had, in the other, torn up by the roots the living force of the nation."[43] That the total exhaustion of the work force was not an improbable outcome of such exploitation was argued in one editorial:

> An appalling mass of human wreckage has been produced by the assumption that legal freedom of contract could be ... when the parties to the bargain were respectively Might and Helplessness. Thanks to that assumption England finds herself with a population so nearly unfit for military service that the mere suggestion of war almost causes panic. She has ground up her men and money. America has made a long start on England's road of folly, as the conditions at Lawrence, for example, bear witness.[44]

The social unrest that would be averted and the physical degenera-
tion resulting from starvation wages were both used as practical reasons
why a minimum wage was in the community's best interests, regardless of
the morality of the issue. If a living wage were paid, one sufficient to
"enable the worker to support himself, his wife, and their children, . . .
you will not have then any more Industrial Workers of the World, or
societies of that type," stated a labor spokesman.[45] Far from leading toward
socialism, as critics of the measure asserted, it would be more accurate to
say that "this and other needed social reforms tend to make outright
socialism undesirable and unnecessary."[46]

RATIONALIZATION OF THE LABOR PROCESS

There were other consequences of a minimum wage, however. Employers forced to pay more for labor would then seek to use it more
efficiently and employ only labor which could operate at a high level of
productivity. It is clear that whether it was considered desirable or undesirable, setting a minimum wage would be a strong impetus to rationalizing methods of production.

Experience in Victoria and in England showed that the dire predic-
tions about wages falling to the minimum had not come to pass. According to Sidney Webb, wages there rose from 12 to 35 percent, hours were
reduced, and the number of employees in the five industries which had
introduced the minimum wage had increased. Moreover, the minimum
rate tended to increase productivity, especially where the rate was fixed
by piecework. It did not eliminate competition for employment, but "transfer[red] the pressure from one element in the bargain to another: from the
wage to the work, from price to quality." When there is no legal minimum, it may actually pay the employer to get inefficient labor (because it
is also cheap), but with a set minimum "he is economically impelled to do
his utmost to raise the level of efficiency of his workers, so as to get the
best possible return for the fixed conditions."[47] Seager also argued that,
with a minimum wage, industries depending on starvation wages would
either have to organize differently, or, being parasitic, cease.

The effect of the minimum wage, then, would be to drive out the
inefficient, incompetent *employer* in favor of those "most favorably situ-
ated, best equipped, and managed with the greatest ability."[48] It was
argued that the minimum wage "positively stimulate[d] the invention and
adoption of new processes of manufacture."[49]

Employers who favored the legislation were those who benefited by the qualitative change in the competition. Edward Filene, a Boston businessman, favored the law. Industry, he said, was under an obligation to pay a living wage, and a minimum wage law was needed to prevent "shortsighted employers" who were greedy and inefficient from setting the standard. He said, "The State has a right to step in, in such cases, and fix a limit beyond which cupidity shall not go," especially when the victims are inexperienced women and children. To the charge that such laws, since they are necessarily only statewide, would drive the industry out of the state with the law into neighboring ones with no law, Filene replied that if a business cannot be efficient and profitable, the state doesn't need it.[50] In this employers' "survival of the fittest," inefficient or wastefully managed firms would fall by the wayside.

These laws were expected to have the effect of driving out inefficient and backward *employers*, thereby forcing firms to use their labor more productively and to introduce new methods of production and machinery. Although this result was seen as a benefit by some, opponents of the laws pointed out that the other side of the coin was that less efficient *workers* would be thrown out of a job as well. Employers argued that they could not afford to pay some workers more money because they were not worth more; masses of poor, aged, and defective workers would then starve. Social reformers argued that these people would then have to be taken care of some other way, but that they were driving wages down when they competed with more efficient labor. These changes which minimum wages were expected to bring about were precisely the kinds of rationalization of production and the labor process described in chapter 2, which were already starting to take place. Minimum wage legislation did not create the impetus for these changes, but did help to further them.

STANDARD OF LIVING: WORKING CLASS FAMILIES

Regardless of the method used—whether a minimum wage rate was fixed by statute or whether it was set for each industry or occupation or for all women—some means had to be used to determine what a "reasonable" rate was. This required determining the standard of living which should be considered a minimum. The laws expressed this standard in various ways: "necessary cost of proper living and to maintain the health and welfare" (California); "necessary cost of living, maintain them in health, and supply the necessary comforts of life," as well as consider the "financial condition of the business" (Colorado); "a wage sufficient to maintain himself or herself under conditions consistent with his or her welfare" (applied to women and minors, Wisconsin); and "experienced adults, $1.25 a day" (fixed by Act, Utah, May 13, 1913).[51]

In the period immediately preceding the passage of these minimum wage laws, a number of studies of family budgets were done by charities, settlement houses, and universities, as well as by state or federal government agencies, including the Department of Labor and the Bureau of the Census. Many of the studies were done to document the wretched living conditions of the majority of workers in a given locale and to argue for ameliorative measures, including workman's insurance and protective labor laws. These studies were then used as evidence in "Brandeis Briefs" to demonstrate the need for legislation. Since this kind of legal argument depends upon substantive economic data, the findings of these various investigations were a crucial component of the legal case for hours laws and minimum wage laws.

Early studies of working class budgets were often done with an eye to determining what level of income was required to prevent a family from falling into "dependency" or to demonstrate the deplorable state of the poor. Allowing for differences in method, accuracy of reporting, and life-styles, all studies showed the high proportion of family income which went for food. Studies done in the time span discussed here showed considerable agreement on budgets and expenditures. Where the case-study method was used, they contained in-depth descriptions of wage earners' living standards. They also expressed the observer's judgments of the different families (neat, sloppy, industrious, indolent), and their view of the proper role of the wife and mother in the household economy.

One study, which is particularly useful for the range of detail and the fact that it included families of varying sizes, was done by Louise More under the auspices of Greenwich House, a social settlement in Greenwich Village in New York City. This was a case study of two hundred families living in the immediate area around Greenwich House. It set no income limits for the purposes of the study, but tried to include "as many families as possible above the so-called 'dependent class'," on the grounds that "the very poor [were] not representative of the normal workingman's family."[52] For twenty-five out of the two hundred families, the wife was the proper head of the family.[53] The largest single occupation of family heads was listed as truckman (22 families); then followed longshoreman (13), washerwoman (9), porter (8), factory worker (13), and others.[54] The size of the family included parents, children, boarders (but not lodgers, who just pay for a room), and other relatives or dependents who lived there six months or more a year. Older children were counted as boarders, since they usually contributed toward the family income but also kept money out for their own use. Therefore, the household budget, rather than the total income of family members, was the unit of study, in recognition of prevailing social conditions.

This study included families with two to ten members and showed income and expenditures separately for each family size. In general, as family size increased, income also increased, since boarders and children contributed to the household. The expenditure for food tended to increase both relatively and absolutely as the size of the household increased, but when there were seven or more in the family, the income also increased sufficiently to permit a smaller *percentage* to be spent on food. However, the larger the family, the smaller the amount of surplus per year, and with ten family members there was an average deficit.[55]

Expenses for food were extremely high for all families—generally from 40 to 50 percent of the total income; only with incomes of over $1,000 per year (the highest income category listed) did food expenses occasionally fall below about 35 percent.[56] The average income for the families was $851.00, of which 69 percent came from the husband, 9 percent from the wife, 12 percent from the children, and 9 percent from boarders and other sources. This study also described in detail the different nationalities represented and analyzed the data in terms of "racial traits". For example, it commented, "as might be expected, the German, French and Italian families were the most provident";[57] and "The characteristic French thrift cannot be well illustrated here, because of the poverty of two of the families studied."[58]

In analyzing the data, More emphasized the potentially negative effect of the wife working. Comparatively few families were completely dependent upon the husband's income—mainly those with young children. As the children grew a little older, the mother could contribute financially to the family's support, but More said, "As soon as he [the husband] sees that the wife can help support the family, his interest and sense of responsibility are likely to lessen, and he works irregularly or spends more on himself."[59] Then, as the children grew still older, *they* worked and the mother could again stay home. For all of the larger families (five or more) in the study, from one to five children were also working.[60] In addition, More stated that "thrift [seemed] to be the most marked in nations in which the preponderance of the income [was] from the husband," since the highest average surplus was reported by three Norwegian families in which 97.8 percent of the income was from the father. This group also had the largest total family income. The absolute and relative amount devoted to "sundries" also increased with income; sundries included medical expenses as well as "spending money," drink, and other expenses.[61]

The case-study method used by More evoked judgments by the interviewer about the character and competence of the wife and the responsibility and morality of the husband, although primary emphasis was placed
upon income level:

> The standards of a well-ordered household in this neighborhood rec-
> ognize the wife as the financier of the family group. It is ... the
> regular standard of respectability that a good husband should turn
> over to his wife all his wages, receiving one or two dollars a week for
> his personal use ... Provided the income is of average size and fairly
> steady, the comfort of the whole family depends upon whether the
> mother is a good manager or not. Hence the character and ideals of
> the women are of the highest importance in determining the stand-
> ard of living of each family.[62]

Sometimes, the woman was "an attractive, ambitious wife" but unable to
do well because of the low or irregular income of her husband caused by
illness, "lack of enterprise," or intemperance. Similarly, if the woman was
"improvident and shiftless, the standard of the family [was] equally so."[63]
This study also described sample family budgets of "typical" families in
each income range, and considered the attitudes and "moral" qualities of
the husband and wife, especially whether the house was clean and neat
and whether the wife could sew, as an indication of "thrift and providence." Aside from their virtues or vices as housekeepers, the women
generally were characterized as having very narrow lives, with "few interests outside their homes,"[64] although some families made great sacrifices
to educate a child or to provide them with cultural advantages like music
lessons. One Italian stonecutter's wife was described as a "stupid peasant,
but ... ambitious for her children, who were pretty and bright."[65]

In some cases, the woman herself was unaware of her buying habits
until she made out the family expense account for the study. One woman
felt she usually spent $7.00 a week for food, but when she was questioned
more closely, the pattern of her actual expenditures was shown to vary
depending on whether the rent was due that week; so the food allowance
in that family actually was $4.00, not $7.00, every other week.

When clothing was needed—shoes or a coat—food also suffered in
many households. This indicates how close the families were to the subsistence level. In fact, the average wage earner's family was "continually
on the verge of dependence," and half the families studied had been so. If,
as More said, the poverty level was put at "that rate of earnings which
puts the family intermittently in the dependent class," then all the families

in this study who had been unable to save for the future were near that line.[66] Only forty-seven out of the two hundred families showed a surplus of income over expenditures at the end of the year,[67] and those were mostly the smaller families.

The advantage of this study was that it included families of all sizes, and the interview data were obtained in a situation in which there was already an established rapport between the interviewer and the family. Although the value judgments of the interviewer clearly led to some families being eliminated from the study altogether, what remains is a sample which is from an established, working-class neighborhood and a close-up picture of buying habits and living expenses.

Another study of New York City wage-earning families, by the Russell Sage Foundation, was done shortly after the Greenwich House study under the supervision of Robert Coit Chapin. Dependent families were excluded, and, as far as possible, only "normal"-sized families were included—that is, those with both parents living at home, with two to four children under sixteen, and with an income of $500 to $1,000. Less than half the families were dependent upon only the father's earnings, while in the More study, only twenty-three out of the two hundred families had only the father's earnings, and none were dependent solely upon the mother's where she was the "head of household."[68] This difference can probably be accounted for by the difference in family composition, since, as noted, it was the larger families in which mother or children also contributed, and the Chapin study excluded those families. Chapin concluded that with less than $600 total income, an adequate food supply was not provided for the families included. One family in three in the $600-$800 income range was underfed, while less than 10 percent of families making $900 or more were underfed. The proportion of families which were underfed was also greater where there was more than one wage earner for a given income.[69] On the basis of food expenditures, as well as clothing standards and housing, Chapin estimated that "an income under $800 [was] not enough to permit the maintenance of a normal standard," since each item in the budget showed a deficiency when the income was in the $600 and $700 range.[70]

Chapin did not use differences in ability or "thrift" to explain why a family fell below the normal standard, emphasizing instead that neither large family size nor improvidence could be used to explain the large proportion of families in the study which were below standard, since family size was limited to the "average," and "there are limits to what can be done by thrift and economy."[71] In addition, he contended that the "ordinary wage-earner's wife" could not be expected to conform to some "ideal" economy:

She cannot spend hours in bargain-hunting, in experimenting with new food-combinations, in making and mending garments . . . She has to take the methods of housekeeping that are traditional in her environment . . . What the exceptional woman might do cannot be made the measure of what the average woman may be expected to do, and if the morale and efficiency of the population are to be kept up, provision must be made for what the woman of average capacity must have to keep her family up to the prevailing standard.[72]

These studies show the living standards that were common among wage-earning families in the early 1900s. Both Chapin and More assumed that the father's wage ought to cover a family's expenses, and they implicitly criticized the low level of wages for men on the grounds that it was patently impossible for him to support a family on that income.[73] Although the More study did include female-headed households, the even lower level of women's wages was not mentioned.

WAGE-EARNING WOMEN

Studies which focused on working women, whether single, married, or mothers, all indicated the low standard of living a woman could expect from her own earnings. They often emphasized the detrimental effect of long hours on women's health and childbearing. Although they recognized that women worked from "necessity," attacked the "pin money" fallacy, and generally recognized that women were in industry to stay, they all expressed concerns specific to womens' functions as the "mothers of the race." Earlier studies tended to be more moralistic in tone, while studies after World War I mentioned the value of "independence" and noted that many women continued to work even after marriage.[74]

One study of working conditions of mothers, conducted by Katherine Anthony and sponsored by the Russell Sage Foundation, covered the middle-west side of Manhattan. This neighborhood was composed mainly of Irish and German "Old Stock" families with "no local tradition favoring wage-earning by married women." Not to work in this neighborhood was "a mark of the middle-class married woman, and the ambitious West Side family [coveted] that mark."[75] Sometimes, therefore, they tried "to conceal the mother's employment," an attempt which was, Anthony stated, "one of the little snobberies of the poor." But, the author continued, these were working women, which "qualified them at once for [our] respect . . . They represented the best standards and best elements of West Side Life."[76]

Fully one-third of these women were widows, and the chief cause of death of husbands was tuberculosis (35.4 percent).

The mothers were generally limited in their work area to the immediate neighborhood. Of the 370 families in the study, 46 percent had working children (28 percent of these working children were under sixteen years of age).[77] There was a sharp contrast between the occupations of the mothers and the daughters, since 70 percent of the mothers but only 5 percent of the daughters were in domestic service. Ninety-three percent of the girls entered the "newer occupations — stores, shops, factories." Most of the mothers did do housework before their marriages — 46 percent for wages, and 16 percent in their own houses. Thirty-two percent of them had been in manufacturing, while 23 percent still were (the textile mills had left the area).[78] Although it would be easy to assume that there was a split between the two periods of wage earning for widows, in fact many widows had been intermittent or constant wage earners even when their husbands were alive. Forty-two percent had worked at intervals during their married lives, while 51 percent had never worked before their husbands died.[79] One of the main occupations of this group of women was laundry work, one of the hardest and lowest paid of women's trades.

Of this group of women studied, only the 23 who worked in factories came under any laws regulating hours. Almost half of the 159 women for whom the study had information worked nine hours a day or more.[80] Almost one in five worked over ten hours a day, while almost a third of the women worked "part-time," meaning less than eight hours a day. Many of the "short-day" workers were public cleaners, a job which frequently involved "split-time" working hours.[81] Hours of scrubwomen were, as Anthony said, "inhumanly long." She continued: "They are on duty from 12 to 14 hours a day . . . That the women are perfectly submissive to these conditions is undoubtedly due, at least in part, to the complete stultification of spirit to which a life of monotonous toil has reduced them."[82] Waitresses also worked twelve-hour days with time out in the middle, and many were employed as part-time help.

The wages of women were generally about half those paid to men. Anthony did not attribute this fact to differences in the skill or intelligence required, but rather to a general practice of paying women less, as was found in a British study in which women had replaced men on a job and received about one-third to one-half of what the men had previously earned. No such comparison was possible on the West Side, however, since women's occupations were completely different from men's. As Anthony said: "Women's wages on the West Side are not affected by competition with men . . . the women follow the traditional domestic occupations of their sex and the men the traditional outdoor occupations of theirs. They work in separate, non-competing worlds."[83] Those women who worked in factories did not "replace" men either.

Fifty-six percent of the women in the study earned between $4.00 and $8.00 per week. The earnings of widows (an estimated $353.08 per year) accounted for almost 90 percent of the total income of the household if there were no children in the family at work. Where there were also working children, the family income increased to $785.20. Deserted women and women with idle or sick husbands were also sole adult wage earners. The more other members of the family contributed, the lower the earnings of the mother in the house were likely to be.

> Apparently, the mother works when she must, and when the necessity is less stringent she relaxes her efforts outside and gives more attention to her home. But to give her attention entirely to her home is a luxury which she cannot afford ... Too often we hear these women spoken of as if some perversity of instinct drove them to neglect their homes and go to work at the expense of their homes and children. It is for the sake of their children that they work, as mothers have done from time immemorial.[84]

The subordination of a woman's working life to her primary function in the home is expressed very clearly here. The average income of the ninety-six families with both parents working (with an average of 4.96 members in the family) was $705.12. By Chapin's standards, this figure meant that they could barely support themselves.

This study disputed the claim that the small earnings of the mother were offset by the greater expense and waste caused by her inability to manage the home. Rather, it leaned toward the view that the habits of both working and nonworking mothers were about the same and were conditioned by the same factor—not what was more convenient, but what cost the least.[85]

Anthony was gently critical of the patronizing, moralizing attitude of philanthropical institutions, and mentioned several instances where social agencies showed a lack of understanding of the conditions under which these women led their lives:

> In our efforts to help her with her children, we sometimes overlook the fact that it is the mother who bears the brunt of our well-intentioned requirements. She is summoned to school, to the juvenile court, to the clinic ... These apparently simple errands cost her a half or a whole day's work.[86]

If she complained, she was told she ought to be grateful for the assistance.

This study stressed the "heroism," determination, and courage of these women, who, far from shirking their responsibilities as mothers or doing irreparable harm to their children, were contributing as best they could to their children's welfare, making every effort to keep the family together wherever possible. Anthony concluded: "Not one of the mothers could afford not to earn. They had become wage-earners in obedience to the most primitive of maternal instincts." Otherwise "their children would have suffered seriously."[87]

In comparison with this study of wage-earning mothers, Louise Odencrantz's study, *Italian Women in Industry*, done from 1911 to 1914 (also by Russell Sage), focused mainly on single women. Most of the 1,095 women interviewed in this study were very young (two-thirds of them were under twenty-one), and only 150 of them were living outside a family group. Earnings from women only supported 50 of the 544 families. The father added to the family income in 383 out of 544 families; regardless of whether he contributed financially he was usually considered the head of the household.[88] Odencrantz stressed the reliance of these families on the wages of their women workers, 86 percent of whom turned over their paychecks unopened to the family household manager. By contrst, "it was not unusual to find families in which the sons were not giving a cent to the support of the home."[89] In these families, wage earning did not contribute to the women's independence, since she contributed her wages to the family and received only a small spending allowance — less than the sons. Her wage earning was considered a necessary evil. As Odencrantz said, "In this way, the women are kept in the paradoxical position of simultaneous wage-earning and dependence."[90]

Although it was said that in Italy women did not go out to work as they did in America, one-fourth of them had worked even there, and many of them had done work at home or had helped in a family store.[91] Manufacturing was the main type of employment for the Italian women included in the study. Odencrantz felt that part of the appeal of the needle trades to Italian women was that "their idea of the woman [was] primarily as a home-maker": since sewing was an important skill, they thought they would learn to sew their own clothes. This was not very likely, however, because of the specialization in the industry, where a woman might work doing only one small part of a dress or do something that was not sewing at all.[92] Moreover, fine, careful work was not encouraged by the work organization in the garment industries. Other occupations included flower and feather working, paper box making, tobacco (this industry had the largest proportion of foreign-born workers), and candy dipping (which was considered an undesirable, unusually low-paid trade with long hours). But Odencrantz disputed the view that Italian women undercut wages for other labor and were willing to work for less.[93] The Italian women at work in the establishments visited in the study worked at the "same processes and at the same wages as their fellow-workers." She continued:

> Any attempt, therefore, to understand and improve conditions for them will forward the movement for women workers as a whole . . . [These conditions present] an indictment, therefore, not of their personal standards but rather of the social and industrial conditions that are permitted to exist.[94]

Another, less systematic set of case studies of "self-supporting women living away from home in New York [City]," done by Clark and Wyatt for the National Consumers' League, discussed budgets for a number of saleswomen, shirtwaist makers (who had just had a long and impressive strike), other machine workers, and women in industries requiring a great deal of physical strength, like laundry work. One salesgirl, who at age seventeen had been working in stores for three-and-a-half years, earned $2.62 per week for a normal working day of nine-and-a-half hours, but during Christmas she worked twelve to thirteen hours per day without extra compensation. She lived at various times with an aged grandmother, an aunt, and in a dormitory in a charitably supported home for working girls.[95] Another seventeen-year-old girl, "Sadie," earned from $2.50 to $6.00 per week, depending upon the season and the job. When earning $3.00 per week, she had only 90¢ a week for the two meals a day she did not eat with her landlady, whose suppers cost 20¢ per day. Considering that 22¢ per day was considered a minimum food budget for an adult man living in a family in 1905, it is clear that Sadie paid more for being alone and also that her food budget was almost unbelievably small. Dire poverty was evident from the budgets of many of these women. Skilled labor did not seem to fare much better.

This account gave considerable attention to the two major strikes in the clothing industry and noted the major benefits of unions—not only in pay, but in reduction of hours, in better working conditions, and in dignity. Clark and Wyatt concluded, however, with a generally optimistic account of Taylor's system of scientific management and its potential applications to the needle trades, as discussed in chapter 2.

A FAMILY WAGE?

All the preceding studies, which discussed budgets and standards of living for families or single women, showed the extremely low wages of women workers throughout the period. Frequently women did not earn enough to support one woman, and almost never was their wage alone sufficient to support a family. The assumption on which relative wage rates of men and women were based was that the man should be the wage earner in the family and his wage alone ought to be enough to support it, while the wife "produce[d] economic and spiritual values within the home." This belief assumes, as Gwendolyn Hughes put it, that "first, every man's wage is a family wage and, second . . . a woman's place is in the home." She continued: "According to this theory . . . every woman is regarded as dependent upon the wages of some man, either husband, father or brother. When she finds it necessary or expedient to work outside her home she is regarded as a temporary worker with no one but herself to support."[96] Accordingly, women's wages were as a group lower than men's, with dual wage scales for men and women doing essentially the same work. But, as Hughes said, "the struggle to live on the husband's wage, in most industrial families, [was] a failure."[97] This and other studies bear out the fact that, for the majority of families, multiple wage earning was the rule and not the exception. And even with several members working, three-fifths of the families of the wage-earning mothers studied by Hughes had incomes below the official Philadelphia standard set by the Bureau of Municipal Research, which was $31.42 per week for a family of five ($1,634.00 per year).

The "solution" to the "problem" of women working outside the home, then, for some observers, appeared to be simple: insure a "living wage" for men. Testimony was given to that effect before the New York State Factory Investigating Commission by Dr. Woods Hutchinson, who stated that rather than emphasize issues concerning working women and child-bearing, the best thing was "to give a decent living wage to the woman's husband."[98] When asked, "You think a man's wages ought to be enough to support his wife and children?" the doctor answered, "Yes, emphatically." Florence Kelley testified that a woman ought not to be allowed to work at least three months after childbirth, and if she did go back to work sooner,

it [was] done largely through a mistaken idea of thrift on the part of the family, or by the shiftlessness and selfishness of the husband drinking up the family earnings, and largely encouraged by the manufacturers . . . for the purpose of reducing the wages by having both heads of the family and all the children contributing to the family purse . . . A man who is in the position of the head of the family which is increasing ought to be held up by the community rigidly to his duty in supporting his wife and children.

When asked what would happen if he could not do it, she replied, "I think he ought to go to the workhouse."[99] A similar sentiment was expressed in testimony before the commission concerning the evils of "home work," for which earnings of women were seldom more than $6.00 per week, with all the expenses of rent and equipment paid by the worker. Dr. Annie Daniel's solution was to abolish home work: "The women would work in factories and get better pay. I am pretty sure it would result in making the husbands work in some cases."[100] In a discussion entitled "How Nightwork of Women is Menacing Maternity," one writer commented, "Women do not work in the mills at night because they want to, but because they have to, because their husbands are getting so little."[101] Her solution was not as harsh as Kelley's, since she advocated maternity care and higher wages (presumably for the men primarily).

Another proposal for insuring a living wage was to use a legal minimum *family* wage as enacted in Australia (distinguished from the United States where, as noted, the minimum wage was only for women and minors), which established a minimum wage for men which was intended to be sufficient to support a family. "Men who have no dependents and women who have dependents are disregarded as unusual cases of which cognizance cannot be taken in the law. The law assumes that all men do or eventually will have someone dependent upon them and that women do not and never will."[102] Beatrice Webb, as a member of the British wartime commission on Women in Industry, criticized this differential minimum, and stated that it assumed "that industry is normally a function of the male,"[103] and that women and children are only permitted to work under special conditions. The legal minimum should be identical for either sex, she went on, with no separate occupational rates for men and women; instead, wages should be determined by the "aptness and fitness of each individual."[104] Webb favored a plan of providing a grant to parents, which Hughes also seemed to consider a possible future solution to the problem. Hughes would drop "the fiction of the husband's wage as a family wage," and would meet the family needs of workers by subsidy either from industry or the state.[105]

Another writer, who agreed that you cannot discuss budgets and wages by assuming that the man's wage is the only one, cautioned that employers had also used this argument to maintain that a very low minimum wage was adequate precisely because it did not take into account other contributions to the family. Therefore, she said, those who want to determine the wage rate by whether the worker is supporting a family, and who would pay a family head more than an independent person, "avoid the real issue of wage for service, or wage as a fair proportion of production in a competititve economic system."[106] She concluded, "The proper basis [is] equal wage for equal time and equal service . . . the amount necessary to maintain a family in health and at least the minimum of comfort should be regarded as the minimum wage for every adult wage-earner, and no allowance should be made for contributions from other family members."[107]

A slightly different approach was taken by Scott Nearing, who was critical of the whole wage system, but who argued:

> Under the present social system, a man's wage must be a family wage. The home is looked upon as the basic social institution. Each man is expected to make a home, and having made it, to earn a living sufficient to allow the wife to devote her time and energy to the care of the home and of the children.[108]

By comparing a number of different budget studies, including Chapin, he estimated that 90 percent of wage earners (male) were paid less than $1,000 per year in 1912, and that 70 percent of them earned under $750 per year. During this same period, estimates of the minimum required for a family of five ranged from $750 to $1,000 per year. Nearing stated, "Nothing could show more conclusively the frightful inadequacy of American wages."[109] He concluded:

> The employer does not even put himself to the trouble of asking whether the prospective employee is married or single, because that makes no difference if a man is handy with his tools . . . There is no relation between the social [family] needs of a man and the wage which he receives. Wages are fixed wholly independent of social relations. The American wage is anti-social.[110]

Here, Nearing used the idea of the "family wage" to say that, judged by its own social standards, the system was deficient because it manifestly did not provide its male wage earners with a minimal wage. The pitfalls of this approach—even when used to criticize, as Nearing did—are that it ignores the issue of women's wages completely, and the assumption that the man is head of every family goes unexamined.

During the period 1905-25, important changes were taking place in working conditions. John Commons stated that "the net result of the changes in hours which occurred between 1890 and 1930 was to reduce the average week's work by approximately a day, i.e., by about eight hours."[111] (Whitney Coombs also noted in passing the decrease in hours of labor between 1890 and 1924.)[112] At the same time, productivity did increase materially. But from about 1905 to 1925, labor fared rather poorly and real wages declined slightly, at least until the war period.[113] The majority of working-class families did not earn enough to reach the minimum accepted standard of health and decency. Unskilled labor fared especially poorly.

The beginning of this period was characterized by long hours, overwork and a high level of industrial accidents, and irregular or seasonal employment in many trades. It would appear that by the end of the postwar period some of the worst abuses had abated somewhat. The shorter workweek resulted in somewhat lower weekly wages, which offset the increase in hourly wages but also meant more time to recuperate from fatigue on the job. Interest in "scientific management" by social reformers was combined with concern for the harmful effects on the worker of industrial overwork. Although overwork was a problem for all workers, it was considered especially damaging for women and for their important function as future mothers.

CONCLUSION

The arguments centering on a legal minimum wage show a concern for the potentially disruptive consequences of unlimited exploitation of workers: the damage to the "community" by having a large class of dependent wage workers, and the potential for social unrest and radical activities. The minimum wage laws were intended to place a floor on employers' ability to develop their business by depressing wages as low as possible. But this option was only one of several available to businesses, and firms which saw different means of cutting costs and increasing productivity sometimes had a real interest in preventing other competing firms from cutting wages. They could achieve the same objective by increasing the efficiency of production by more effective control methods like "scientific management" or by developing less labor-intensive technology.

As will be shown in chapter 7, organized labor generally opposed minimum wage rates for men workers and did not particularly support them for women either, at least throughout the pre-World War I period.

The debate over this kind of regulation of the labor processes, by touching directly on the "wage bargain," also shows the dilemma of social reformers, who wished to improve conditions of life for workers, especially the unorganized and powerless, but who, because of constraints upon their view of possible solutions, were led to support these laws for only women (and children). Their views of women were intended to serve as arguments against the prevailing industrial conditions, but in the process these views also helped to set women apart from men in their need for protection, reinforced the positon of women as primarily wives and mothers, and contributed to the segmentation of the labor force by limiting women's participation in it.

The issues surrounding these laws reveal the tensions between the employers' desire to treat wage labor as a commodity without regard for the health and reproduction of the workers as a class, and the demands of social reformers that conditions of life be improved for the lowest sector, under pain of its possible extinction, or also, of social disorder and revolution. But since this legislation affected women workers specifically, whose wage scale never approached subsistence, the relative failure of minimum wage laws can be attributed in part to the fact that, although they were aimed at insuring the preservation of workers as a class, as Brandeis stated, working was not the primary way in which women contributed to the reproduction of the labor force.

Although, as workers, women did help support the family, their wage labor never was supposed to make them *self*-supporting. Therefore, where minimum wage scales for women were set up, they did not come close to insuring the support of a family, and generaly not even of the woman herself. On the contrary, it was felt that an equitable wage structure was one which would allow the *man* to support a family unaided, and women's wages were sometimes considered a potential hindrance to such support. Under these conditions, then, the Supreme Court could continue to uphold hours and no-night-work legislation (in 1923 a night work law was again upheld by the court) while disallowing minimum wage legislation for women on the grounds that it interfered with freedom of contract. Legal precedent and substantive evidence served to establish the constitutionality of labor legislation, allowing the laws to be upheld in the one case and struck down in the other.

Part Two

WHOSE STREETS ARE THEY?

The Law: "Streets are not safe for working women at night."
Working Woman: "Well, then, make 'em safe."

Chapter Five
The Suffragists: The Feminist Opposition

The women suffragists in the early twentieth century saw protective labor legislation for women as a side issue to their main concern—giving women the vote. Although working women were not the mainstay of the suffrage movement, the vote was intended for all women regardless of class, and suffragists combined their push for the vote with examples of the public interest in matters like temperance or labor laws for women, which they assumed all women could be expected to support regardless of class.

The connection between the suffrage movement and protective legislation for women illustrates the way middle-class social reformers who were not primarily labor oriented like the Women's Trade Union League viewed working women. Their position changed as the broader issue of equal rights for women emerged in the postwar period. The suffrage movement eventually became the source for the only principled feminist opposition to protective labor legislation for women which emerged in this period.

The Fight for the Vote

The successful drive for suffrage had been preceded by a long, unsuccessful fight for the vote both before and after the Civil War. In the antislavery movement in the midnineteenth century, women abolitionists discovered that they were hamstrung in their work against slavery because they did not have either the power of the vote or the right to be heard on the key issues of the day. Women abolitionists frequently compared their own status to that of slaves.[1]

With the granting of freedom and citizenship for former slaves, the question of who was to be included in the newly extended suffrage split the abolitionist and the women's movements. Women abolitionists were incensed that the newly freed male slave was to have the vote under the Fourteenth Amendment while their own demands were to be put aside. Former abolitionists like Elizabeth Cady Stanton campaigned and petitioned *against* the vote for former slaves. For the first time, the word *male* was included in the Constitution, and the women who had fought for freedom from slavery felt betrayed. The justification for excluding women was that the amendment would not pass otherwise, and to push for woman suffrage at the same time as the vote for former slaves would mean that both would go down in defeat.

Frederick Douglass, former slave and also a strong supporter of women's rights until emancipation, declared his opposition to striking the word *male* from the amendment on the grounds that the need of the black slave was much greater than the woman's for this right.[2] Women felt that this setback would delay the cause of women's rights fifty years, and in this they were quite right.

In the years following the passage of the Fourteenth Amendment, the struggle for women's suffrage continued. The women's movement soon split into two groups—one, the National Woman Suffrage Association, favored working to secure a federal amendment to the Constitution for the vote, while the American Woman Suffrage Association worked for state-by-state action. By 1890 these two groups had joined again, forming the National American Woman Suffrage Association (NAWSA).

The years from 1896 to 1910 were "the doldrums" of the suffrage movement, according to Flexner. Susan B. Anthony died in 1906, and Anna Howard Shaw, who succeeded her, did not arouse the movement to great activity.[3] By 1907-10, there was a proliferation of suffrage groups and a rift in the older one; the outcome was that Harriot Stanton Blatch succeeded Shaw as head of NAWSA, and a period of intense activity followed.

During this period there were two main groups in the suffrage movement—the older organization, NAWSA, which was the more conservative in method, and the more militant National Woman's Party (NWP), which was formally founded in 1916 by Alice Paul. Paul had experienced the militant phase of the suffragist movement in England. Returning to this country, she became active in the congressional committee of the established organization, NAWSA. Upon Wilson's election to the presidency, Alice Paul helped organize a major demonstration in Washington on the eve of his inauguration, and the suffragists did not give him much peace thereafter. They sought support from both major political parties, getting either a vaguely worked plank (from the Republicans) or a statement in support of "extension of the franchise to the women of the country by the *states* upon the same terms as men," which amounted to denying support for a *federal* amendment.[4]

Following their policy of holding the party in power responsible for the failure of suffrage, the NWP promised to work actively *against* national Democrats in those states where women already voted (mainly the West); this tactic seems to have jarred representatives of Congress considerably, since they had no experience with the potential power of women voting as a bloc on the suffrage issue and they were not sure how much real voter strength lay behind the threat.

As Wilson's polite intransigence continued and the issue of war became paramount, the women began to attack him openly. In 1917, in the midst of the war, the NWP used his alleged concern for democracy abroad to pressure him into support for democracy at home, and he frequently was placed in the embarrassing situation where visitors and foreign envoys to the White House had to pass by the women's pickets. When these tactics seemed to get nowhere, the women formed a daily picket line in front of the White House, starting on January 10, 1917, which continued with general tolerance from the president until June, when the Russian war mission to the president was met at the White House gate with the following statement:

> TO THE RUSSIAN ENVOYS: President Wilson and Envoy Root are Deceiving Russia When They Say "We Are a Democracy, Help Us Win The World War So That Democracy May Survive." We the Women of America Tell You That America is Not a Democracy. 28 Million American Women are Denied the Right to Vote. President Wilson is the Chief Opponent of Their National Enfranchisement.[5]

The women were informed that if they continued to picket they would be arrested, to which they replied that they had been picketing for six months without interference. Although peaceful picketing was plainly within the law, the following day two suffragists were arrested, charged with obstructing traffic, dismissed on their own recognizance, and never tried. As the women persisted, however, sentences of thirty days, sixty days, and longer were served, since the women refused to pay the fines as an alternative. They were sent to Occoquan Workhouse, and the issue of suffrage became also the issue of the treatment of the suffragists.

The women arrested were frequently prominent persons, wives of wealthy men or presidential supporters like Mr. J. A. H. Hopkins, who went directly to President Wilson, and asked, "How would you like to have your wife sleep in a dirty workhouse next to prostitutes?" The president was "shocked"—the Hopkinses had been his dinner guests and had supported him politically and financially.[6] Mr. Hopkins then informed the president that the only solution to the present dilemma was the "immediate passage of the Susan B. Anthony Amendment."[7]

Wilson was met by more pickets and women with signs reading "Kaiser Wilson . . ." The crowds surrounding the arrests were allowed by the police to become more and more violent, and the police participated in attacks upon the women pickets. In October a large group of suffragists, including Alice Paul, were arrested for picketing. They refused to post bail as usual, when taken to court refused to rise when the judge entered, refused to speak when asked to identify themselves, and when asked whether they chose to plead innocent or guilty, did not answer. They were convicted and sentenced to seven months in the Occoquan Workhouse, where they demanded to be treated as political prisoners and went on a hunger strike to protest conditions in the prison; a few women were force-fed. Alice Paul was sent to the prison hospital and seen by an "alienist," who declared her sane; nevertheless, she was sent to the psychopathic ward of the hospital.

Upon their early release from prison, these women organized the "Prison Special" of the Woman's Party—a train that whistle-stopped the country, bringing the suffrage message and news of the treatment of women in prison throughout the South, West, and Northeast. Former NWP prisoners wore the prison garb as a badge of honor.

Toward the end of the campaign, the NWP picketed the White House nonstop and persisted in lighting "watch fires" on the White House lawn, which they managed to light and keep going despite the best efforts of the police to stop them and to arrest all the perpetrators. From all accounts, these women were well-dressed "ladies," evidently well-to-do. This fact in itself was enough to gain them sympathy from some observers, who saw the "low element" in the crowds that harassed them, in contrast to the genteel, middle-class, educated group of women who carried picket signs.

In addition to using direct action and militant activity in the streets, the NWP also organized an extremely effective method of lobbying which involved a complex index-file system containing information on each con-gressman, his personal habits and preferences. The person closest to him, whether it was his mother, wife, or someone else, was noted in the file, as well as constituents from his home district who were likely to impress him. These secondary people then became the target for a barrage of prosuffrage propaganda. It was an extraordinarily well-organized and sophisticated lobbying machine, and an effective one as well.

As expected, the great majority of these women's energies and thoughts were devoted to the suffrage cause alone. Before women got the vote, any other issue, like labor legislation for women, was considered solely in terms of its relation to women's suffrage. The suffragists frequently made the point that when women got the vote, one of the things they would be able to do with it would be to pass legislation favorable to women and children.

RATIONALE FOR THE VOTE: TO PASS "GOOD" LAWS

Before the U.S. involvement in the war, suffrage propaganda by both suffrage groups, NAWSA and NWP, took the positive value of protective legislation for women as a given, in the same way as it did child labor legislation. The differences between the two suffrage groups before 1920 appear to have mainly concerned method. Both groups were composed primarily of middle-and upper-class women, and the advertising, feature articles, and other aspects of both groups' journals reflected this status.[8] NAWSA, which became the League of Women Voters (LWV) after the suffrage amendment was passed, continued to favor the protective laws. The National Woman's Party gradually changed from unquestioning endorsement to opposition to any "special legislation" for women, favoring instead an equal rights amendment which would prohibit all sex-based differential treatment in the law.

The official organ of NAWSA was the *Woman Citizen*, which grew out of their *Headquarters News Letter* and *National Suffrage News* around 1917. These journals indicated their concern with "good" legislation, including abolition of child labor, compulsory education to age sixteen, an eight- or nine-hour day for women, abolition of night work for women and minors, the right of labor to organize, a women's bureau, prohibi-tion, mothers' pensions, and guardianship of children. It was assumed that these were matters on which all women could agree, regardless of their political affiliations, and that their passage was almost insured once women gained the vote. The women presented statistical comparisons to show that "good" laws were almost twice as likely to be passed in suffrage states than in nonsuffrage ones, and maintained that, "by social legislation, women and children [were], therefore nearly twice as well-off in suffrage than non-suffrage states."[9]

The period of intense suffrage activity coincided with World War I and after, and one of the fears of labor reform groups was that the war effort would erase all the gains in legislative reforms: *The Suffragist* noted that "the attempt to break down protective laws for women and children in industry was almost the first move made by some state legislatures after war was declared ... The Department of Labor of course opposes any of these retrogressive changes."[10] At the same time, the economic status of women changed drastically with the war, since women were hired in large numbers for previously all-male jobs as part of the war effort.[11]

EMERGENCE OF THE "EQUAL RIGHTS" ISSUE: THE POSTWAR PERIOD

In 1919, directly after the war, NAWSA noted that women "in men's jobs" did not get the higher wages of men. Only 20 of the 117 plants studied by the New York Bureau of Women in Industry gave "equal pay" to women replacements; that is, only 9 percent of the women employed to replace men received equal pay. NAWSA commented: "The problem of whether or not the woman in man's work is to be a menace to skilled labor thus becomes a problem of equal pay and equal opportunities, regardless of sex."[12] The position of "colored women" industrial workers in New York City was even worse than that of white women, since they took work a white woman wouldn't take at wages white women would not work for, and were the last to be hired in industry. NAWSA recommended education of these women and "better understanding on the part of white people."[13]

NAWSA also attempted to counter the antagonism of men workers to women "taking over" men's jobs. Women were evidently in those jobs to stay; one study showed that only 3.9 percent of women (6,771 women) were actually laid off their wartime jobs. Equal pay for equal work then became essential:

And the truth of this is seeping into the minds of laboring men, whose earlier reactions against women in industry tended towards limiting her opportunities and her pay. They now see that it is not the working woman but her exploitation which menaces them, and that safety for both sexes lies in equality of pay. They have not yet come all the way to the point of acknowledging equality of opportunity for women. Some are still for giving women only the left-overs of men's labor. But war has shown even the dullest the fallacy of having woman as an industrial under-bidder.[14]

NAWSA also resented the way in which women were being played with concerning work outside the home:

"Come hither," said mere man to mere woman when the jobs were yawning empty. "Back to your kennels" snaps the master's whip when the need is over. "The country will care for your children," cry the sociologists when the mother is needed at the factory. But they snear at her lack of maternal feeling when "with children who might reasonably be expected to need her care," she still sticks on her job to which they called her only yesterday.[15]

They editorialized further than no one ever objected to the lack of maternal care when the woman's job was charwoman and she worked all day "and [did] the family washing at midnight in order that she [could] get up and char some more the next day." They continued: "All that society ever does about that kind of woman in industry is to call her 'my good woman' and prove to her that her children are ill brought up ... it is only when these women get real jobs with steady wages and the power to unionize themselves that the male's right to have and to hold all industrial posts comes to the surface."[16]

In the immediate postwar period, NAWSA upheld the view that women were physically capable of industrial labor. A brief note mentioned that a study of women's muscular strength concluded that it was more a question of use than of sex, and that there was "no difference in muscular strength of women and men which is due to sex as such."[17] The purpose of the study was to see whether women had been harmed by their work in men's jobs during the war.

NAWSA also toyed with possible reorganizations of home life to suit women's growing interest in the world outside the kitchen. Charlotte Perkins Gilman, known for her radical ideas on domestic arrangements, said that hiring someone to care for children was as old as Pharaoh's daughter and should not be condemned. "The 'Hired' Mother versus the Tired Mother," written for the *Woman Citizen* in 1919, criticized the prevailing custom of having domestic work be the exclusive occupation of women, and contended that the community ought to help out by offering hot meals and child care.[18] This suggestion was not quite as radical as it sounds, for shortly after, Gilman proclaimed, "Whatever else we lose, we must keep the home." She said, "Working women do not wish to be servants" because their "status" is so low, [but] we could have a kitchenless house, with food delivered to the door (by motor to eliminate horse litter)." She saw the dilemma in the following terms: "As women, [women] should all, if normal, be wives and mothers, but as workers each should do the work she likes best and can therefore do best . . . The women of our time are torn between the universal duty of motherhood, and the special duty of each human being to do his or her best work in the world."[19]

This kind of open exploration of alternative arrangements of women's lives to include both family responsibilities and wage-earning work faded into the background in the next few years. Discussions of housework became "the servant problem" and emphasized the emotional drain that housework entails. They did serve notice that women intended to have careers and homes too,[20] although they were unclear how this combination was to be managed, or even whether married women ought to be working at all.

THE SPLIT EMERGES

A few years after the postwar period, the emphasis had shifted; NAWSA's main activities, through the League of Women Voters, were political discussions of elections, and they had refined the distinction between simple "equality" before the law to "equality of method" versus "equality of result." An earlier (prewar) position had claimed that of the laws alleged to "favor women," "not one of them present[ed] a substantial instance of discrimination in woman's favor, and if they did so, the women would be the first to protest, *for they do not desire to be a favorite of the law*, but merely ask for equality under the law."[21] There was no specific carryover in this earlier article to protective labor laws—these had not yet become a bone of contention. By 1922-23, with the introduction of the "blanket amendment" to grant complete equality under law to women, the lines had been drawn. NAWSA (now the League of Women Voters) argued against a federal equal rights amendment and in favor of action at the state level to remove those laws deemed unsatisfactory. They justified support for special labor legislation for women as, first, an expedient way of protecting women since the laws seemed to be constitutional when applied to women only, and secondly, by maintaining that there were basic biological differences between men and women that would always require differential treatment of women in industry. They also began to accept the notion that married women ought not to be working at all, and suggested various measures toward that end.

In a discussion at a conference on women in industry, all participants agreed that married women ought not to be in industry at all, but differed about how they should be excluded. Sophonisba Breckenridge of the University of Chicago suggested that "a living wage for men" for a family of five was what was needed, with "disciplinary measures for husbands who [were] unwilling to work, and state aid for the wives of those who [could not] work." Only the employers' representative at the conference was opposed to legislation for women only and for having any future legislation apply to both men and women, though she was not in favor of repealing all past laws. She added that if women are to do a double job (home and work), men should share in the housework.[22]

The League of Women Voters own position regarding the "blanket amendment," was that they "believed that biology is against the theory, and that for the sake of the whole race certain protections must be thrown about women, especially in industry, at least until the standards for both sexes are raised to a point far beyond present possibilities." They added that they believed the piecemeal method would "bring equality safely."[23] The LWV also believed that protective labor legislation was not responsible for low wages and limited opportunity for women and did not aim at removing the causes of their economic disability, but was remedial in nature. The causes of that disability, they said, "in addition to the physical limitations of women," were "lack of organization, lack of training, and persistence of the traditional attitude toward women's work and education." Further, they argued that the more "liberal" view, which would extend legislation to both sexes, overlooked the fact that doing away with existing laws would not improve conditions for both men and women, that men preferred to unionize rather than get laws for themselves, and that "certain existing legislation for women [was] based on their physical characteristics and could not apply equally to both sexes."[24]

Part of the dispute centered around the effect of the one equal rights law which had already passed in Wisconsin. The Wisconsin law included a provision which gave women equal rights before the law and removed discriminations, while reserving to women the "special protection and privileges which they [then enjoyed] for the general welfare." The law in Wisconsin certainly did not succeed in removing the legal disabilities of working women completely, and the attorney general at the time refused to apply it to women working for the state legislature. The existing statute which barred them was still in effect despite the equal rights amendment, he argued, since "legislative service necessitates work during the very long and often unseasonable hours and . . . it was not the intention of the legislature to change this practice, as would be required under the statutes relating to the employment of women." He continued: "I feel all the more free in so holding for the reason that the legislature is in session and can readily change this by specific enactment if this should be thought desirable."[25] Opponents of the federal equal rights amendment were quick to note the conditional nature of the Wisconsin law, which allowed for "special privileges and protections" to continue which the federal amendment did not. The law also had the immediate effect of making a woman liable for notes she had cosigned with her husband. Those opposed to the "blanket amendment" concluded that the bill had nothing good in it which could not be obtained without endangering the provisions already existing for women, and that it had already caused demonstrable harm, according to the *Woman Citizen*.[26]

Thus, NAWSA remained consistent in its support of protective labor legislation for women. At first there was unquestioned acceptance of the laws' positive benefit for working women; as the economic situation changed with the war and women went to work in large numbers at previously male jobs, however, the need for such legislation began to receive closer scrutiny. This forced a gradual reconsideration of position by the National Woman's Party, but confirmed NAWSA in its original stand. Both of these groups favored "equality" for women, and certainly suffrage. Both groups consisted of articulate middle-class and wealthy women. They differed regarding the methods to be used, both for suffrage and also for "equality" of women, and consequently in their definition of what "equality" consisted of—formal equality before the law, or "substantive" equality ("equivalence of result," as NAWSA put it). The NWP was consistently the more militant of the two groups, and direct action was their style, as has been shown.

Neither group was above racist appeals; for example, in order to get the Southern vote on the suffrage amendment, both groups argued that the increased number of white (women) voters would insure white supremacy in the South even if the Negro should one day be permitted to vote. They also pointed to the injustice of letting ignorant (though naturalized) foreigners vote if they were male while denying literate native-born women the same right.

Once their positions on protective labor legislation had diverged, both groups claimed the support of *real* working women for their positions and accused the opposition of being a bunch of non-wage-earning women with no right to decide for others what they ought to want. This theme was common in arguments on both sides—that those who argued the other position were wealthy women who had never worked for wages, or else were privileged professional women who had no need of such laws and were attempting to force their own views on working women.

These were the justifications used by the group of suffragists that consistently maintained their support for protective labor legislation. I will now turn to the group which, after initial support, changed its position and became one of the strongest and most articulate opponents of such legislation—the National Woman's Party.

THE BEGINNINGS OF THE FEMINIST OPPOSITION TO "PROTECTIVE" LAWS

The NWP was sympathetic to protective labor legislation for women right through the war period. Following the war, in 1919, they noted in the *Suffragist*, "Women in industry demand labor laws," quoting Mary Dreier, spokesperson for the lobbying group in Albany for protective labor legislation.[27] Their position is unstated here, though it appears that they concurred. A few months later, they noted that an Indiana study showed some women working eighty-eight hours per week and commented, "Indiana is, moreover, not the only state with inadequate laws to protect working women and children." Using this evidence as a further argument for the ballot for women, they added, "There are still Senators who maintain that each individual state has made such provisions for the protection of its women that it is unnecessary for the U.S. Senate to put a ballot in the hands of women."[28]

The NWP preferred to emphasize the need of both sexes for the legislation, as is demonstrated by their comment on the minimum wage campaign in New York State, in which they described the wages for women as "almost unbelievably low." Sixty-five percent of the women in 417 factories surveyed received less than $10.00 per week, when $15.00 was the minimum cost of living for one person in New York. The NWP (as well as the NAWSA) were sensitive to the fact that the minimum itself was usually calculated differently for women than for men, since the minimum standard for men was estimated not for an individual, but included dependents. They concluded:

> Employers should be forced to pay all workers at least enough to live upon decently . . . A further effort to equalize the position of women and men in industry is being made in New York through the effort to secure a law granting an 8 hour day to women. Men workers have set up this rule . . . through their organizations. The women up to the present

have been unable to do this. We look forward to the day when obviously just regulations like a living wage and a short working day will be granted to men and women alike without discrimination of sex.[29]

These arguments either accepted the legislation or linked it to the vote for women. It was not until May 1919 that any hint of unfavorable consequences of these laws found its way into print in the NWP newspaper, although women printers had been fighting to have themselves exempted from the no-night-work law for years. The immediate issue that brought the question to the fore was the wholesale firing of women railway workers. These workers had worked as subway guards, "conductor-ettes," ticket sellers, and ticket collectors for a brief period during the war. The Brooklyn Rapid Transit Company dismissed nearly three hundred "conductor-ettes" and ticket agents without notice and without refund for their uniforms, which had cost them $18.00, and blamed their dismissals on the law prohibiting night work for women from 10:00 P.M. to 7:00 A.M. The NWP article in May commented cautiously, "Whether or not the women will make a fight to retain their jobs has not been determined. It is a question whether the law was in favor of women or just exactly the opposite."[30]

In March 1920, columnist M.L. Obenauer aired the dispute fully for the first time, although she was cautious regarding her conclusions. She noted that the controversy over protective labor legislation had grown because during the war women had entered many previously male fields, and the past uneasiness over the "bracketing of adult women with children" had broken out into the open. She said that "a certain class of wage-earning women [were] making an insistent contention that a woman's chance to learn a living is as essential to her welfare as protection while she is earning it," and that they demanded that laws not jeopardize it. These working women were backed, she claimed, by certain groups of non-wage-earning women whose political slogan was "No favors, no handicaps." Before the war, two-thirds of the women in manufacturing worked in about six industries, where "the restrictions imposed on the employment of woman labor were not such, on the whole, as to make it profitable for such industries to substitute men for women." In the rest, women were

regarded as interlopers by their brother workers, [and the] laws that put the grown woman in a losing race with a grown man for a job were passed usually with the sanction of the public, frequently with the approval of organized labor, and without much protest on the part of the employers, who depended principally on men.

There was not much opposition from women workers either.

Obernauer stated that protective labor legislation did not distinguish between conditions which were dangerous to both sexes and those which were a danger to women specifically "because of a woman's physical organization." For instance, grinding or buffing trades did not involve heavy physical labor, but the metallic dust particles were dangerous. Most states therefore had guards required for such machines, "yet women [were] forbidden in some states from operating them." On the other hand, foot treadle ironing machines commonly found in steam laundries were an especial health hazard for young women because of the weight required and the awkward leaning position which the workers had to assume for hours on end without respite, and yet no law barred these machines nor limited who (that is, by age or sex) could use them. Similarly with the mangle in such laundries. This work was unskilled and low paid, and the women operators were "not in competition with men" for these jobs. In other occupations, employment of women was prohibited where they *were* in competition with men, and in that case, protective legislation for women "only [served] to bar them out of the occupation in many places," instead of placing restrictions appropriate for both sexes to "do away with the conditions prejudicial to health." Noting other inconsistencies and incongruities in state laws, Obernauer concluded that there was a need to question "the basis for determining the degree of protection essential to the health of the adult woman without unnecessarily curtailing her choice of employment or needlessly handicapping her in competition for advancement."[31]

Thus, by the time the woman's suffrage amendment to the Constitution was ratified, the NWP was in the process of changing their position regarding protective labor laws for women. While it was unclear whether an equal rights amendment would do away with these laws for women, the NWP had turned their attention from getting the vote for women to the passage of the amendment, which would have prohibited any discrimination or distinction on the basis of sex. When challenged by the Women's Trade Union League to clarify their position, Alice Paul apparently equivocated, saying first that the equal rights amendment would not do away with protective labor laws for women, and then, that it would do so and that that would be all to the good.[32] There was evidently some division of opinion within the executive committee of the NWP, because they refused to commit themselves publicly during this period.

By 1923, the NWP had resolved the conflict over their position and had begun an intensive campaign for the equal rights amendment and against all protective labor laws for women. The NWP had to clearly distinguish their position against all such legislation from opponents on two fronts. Organized labor and social reformers attacked them for being unrealistic with regard to the needs of the working woman or for being outright antilabor. They were also accused of ignoring innate biological differences, especially motherhood. Their weekly journal, *Equal Rights*, documents their legislative efforts, as well as their responses to criticisms of the proposed amendment in clear, cogent arguments that appear very modern in tone. They also came out in opposition to various bills for minimum wages, special working conditions, and prohibitions that applied to women only.

EQUALITY, NOT RESTRICTIONS, FOR WORKING WOMEN

The NWP Declaration of Principles states: "Women shall no longer be barred from any occupation, but every occupation open to men shall be open to women, and restrictions upon hours, conditions and remuneration of labor shall apply alike to both sexes."[33] For each specific issue involved, the Woman's Party responded on two fronts. First, they argued that the concept of special privilege for women was inherently unjust, no matter how benevolent the measure appeared to be, and secondly, they demonstrated that the particular measure in question was a handicap and a disservice to women in ways which they then specified.

The principle of equality for both sexes in labor legislation, as in other issues, is opposed to the idea of privilege, which contains the assumption that women are incapable of defending themselves. To those who claimed that the inequality, frailty, and dependence of women was innate and could not be legislated away, the answer came in a heavily sarcastic editorial:

> Those who would maintain the status quo forever invoke either Nature or the Deity to prove their case. Particularly in connection with the emancipation of women, Nature, both human and otherwise, has been put under a terrific strain. "You cannot obliterate the natural differences between men and women by act of legislature," people used to say, in combatting woman suffrage, and then they would go on to show how Nature herself had ordained the home and not the polling place as the sphere of woman. Very discouraging, very upsetting, for Nature is a hard thing to overcome.

Then, after women got the vote, they pointed out, "The sun rises and sets just as if the eternal order had not been disturbed at all!"[34] Noting that the focus had now shifted to married women's alleged need for protection, they advised the "naturalists" to "take a little of their own medicine; to open their biological eyes a trifle wider to the facts of Nature and to see if the female of the species necessarily becomes a parasite as soon as she takes unto herself a mate."[35]

The often-repeated argument that women's natural biological functions make her weaker was mocked in an editorial entitled "Invalids?" which stated that the natural bodily functions (estrus cycle) of women should not be looked upon as pathological. The article noted that arguments against equal rights saw woman as a "semi-invalid":

> Maternity of course accentuates the malady, but even in the unmarried it is there, obstinately, persistently, recurring as does the moon at regular intervals. Womanhood is regarded as a sort of intermittent malaria, or relapsing typhoid, or chronic gall-stones, keeping steadily on in cycles until it is time to buy a coffin.

Noting that women athletes could compete successfully without interference from their normal bodily functions, the article concluded: "In no other animal than the unnaturally clothed, unnaturally repressed human female does the oestrus cycle parade under the guise of invalidism. Nor does a normal function appear as abnormal save in the minds of those who have been educated to so regard it."[36]

Arguments of the NWP during this period unequivocally rejected the notion of any inherent, genetic disability that might form the basis for "protecting" women through law, as the more conservative NAWSA had argued. They also refused to concede that man's greater physical strength justified such measures. An article written by a doctor addressing the issue of physical strength contended that although men are usually stronger than women in industrial countries, the difference is probably environmental, since "girls do not have the opportunity for the hyperactivistic life that small boys lead." He continued: "With the astounding development of automatic machinery physical strength by and for itself is rapidly losing its former important position as a significant aspect in homo industrialensis." The logical thing to do then, would be to determine the strength necessary for the job and then hire individuals who conform to these limits.

The main thrust of the doctor's discussion was the relative physiological limitations of each sex in industrial conditions. He pointed out that inguinal hernias, for example, do not occur in women, although others do, especially among multiparous women, and this fact constitutes a real difference in physical capacities which affect job performance. He said that menstruation does not impair mental functioning and only affects about 5 percent of a woman's physical functions, a weakness which could be overcome. The "psychological" difference—that women can do "rapid repetitive motions" better than men, again, the doctor advised deciding on an individual basis. He concluded, "The physical, physiological and psychological differences between men and unmarried women do not demand special health standards for women." The doctor cautioned, however, that the conditions of "potential or actual motherhood wholly prevents absolutely equal competition in industry of married with unmarried women as well as with men." He concluded, "An intelligent solution of this problem is neither simple nor obvious."[37] He was referring here to the practical difficulties faced by women with small children before and after childbirth, however, rather than to any innate disability. This testimony was closer than most of the articles that the journal printed in justifying any limitations upon the work of married women at all.

Although they favored equal treatment of men and women in general, the NWP were not blind to the special problems facing married women with children. They saw this condition not as an individual handicap to be faced by each woman separately, but as a social cost that ought to be taken into account by intelligent social policy, which, they contended, had nothing to do with the principle of equality before the law: "There is an overwhelming social need for an intelligent treatment of maternity as a fixed social charge . . . The Equal Rights amendment will not hinder the progress of true maternity legislation any more than it will interfere with soldiers' bonus measures." Maternity legislation would not be inequality of treatment between men and women. "It merely involves inequality of treatment between the mother and non-mother, just as the soldiers' bonus involves inequality of treatment between the veteran soldier and the civilian but not between men and women."[38]

> [Since] women make a significant contribution in motherhood . . . [it is time that] we now recognize that the welfare of the race demands special pre-natal care and it may not be long before we grant women compensation for the burdens involved in maternity. But how unjust to hamper all women at all times in securing economic freedom under the guise of protecting motherhood.[39]

Motherhood itself was sometimes seen as an almost sacred, mystical state:

> The contribution which women make to the race through motherhood is greater than any gift that men can bring. This fact is eternal

and should be recognized . . . Soldiers have received pensions and even bonuses not applicable to men at large. Why should not mothers receive adequate compensation, also?[40]

They then came out in favor of some measure like an "Endowment of Motherhood" which would be available (but not compulsory!) to mothers who wished to stay home with young children.

The NWP thus maintained a logically consistent position that women were to be considered the equal of men regarding jobs in a competitive market. At the same time they defined pregnancy and childraising as a specific condition that affected some but not all women and that merited appropriate measures. Although the NWP usually stuck to this position, on occasion they were not above capitalizing on the notion that women had *superior* qualities by virtue of their sex which were too valuable to be confined to the home sphere: "It is as if within their very fiber women had certain instincts that are not yet developed in men, and these instincts are at the moment of the greatest possible importance to humanity, for they represent the concerns of civilization, and they repudiate brute force."[41] The specific issues which the journal discussed—night work laws, minimum wage legislation, prohibitions against women working for a specified period before and after childbirth—were discussed with all these assumptions often only implicitly present; explicitly, the NWP combatted the legislation on its own terms, arguing that it was in fact no protection, but a genuine harm to the group it purported to help.

In response to various state laws which prohibited night work for women, the NWP's position was that if this restriction were desirable it must apply to both men and women. The Woman's Party officially took a neutral position regarding the desirability of any kind of labor legislation in general, whether for men or women:

> The Woman's Party is not a labor organization and does not presume to say what is the best method of improving labor conditions— whether by organization, by legislation, or by reconstructing the form of our society. The Woman's Party simply demands that whatever the method adopted it not include any discrimination based on sex.[42]

Labor laws assume women are weaker, and in the present system, to be weaker means to be exploited:

To conceive that in the sharp and bitter competition ordained by the present organization of industry [the weaker] will get the preference in salary, hours or position is to admit a complete mis-apprehension of the mainsprings of business. Weakness predicates exploitation. This is an axiom of the capitalist system.[43]

The NWP also accepted "freedom of contract" as an argument against protective laws, an outlook which tended to weaken rather than strengthen their position, since they thereby admitted the competitive, exploitative nature of work under capitalist industry. They cited favorably one assemblyman's opposition to the New York night work bill on the following grounds:

The right to work is one of the human liberties that should not be infringed in the case of a woman any more than in the case of a man . . . We must not consider the adult female as a ward of the state, but we must give her the same freedom of contract and the same right of selection or choice that we give to men.[44]

The NWP in the two arguments just cited were standing on both sides of the fence. They were arguing that the weaker party is always at a disadvantage under capitalism (and thus *not* equal), while at the same time they were arguing for "freedom of contract" for women and men (which is predicated upon formal equality between the bargaining parties — the individual worker and the employer). By 1924, the "freedom of contract" argument and the laissez-faire doctrine associated with it had been almost abandoned by the courts even for labor legislation intended for men.

The NWP argued that the legislation regarding night work had been a hardship for women. The New York law forbidding work in various occupations for women after 10:00 P.M. had succeeded in having women at soda fountains and candy counters replaced by men for the night shift. Women proofreaders and linotypists were similarly put out of their jobs, and only "after untiring effort, the women got themselves exempted from the law and were then able to regain their employment."[45]

These laws were also condemned for their overall effect on the labor force, since they meant "narrowing the labor field which women [could] enter and forcing them to compete with each other in an even more restricted area than that formerly open to them." If these night work laws are justified on health grounds, they stated, then the Scandinavian example of restricting night work for both sexes was the best answer. If it is claimed that it is unsafe for women to be out alone at night, then "the solution is to make the streets safe instead of barring women from night occupations."[46]

As further evidence for the harm done to women by exclusion from certain employments, the NWP cited the Wisconsin law prohibiting women from working in the state legislature. "When we examine one by one each of the 'privileges' and 'the protection' women are supposed to enjoy, we find that in practically every case it is really the man, not the woman, who is protected." Under the Wisconsin law, "men holding paid positions under the legislature [were] 'protected' from the competition of women for these positions." The NWP argued that legislators, as males, could be expected to continue to defend their own groups' self-interests, and that "so long as men are in control, they will continue, often unconsciously, to legislate in their own interest." Therefore, women need not fear equality with men under the law, since they "may rest assured that this difference will be to their advantage, even though the different law is passed ostensibly for their 'protection.'"[47]

Minimum wage legislation for women was another area that was opposed by the NWP, as discussed in chapter 4. Although several states had minimum wage laws for women, their constitutionality was never clear. One of the main arguments in favor of special legislation for women, including minimum wage, had been the lack of unionization of women compared to men. Since unorganized women workers were weak and at the mercy of employers regarding wages and hours, the legislation was justified as a substitute for their own collective action, while men were expected to gain improved conditions through self-effort. The basis for this argument—that women were less organized then men—was attacked as factually incorrect, and the NWP attempted to refute the "fallacy" that a significantly greater percentage of women were unionized.[48]

Who benefited from the alleged protection was also at issue. One writer noted that Commons and Andrews (noted experts in labor laws) referred to protective legislation as laws that "protect men in their bargaining power," that is, that favor men, not women and children. The effect was to severely limit women in "their competitive industrial life." The author preferred to stress the cooperative aspect of labor: "Now what the worker really needs is not less competition, but greater solidarity. If men and women stood together they would no longer be competing with each other."[49]

The NWP's opposition to protective labor laws for women placed them in the camp of the employers when legislative hearings on labor bills affecting women were being debated, and provided employers with ammunition in their fight against the bills. Nowhere in the NWP's literature is there recognition that this position might place working women themselves in a dilemma, or that it might present a conflict of interest in their own support for working women's rights. Instead, they joined forces with the Women's League for Equal Opportunity, which was led by women printers but which had a conservative, laissez-faire approach to labor issues (see chapter 6).

By contrast, the group of women reformers which did have a labor orientation, the Women's Trade Union League (WTUL), developed their position from the starting point of working women's need for unionization. Gradually, they came to emphasize at least as strongly the need for labor legislation for women, and came into direct conflict with the NWP supporters as well as with the one group of working women which opposed protective legislation for women. The WTUL will be considered next.

Chapter Six
The Women's Trade Union League and Protective Labor Legislation

INTRODUCTION

The Women's Trade Union League (WTUL) was one of the most active proponents of protective labor legislation for women. It occupies an interesting position with regard to the labor movement and the women's movement, and many of the tangled relations between the two are reflected in the internal inconsistencies and dilemmas which the WTUL faced.

Formed in the United States in 1903 as a group devoted to the goal of organizing women into trade unions and making unionism "respectable" for women at a time when it was only quasi-legitimate for men, the WTUL's membership consisted of "wage-earners and also women of independent means."[1] By recognizing and incorporating two classes of women as members, the league (both here and in England) claimed to have "cut across the classes," and was "a women's organization" which included trade union consciousness as an integral part of its purpose. WTUL membership consisted of working women and "allies," and the conditions of membership for the two differed: working women had only to show a paid-up union card to be members, while the wealthy "allies" paid dues.

The impetus for the league came from the middle-class social reformers; settlement house workers like Jane Addams were among its founders. These women faced all the problems inherent in a reformist middle-class organization which nonetheless wished to maintain the support of working-class women. They recognized the dangers inherent in trying to be an organization *for* working women which was not also *of* them, and throughout their history the WTUL sought out members from the trade union movement and working women who might assume positions of leadership within the WTUL.[2]

An organization with the class makeup of the WTUL is always open to the charge that it does not represent the "real" interests of the working woman, and one of the most frequent attacks against it was that it was a bunch of upper-class women who purported to speak for working women without the vaguest notion of what their problems were. This argument came to a head after World War I over the issue of support for protective labor legislation for women when the equal rights amendment was proposed.

Although the main purpose of the WTUL was to support working women in their efforts to organize themselves and to strike when necessary, the WTUL also came out very early in favor of legislation to achieve better conditions for women. Their energies were increasingly devoted to lobbying in state legislatures for "welfare bills" like minimum wage and hours restrictions for women.

The WTUL also participated in the growing push for women's suffrage, an issue which seemed peripheral to the lives of working women but which nevertheless affected them directly as workers. Since the suffrage movement was overwhelmingly middle class but lacked the WTUL's specific commitment to working women, class differences eroded "feminist" concerns, and although working women connected with the WTUL may have agreed with the aims of the suffrage groups, they never felt comfortable working with them. The middle-class members of the WTUL were also frequently active suffragists, and on occasion could provide a link between the trade unionists and the suffrage movement.

From its organization in 1903 to 1925 and after, the WTUL retained its commitment to organizing women workers and offering them strike support. However, its focus increasingly shifted to promoting labor legislation for women. The basic perspective of the organization emphasized the responsibility of middle-class members of the community for industrial evils, which were becoming increasingly apparent, and their duty to help ameliorate the exploitation of women workers in particular. The WTUL's reasons were sometimes explicitly stated in terms of preventing a possible revolution if conditions were not improved within the existing system: "If the whole burden of remedying unfair industrial inequalities is left to the oppressed social group we have the crude and primitive method of revolution. To this the only alternative is for the whole community through cooperative action to undertake the removal of industrial wrongs."[3] The WTUL's platform as stated in 1908-1909 favored equal pay for equal work, the eight-hour day, minimum wage, full citizenship for women, and "all principles of the economic program of the AF of L," but they were generally ignored by the American Federation of Labor (AFL). Most unions apparently ignored the WTUL's invitation "to send two women delegates from your local union to the National Convention."[4] This was not necessarily a deliberate slight of the WTUL in particular, however, since the AFL was generally disinterested in organizing women workers. It was the New York shirtwaist makers' strike in the winter of 1909 that brought the WTUL its first real recognition from organized labor.

The WTUL and the Shirtwaist Strikers

Frequently the AFL did not step into a trade until the women had already organized themselves or had proved themselves worthy by conducting a successful strike. Alice Kessler-Harris noted, "It could be said of the early 1900s that Jewish women courted the unions that should have been courting them."[5] Before the strike the Ladies' Waist Makers Local Union Local 25 had a thousand members. Two hundred women workers were "locked out" when they tried to organize a union, and when they picketed (legally), they were harassed and arrested. When it actually came to a strike call at a Cooper Union meeting on November 22, Gompers and other "official" speakers were the voices of moderation and caution: it was an eighteen-year-old striking worker, Clara Lemlich, who moved the assembled women to action and who literally established the strike by popular acclaim, and the strike became known as the "uprising of the thirty thousand."[6]

Even before the strike was officially declared, however, the WTUL had begun to support the picketing women. Upon hearing of the harassment by police, the WTUL women joined the picket line. Mary Dreier, "a woman of large independent means," Margaret Johnson, and others were arrested by the police.[7] (They were let go with apologies when it was discovered "who they were.")[8] As soon as the strike was declared, the WTUL set up an information bureau in union headquarters and provided speakers, financial support, and good press throughout the strike. Through the participation of these wealthy women, the cause of the "working girls" (and their plight during the winter strike) was well publicized.

The issues in this strike were not primarily wages, but union recognition, and also an end to some of the more galling practices in the trade. These included complaints by the women that they were not allowed to lift their heads from the machine even for a minute, that they had to eat while running the machines, and that they were locked in to do overtime. Many such "little" aggravations "produced such a state of chronic irritation" that, although many girls had no personal complaint, they joined the strike on behalf of those who did.[9]

Sympathy for the strikers was won on a variety of different grounds, from simple class consciousness to community responsibility. The fact that they were such young women who displayed such steadfastness and militancy was emphasized, and a number of articles described the heroism of individual strikers.[10] The fact that the strike was run by women and for women, with a minimum of male intervention, was also noted. William Mailly observed that in each shop a few girls were the leaders, mostly those who were better paid and had *fewer* grievances, and that although most strikers were Jews, who predominated in the shirtwaist shops, nonetheless three thousand Italians struck with them. He particularly noted the minor role played by men, "both in numbers and direction," a phenomenon which, he contended, was something new (although the union officials were men). This fact, he felt, was symbolic of how deep was the movement of women for greater political and economic recognition.

The contemporary analyses of this strike could not avoid seeing and being impressed with the dedication, solidarity, and spirit of the women workers, and the inescapable conclusion was that they were quite capable of sustained, organized efforts in a strike situation without assistance from male trade unionists. Support from middle-class reform groups, especially the WTUL, was frequently emphasized as a factor in their success.[11]

College students from Vassar and other elite colleges also joined the picketers. They defined their concern for the women workers in terms of community interest in having healthy citizens, but also stated that the "mothers of the future generation" needed to be supported in their struggle for better conditions. The workers' own interests and their *class* consciousness was played down.

Unions and the WTUL Reformers

Organized labor was less congratulatory of the WTUL, however. The *American Federationist*, the official journal of the AFL, viewed the shirtwaist strike in New York as a sign of the times for unionization, since these workers had not responded to union organizers in the past. The journal noted that it was the better workers who were the best strikers, and that help from "prominent people" was a factor.[12] It made no mention of the WTUL.

The AFL journal also gave space to the views of reformers like Ida Tarbell, who saw a "new solidarity of society" in the strike. Impressed with the strikers' unity, she stated that by striking they were "working not merely for themselves but for society as a whole,"[13] and also saw the strike as an example of women aiding women. By coming together gradually and forming into unions, thousands of girls could obtain shorter hours, more pay, and better sanitary conditions. This victory was important because "these girl workers of today [would] become mothers of tomorrow"; therefore the unions were protecting the life of future generations as well.[14] Unions, in this view, take the place of disruption and disorder; this position in fact mirrored the accommodations the unions were making as they successfully organized in the garment industry.[15]

This view of unionism, according to which the "worker has just as much right to bargain collectively as the employer has,"[16] stressed the disciplinary effect that unions had on worker output and reliability, which could easily be shown to benefit the employers in the long run as well as the workers. The emphasis of the reformers on the "community benefits" of better working conditions was not necessarily at odds with the union's own rationales.

There was always considerable resistance on the part of labor to bargaining away their "right to strike," however, and throughout the protocol era this issue evoked the most resistance to arbitration from both sides. The leadership of the WTUL did not always view the strike weapon as a necessary aspect of collective bargaining. Margaret Dreier Robins, for instance, while extolling the virtues of unionism because it fulfilled the need for self-government in industry and promoted fellowship, felt that the strike was "the only weapon of unorganized workers" but that "union men and women should use the strike weapon only as a last resort."[17]

Since the league was committed to furthering the AFL and no other labor organization, they sometimes were put in the embarrassing position of denying assistance to striking workers who were outside the AFL or else of supporting an unauthorized strike which the AFL was trying to end. This was what happened in the Lawrence textile strike in Massachusetts.[18] It was organized by the Industrial Workers of the World (IWW), while the AFL union leaders counseled moderation and a return to work. The WTUL organizers had to either break with the AFL leadership and side with the strikers, or refuse relief to the strikers, whose position was desperate. Their dilemma was that the IWW was an important part of the strike, and although the local WTULs were affiliated with the AFL, the national organization was not.

After four weeks of the strike, when the WTUL did decide to act and relief headquarters were established, they were hampered by their affiliation with the AFL. According to the Boston league members, they "withdrew from relief work . . . because they felt pressure was being brought to bear upon the strikers to go back to work as a condition of relief." They had "given aid to people who had not accepted the settlement if the need was great."[19] There appears to be confusion about whether, after the United Textile Workers Union accepted the settlement, relief was given to all or just to those who returned to work.

The league was conscious of its ambiguous position regarding the labor movement in another instance. After the Triangle Shirtwaist factory fire, which claimed up to 145 lives of young girls who had been locked into the factory when the fire broke out, the WTUL visited girls in the hospital and worked with the unions around the issue. However, the league secretary reported that she felt she had made a big mistake in acting as a member of the league and helping to call a citizens' meeting which was not initiated by organized labor. She felt that this action might have compromised the integrity of the league in its relations with organized labor: "The League composed as it is of two groups of people, unionists and sympathizers, is in danger of creating a feeling that the latter look for strength to other forces than labor and thus by interference deny the very reason of the League's existence to help labor meet its situations."[20]

This sensitivity to labor issues was unusual among reform organizations of the period, and the WTUL seemed to take delight in pointing out other organizations' derelictions. The WTUL frequently received publicity notices from groups like the New York League of Women Voters. The WTUL notified these groups that they refused to post the notices because there was no union label on them.[21] But the WTUL also found itself on the receiving end of this criticism during the WTUL National Convention, when they were criticized for not having a union label on printed matter used by delegates. They appealed to the Brooklyn Union Label Department to get them women's apparel for their delegates that did have the label. (This request proved impossible to comply with, since only women's shoes had the label and this outlet only carried men's clothing.)[22] The Brooklyn Labor Council duly reported this lack of a union label to its organization.

THE WTUL AND THE SUFFRAGE MOVEMENT:
RELATIONSHIP WITH WORKING WOMEN

A more serious issue, which highlighted the labor orientation of the WTUL, was the question of their support for the women's suffrage amendment. There was no liberal, labor, or radical group which openly opposed votes for women (although some felt that the vote was barely relevant to real change for the working class). Since both wings of the suffrage movement were overwhelmingly middle class, they recognized their limited contacts among working-class men and women, and sought the support of labor-oriented groups like the WTUL. Sometimes the women trade unionists agreed to support an organized suffrage campaign, and this arrangement, considered a "loan" of the trade unionists to the suffrage cause, was undertaken with a kind of mutual recognition of the ways in which each group could further its own ends. Thus the New York league suggested that one of its working women members, Margaret Hinchey, "be given the [suffrage] campaign for . . . October to work for suffrage."[23] Hinchey was distinctly uncomfortable when she attended the Suffrage Convention, and wrote to Leonora O'Reilly that the whole convention consisted of "ladies," and that "not a word of labor [was] spoken at this convention."[24]

Working women were rarely active in suffrage groups, although some, like Rose Schneiderman, were better able to bridge the gap and attempted to act as an interpreter of working women. Schneiderman said that her primary reason for wanting the vote for women was to make politicians listen to women. When striking shirtwaist workers asked the mayor to stop police brutality, they were not listened to, but the men chauffeurs were heeded, and the difference was the *vote*, Schneiderman contended. She said she was "a Socialist and a Trade Unionist who looked upon the ballot as a tool in the hands of working women with which, through legislation, they could correct the terrible conditions existing in industry."[25] Schneiderman added that she "did not expect any revolution when women got the ballot, as men had had it all these years and nothing of great importance had happened. But women needed the vote because they needed protection through laws."[26]

Schneiderman did attempt to make the suffragists understand what working conditions were like in a factory so that they might better understand the apparent lack of interest of working women in the vote. She spoke before the Suffrage School in Washington, D.C., describing what industrial working conditions were like with examples of industrial diseases in chemical industries, fumes, and lead poisoning. She said, "I hold that the humanizing of industry is woman's business. She must wield the ballot for this purpose."[27] Schneiderman maintained that the long hours which women worked, the "nerve exhaustion" which resulted from modern inventions, piecework, and homework were the reasons for working women's absence from suffrage meetings. She said:

> Some of you . . . are saying that the working women are not taking part in this great suffrage movement, and that they are not coming to the fore as they should . . . how can they? Working nine, ten hours a day and then on their return home attending to their home duties, where is the time for them to take active part in even a suffrage movement? Many times they have to stay in the factory and work through the evening, they cannot make engagements without the reservation that they can break them if work calls. And when these women join their union, attend their meetings, and pay their dues, they are doing more for social betterment than any other group that we know of. They are getting their suffrage training [i.e., in leadership].

Schneiderman here is obviously trying to interpret the lives of working women to this group of suffrage women, whose ignorance of the conditions of daily life for poor, unskilled working women was nearly complete. She concluded: "So once again I call upon you women to stand ready to help the working woman. Not to ask her to come out and help you get woman suffrage, but to go to her and offer her your help to win woman suffrage."[28]

Although Schneiderman was a union organizer and official in the WTUL (and later WTUL president), she contributed actively to the suffrage cause, and if this involvement did not seem to bother the women unionists, it did bring her some criticism from the left. The socialist, Max Fruchter chided her for her emphasis on suffrage to the neglect of socialism, claiming that trade unionism, suffrage, and socialism all wanted the same thing, and that socialism was the most "far reaching" of them all. You cannot serve two gods, he told her:

> You either work for socialism and as a consequence for the equality of the sexes, or you work for woman suffrage only and neglect socialism. Then you act like a bad doctor who pretends to cure his patient by removing the symptoms instead of removing the disease itself . . . If the question of woman suffrage is not a sex question, but as you stated a class question, where is the logic of class consciousness to ask a professional politician for aid?[29]

His letter assumed that they were in agreement on all three aims, including socialism. In fact, Schneiderman moved further away from socialism and closer to the "trade unionism pure and simple" of the AFL as her official involvement in the labor movement and the WTUL deepened. She increasingly emphasized the need for legislation to improve the working conditions of women, and also emphasized their frailty and the need for such legislation specifically for women.

The WTUL journal, *Life and Labor*, consistently supported suffrage causes and reported suffrage activities in its pages, making the connection between suffrage and the needs of working women.[30] The WTUL's activities in suffrage organizations were frequently on behalf of NAWSA, and its members criticized the more militant wing of Alice Paul, siding with NAWSA when the split over the equal rights amendment finally came.[31] Middle-class members of the WTUL may have felt more at home with the suffragists than did women of working-class origins, but some of the working women clearly felt an obligation to work for suffrage even though the suffrage organizations may have regarded them as something akin to noble savages. The connection between the powerless condition of women in general with no vote, and women as workers needing specific kinds of legislation but with no vote, was too obvious to miss. The suffrage issue, then, was the intersection of the needs of women as women and women as workers, and the WTUL, which contained woman of all classes, could help bridge the gap.

THE WTUL AND MALE UNIONISTS

The primary focus of the WTUL, however, was to work on behalf of women as workers; therefore the relationship between working women and men workers and unions was an unavoidable concern. The WTUL's stated aim was to organize women into trade unions and the AFL, but the existing male unions frequently discouraged or outright forbade women from joining them. (The position of organized labor will be discussed more fully in chapter 7.)

The opposition of men seemed especially incomprehensible to the WTUL organizers when women were undercutting wages and being hired as a source of cheap labor instead of men. The WTUL organizer Agnes Nestor reported to the New York league her experience of speaking with 150 men cigar workers at one of their union meetings:

> There was a great deal of opposition to the organization of women — the same attitude we find so often in the New York locals — an attitude of resentment to the women entering the trade, and a want of confidence of the women's ability to organize. We urged on the local the fact that the women were capturing the trade, and the only way for them to protect themselves was to organize. They at last agreed to form a committee for consultation. We have heard nothing from them.[32]

By contrast, any evidence of interest on the part of men workers was eagerly related. A letter from the WTUL secretary informed Nestor that the secretary and Schneiderman had had a "special meeting with the trade union men, which was very well attended." The secretary continued, "We believe that for the first time, we are going to be able to get some real cooperation from them."[33]

Efforts to organize women on the part of the AFL unions were frequently half-hearted when attempted at all; the lack of success which sometimes followed was used as further evidence that women were unorganizable. The WTUL exploited every chance to prove otherwise—and the conduct of women strikers gave them plenty of evidence of the courage, dedication, and spirit of women involved in union organizing and strikes.

The problems came after all was quiet again—the newly formed locals had most trouble staying together in times of relative peace. Schneiderman, struggling to keep the White Goods Union organized after a strike (1908-1909) was settled, commented that organizing women was different from organizing men, and suggested that they had not "considered seriously enough the joyless life of the working woman." She added, "Perhaps, we have not done all that is necessary to make the labor organization a social as well as an economic attraction."[34] This idea was picked up by others, and the International Ladies Garment Workers Union (ILGWU) did found Unity House, a country resort for its members which was initially scoffed at by male unionists but who then asked to use it.

Organizing women into trade unions was sometimes considered the main means of forcing improvement in working conditions for women, and sometimes also seen as a means of getting legislation passed that would then benefit all women workers, organized and unorganized. In an uncharacteristic gesture of support, John Mitchell of the AFL sent greetings to the WTUL 1909 convention, stated his conviction of the need to secure more protection for women workers, and added:

> I am equally convinced that the solution of the problem depends entirely upon the organizing of women workers in trade unions. While splendid work in their behalf is being done by various associations, yet permanent relief and permanent remedies must come from the actions of the women themselves . . . As their numbers increase, the struggle for existence and for tolerable conditions of employment becomes more intense.[35]

Gompers also preferred to emphasize the need to organize women workers into unions rather than to use legislation. And Schneiderman, although a staunch supporter of all protective legislation at the time, commented bitterly on the failure of a large part of these laws to pass the New York legislature:

> Trade Union organizing, with collective bargaining and strikes if necessary, will do more to protect the women workers of this State than appeals to a reactionary legislature led by an 18th century manufacturer . . . A two-week strike of all women laundry workers would accomplish wonders . . . Personally, I shall advise the executive board of the TUL to make no more appeals to the Legislature as it is constituted at present. It is humiliating.[36]

Appeals to unionize stressed the similar situation of workers as a group rather than the differences between men and women. Frank P. Walsh, in an editorial in the WTUL journal, reaffirmed the primacy of trade unionism: "I believe all legislation and all political 'reforms' are pretty hopeless and meaningless without it."[37] Gompers asserted: "Women work in industry side by side with men. Their relations to industry and their relations to employers contain no elements different from those of men's relations. Industrial protection and industrial betterment with freedom involve no element that differs from problems of men. Economic organization is the hope of all."[38]

Thus, unionization was sometimes seen as the common factor uniting men and women workers, and appeals for women to organize were not made on the basis of their sex, but to them as members of the working class with interests in common with other workers. As can be seen, this "solidarity" of workers (especially women and men workers) was frequently more mythical than real, and differences in method of organizing as well as the fact that women were seen as competition for "real" workers, that is, men, tended to undermine this view.

LEGISLATION AS A COMPLEMENT TO UNIONIZATION

Unionization for women was seen by the WTUL as part of a broader effort to improve working conditions, with organization and legislation as two means to the same end. Margaret Dreier Robins made the following comment on an expose of industrial conditions of women workers: "The right arm for this work is union organization and the left arm is social and industrial legislation. The two combined can abolish every industrial evil that exists today."[39]

Although the AFL did not support legislation for men workers, the WTUL supported protective laws for women right from the beginning. In a report to the New York league by the Legislative and Law Enforcement Committee, they pointed out that organized workers were also in a better position to help enforce such legislation: "Speakers have told of the value of organization not only from the point of view of bettering wages and hours of work, but also for its value in compelling employers to enforce Fire Laws and those Factory Laws governing conditions of work."[40]

The WTUL grappled with some of the practical difficulties of organizing specific groups of women, such as workers in candy factories, a particularly low-paid industry which the WTUL tried to organize (generally unsuccessfully) throughout this period. Women in these factories worked from 8:00 A.M. to 6:00 P.M., and longer during Christmas, for $9.00 per week in 1919, while male machinists worked an eight-hour day. Many of these workers were old, Italian women; the rest were young girls, and there was no enduring union. Since the employees did not seek better conditions, the WTUL felt that it would be "through more socialized legislation that the improvement of these factories [would] come, at least for some years."[41]

No potential dangers to jobs of working women from this kind of legislation were foreseen in the earlier period. The only drawback mentioned by Mrs. Raymond Robins at the 1911 convention was the possibility of judicial nullification, that is, repeal of the laws by reactionary courts, and "inefficient and partial administration" of them.[42] The convention recommended extensions of the legal limitations of hours per day and per week, and "legal minimum wage law for sweated industries."[43]

FROM UNIONIZING TO LEGISLATING

Throughout the early period (until about 1914), the arguments for protective legislation hinged upon the need to protect women from exploitation by employers, and since this protection could not be accomplished through unionization alone, legislation was considered a logical alternative. It was not seen by the WTUL as a means of removing women from jobs in which they might be in competition with men.

In fact, during a period of high unemployment in 1914, when the accusation was made that "the entrance of women into industrial life has brought about the appalling conditions of the unemployed," Rose Schneiderman answered indignantly: "The assertion is made without reason . . . why do we not shift the blame upon the child? There are over two million children employed in industrial work in our country today. They have taken men's jobs, so why put the responsibility upon woman?"[44] Women, she countered, were more adversely affected by unemployment than men were, since they were concentrated in unskilled, nonunion jobs and were "not physically strong enough to endure privation so long as men." She maintained that "you could no more put woman back in the home as her sole haven than you could turn back the clock of progress."[45] She stressed the need to find employment for *all* who needed it, male or female. She also argued that even married women, whose employment was frequently curtailed by employers, had a right to work. "Business and matrimony do not go together," said the vice-president of a Chicago bank, who defended the bank's policy of automatically discharging women who got married. Schneiderman charged that one explanation for the policy of the bank in question was that they found that they could pay less to young, unmarried girls. Many employers did discriminate against married women, including the New York Board of Education, to which policy she responded: "And I think it's the most ridiculous thing! . . . [A woman] does not need to spend the entire day with her own little ones. As to the temporary absences that just occur at the time of her children's birth, those have only been seized upon as a pretext for dispensing with her services."[46]

Schneiderman maintained that "marriage should be no bar" to working, and refuted the claim that women were taking jobs needed by married men or unmarried women. She noted that no married man whose wife worked would consent to quit in order that "some poor unmarried man" might work. Rather, she said, "What we do want is shorter working hours, which will give every one a chance, and higher pay, which will mean a living wage for every worker."[47]

The vehemence with which Schneiderman articulated this position in 1912 and 1914 contrasts sharply with her later views on the subject, and is a real index of the shift in focus which occurred within the WTUL. In 1924—after the war period, when women had been employed at a whole range of jobs previously closed to them, after women had won the vote, and at the height of the debate over the equal rights amendment—Schneiderman, speaking at an Albany hearing in defense of protection for women in industry, stated that women cannot do "the same work as a man," and that "equal rights cannot keep them in work for which they are physically unfit." In 1912, by contrast, she had emphasized that individual aptitude should determine the work women do: "It seems to me that it is simply the question of fitness which should decide whether or not a woman should take or hold any particular job."[48] By 1924, she had also decided that women, even if they were individually fit and able to hold a "man's" job, should not be permitted to do so: "And the women who are strong enough to work beside men, and who want to work at the same hours of the day or night and receive the same pay, might be putting their own brothers, or sweethearts, or future husbands, out of a job."[49] Schneiderman was at that time vice-president of the National Women's Trade Union League and president of the New York organization.

Initially, the WTUL had concentrated on unionizing women. Gradually, they came to define their mission in terms of lobbying for protective laws, including those which prohibited women from working at certain jobs.[50] These laws began to be justified by women's relative weakness, as health measures that were needed more by women than men, and by stressing the importance of healthy women for the future of the race.

At the same time, the effects of these laws, which did displace women from industries they had previously been in, came under increasing attack from the women affected. As a result of the no-night-work laws, women printers were thrown out of their jobs; this group of workers then formed the most contentious opposition to protective labor legislation and were a constant thorn in the side of the WTUL. After the war, women were also fired to make way for returning men in a variety of jobs, including that of streetcar conductor in several cities.[51]

OPPOSITION TO PROTECTIVE LABOR LAWS FROM WORKING WOMEN

After the no-night-work laws were passed in New York State in 1914, a small but determined opposition developed among women printers. These women succeeded in having the restriction lifted for themselves, and during the postwar years their organization actively opposed all protective labor laws for women. They found support from the National Woman's Party, which, as indicated, opposed the laws, and also from manufacturers who opposed all restrictions on their labor force.

Immediately after the passage of the night work bill, the women in publishing put the WTUL on the defensive. A league representative who spoke before the Bookbinders' Union on January 4, 1914, reported as follows:

> [They] hold us responsible for the enactment of the night law and we were asked to speak on the platform with other people to explain what was to be done with the women who had been thrown out of work. I told them the League had not been responsible for the passing

of the Bill, but when there had been danger of it being repealed one of our workers had gone and spoken in favor of the bill . . . I told them that the one remedy was organization, and that in the case of all good things, the few suffer for the good of the many.[52]

Abram Elkus (lawyer and counsel of the Factory Investigating Commission) was also present at the meeting and promised to see what could be done to save the jobs of those women adversely affected by the law.

The WTUL position, that the laws were beneficial even though a small number of women might be adversely affected by them, was reiterated in the league's support for the Radice v. New York decision in 1918. Radice had employed waitresses after 10:00 P.M. in violation of the law. (He lost on the grounds that "protection of the health of women [was] a subject of special concern to the state," and that night work was bad for health.) The WTUL commented, "The mere fact that in some instances individual hardship is experienced under the statutes is no way controlling as to its constitutionality. Neither is it class legislation because the law applies equally and with the same restrictions."[53]

Frances Perkins, then a member of the State Industrial Commission, argued similarly in defense of the night work bill: "We talked of those who opposed this bill . . . 'Some people always suffer during an industrial change'." Perkins said, "When I investigated conditions immediately after the passage of the bill [three years previous] I found that 100 women were inconvenienced by having their wages cut down. But the other 400,000 were unmistakably benefited by it. Under the circumstances, the 100 inconvenienced should be sports enough to stand it."[54]

The WTUL was consciously calling for sacrifices from a sector of working women for the good of the rest; what is interesting is that this kind of "sacrifice" evoked such impassioned opposition by the women affected, while the "sacrifice" called for by straight trade union activity, like organizing and striking, was greeted very differently by the workers. Opposition from women who were undeniably harmed by the law did not cause the WTUL to doubt their position regarding the positive value of this law. Instead, they hardened their stand and attacked the working women who opposed it, who in turn lost no opportunity to attack the WTUL for being middle class and ignorant of the needs of real working women.

Although the night work restrictions had been passed several years earlier, the effectiveness of the League for Equal Opportunity (the women printers' organization) was felt primarily after the war. In 1919, the Women's Joint Legislative Conference (an umbrella organization which included the WTUL and which lobbied for passage of protective laws), informed the New York league that the opposition to "our bills" had organized a letter campaign to legislators, employers, and working women. Incensed, the WTUL tried to get the women printers thrown out of their union. In a personal conversation with a Mr. Douglas of Typographers Local No. 6, they learned that all they could do was take away the printers' union cards, but that would be difficult because the printers were not claiming to speak for the union in their actions. At hearings for the Lockwood eight-hour bill in Albany during April 1918, Rose Schneiderman and two hundred other people lobbied in support of the bill, while the opposition came from the Telephone Company, the railroads, and members of the Typographical Union. This last group, according to the WTUL, "used all their spare time in speaking against the labor bills or in lobbying for bills breaking down the labor laws for women," and the league notified the Typographers Union of this fact, adding that the women speakers had "made slanderous attacks" on the WTUL itself.[55]

The WTUL also felt it necessary to write to Mary Anderson, a former member who was then in Washington, D.C., with the government, telling her of the three women of No. 6 "and warning her against them, as they had written her relative to night work."[56] During this time, the WTUL itself had been "especially busy . . . with legislative work," and had sent out 677 letters during October 1918 to candidates in the New York election stating their own platform and asking the candidates to state their own position.[57]

That the dissident women were an effective opposition to the protective laws or had at least sown a small amount of doubt in the minds of otherwise favorably inclined lawmakers can be seen from the correspondence with one assemblyman, who wrote asking the New York league "who these persons are and what the organization [League for Equal Opportunity] is in the name of which they speak?"[58] The WTUL responded at length to him, defending their own credentials in supporting working women and attacking the opposition:

> It is an organization started some time ago by the discontented women in the printing industry, who were making more money working nights than they could working days.
>   I think it would be fairly conservative to say they consist of about a few hundred women. The WTUL, whom they spend a good deal of time in reviling, is an organization which has been in the field since 1903. It has an affiliated membership of 60,000 trade union women . . . which [at a conference in January, 1918] went on record as favoring our entire legislative program. It would seem to me that the answer in that is enough.

The writer added that the "very best opinions and minds of the entire civilized world are against them, and organized labor itself, in the person of the State Federation of Labor."[59]

Not only did this maverick group of women workers cause the WTUL problems with legislators, but they also created strains in the WTUL's relations with the labor movement. The Philadelphia Typographical Union No. 2 notified the WTUL that it had "decided to sever its connection with the WTUL, and to withdraw its delegates and all further financial assistance." The letter gave no explanation for the action; the league replied to the union president, William Young, as follows:

> We are, of course, aware of the connection between this action and the fraternal delegate who misrepresented you at our National Convention. Should you really care to know the real character and motives of this woman you could get the information from plenty of the members of your own International who have known the harm she has done the labor movement in New York this long time.[60]

In this instance, the union followed the lead of their women members who opposed limitations on their work. In another case, where the union and the WTUL allied in favor of restrictive laws, the group of women streetcar workers affected accused the WTUL of acting against the interests of women by supporting "the men's union, not the women." The WTUL had contended that the Amalgamated Street Car Workers union had favored the bill, and that it also represented women. The WTUL asked in a letter to Miss Mary A. Murray, president of the Brooklyn Rapid Transit (BRT) Equal Opportunity League, "Is it not true that a BRT official made the statement that bill or no bill the BRT would not employ women as conductors once the war ended?" The league's secretary continued that it was strange to still hear the argument that working women don't want protective labor legislation when a conference in Albany "which was composed exclusively of working women" with delegates from thirty organizations endorsed both an eight-hour day and a minimum wage bill. The WTUL would only believe they did not want such bills when "large representative groups of working women such as these [could] be gathered and [could] go on record as opposed."[61] The women streetcar workers sent an open letter to the *Woman Citizen* making the following charges:

> [The WTUL] well knows of the treachery of the Union of the Amalgamated Street and Electric Car Workers toward the B.R.T. women. Yes, it did favor the Lockwood-Caulfield Bill, it also took the women's

money, asked them to go on strike, and after strike was won, had the audacity to print a pamphlet starting over their own signature that men wouldn't stand for the women coming back on the cars. Did they give the money back that they had taken from the women? No, yet Maud Swartz asks did they not represent women? The history of the Amalgamated in their bitter fight on women all over the country is answer to those question.[62]

Another group of workers affected by the bill, elevator operators, were not organized. Therefore it would have been very hard for them to express themselves on an elevator bill; when consulted, however, they had "complained bitterly" of the long hours and poor working conditions, according to representatives of the WTUL.

During the postwar period, women who had been temporarily hired during wartime were let go afterward, regardless of whether or not they had actually replaced men, or men were rehired in those industries. One writer stated in the WTUL newspaper that women streetcar conductors were hired "not because there [was] a real shortage of men, or to replace employees who [had] gone to war, but to punish men for their strikes in 1916." The writer stated that the women were "getting used as a threat to keep the men 'well-disciplined' and to prevent the spread of union organization among them."[63] The writer, a special investigator for the American Association of Labor Legislation, said that the women were receiving 27¢ per hour, while male "common laborers" were receiving 35¢ per hour. Since the women's work was not regulated, they worked ten-hour shifts or longer and did night work, with its "moral danger," for young girls especially:

> But even if hours were shortened there are many objectionable features in women's work on New York street cars . . . crowds in rush hours are especially large, and . . . are not noted for their good manners. A woman would find it hard to handle disorderly persons. Then there is the moral menace and the health dangers from constant standing.[64]

This writer favored prohibiting women from the job altogether, which the New York league pointed out was contrary to their own position: "The League stands for the protection of women in all industries, rather than their prohibition from some industries."[65]

In Detroit, the women conductors managed to keep their jobs after the war because the men had left for better-paid jobs. The women had been holding the jobs since September 1918 on the same terms as the men.[66] In Cleveland, by contrast, the women streetcar conductors were removed at the insistence of Division 268 of the Amalgamated Association of Street and Electrical Railway Employees, who went on strike to have the women fired. The WTUL protested, saying that the women were trained workers, despite lack of help from the men; that the women did not displace men when they were hired; and that there were not enough men to fill all posts if the women were fired immediately. "The women conductors of Cleveland are all self-supporting women, two-thirds of them supporting, also, children or parents. Twenty-six have husbands or sons in the Army," the league argued. These women had tried to join the union but had been refused because admission would have given them "protection against dismissal."[67] In Detroit also, the men had threatened to strike, but the terms of the contract in that city differed from those in Cleveland.

> This raises the fundamental issue of women's right to equal industrial opportunity with men, trade union women point out, and they add, puts squarely up to the Amalgamated Association once more to choose, on the one hand, between giving the women conductors a square deal by taking them into the union, and on the other hand, forcing them to be scabs or starve.[68]

This issue raised the basic questions regarding a "right to work" for men and women both, as well as the subsidiary issue of whether these jobs were "fit" for a woman. Many of the jobs which had been male preserves before the war, and from which women were excluded on the grounds that the jobs were too physically demanding, were in fact much easier work than what these same women had been doing before, such as factory work. By comparison, ticket taking for a railway looked pretty good and also paid much better. During the short period of wartime, the WTUL took a patriotic stance and declared that women were "thriving on the new jobs." In an article entitled "Doing the Work of Men," they noted that the women working in car yards were strong women and better paid than laundry workers, and concluded that it was a question of individual, not sex, aptitudes. In fact, women could develop "a physique as splendid as that of her peasant sister in Europe."[69]

Although the WTUL supported the war effort, however, they cautioned against using "false patriotism"[70] to "induce women to undertake tasks which [would] injure them as individuals or as future mothers."[71] The war effort was used to try to nullify existing limitations on women's work, and the WTUL was active in lobbying against such bills.[72] In New York State, these efforts against protective legislation were defeated, and at Albany hearings on the bills, Melinda Scott, an organizer for the league, flatly stated, "The chief measure of national preparedness in this country is that which protects the potential motherhood of the United States."[73] She cited President Wilson's message to labor in June 1917, in which he urged that protective labor laws not be lost because of the war.

Although the WTUL appreciated that women were being allowed to enter trades previously denied them, they were aware of the potential for exploitation and frequently felt that this expanded opportunity was detrimental. For instance, girl bootblacks in Boston wore uniforms called "pantalettes"; using illustrations, the league commented that these uniforms were "both immodest and ungraceful," but more importantly, that shining shoes led nowhere, and therefore presented "not so much a case of substitution [of girls for boys] as exploitation."[74]

They also commented on how the war had affected the position of black women workers, with articles sympathetically calling for "a fair deal for the colored folks." Ida Wells Barnett, a black activist, wrote that with men being drafted, white women could work in previously closed occupations, but not "colored women." She stated that the Negro had been "intensely loyal to this country, its institutions," and had done the "hardest and the poorest paid kind of labor," and that now Negroes were being denied even that. She argued: "America cannot afford to treat the Negro so. He is too valuable an asset of the nation . . . he isn't now in a position to assert or demand his rights . . . [but] we should see to it that his family has an equal chance with the white folks" to decent work.[75] Noting the small number of jobs available for black women, the question, according to Mary Roberts Smith (identified as a Negro with the Chicago League on Urban Conditions among Negroes), was whether the black woman would be "permitted to take her place and do her part in helping to win this war"[76]

A later postwar article by Forrester Washington of the Urban League noted that the war's end meant a loss of jobs for "colored girls," who were the first to be fired. Chicago, with the third largest Negro population, was "most inconsiderate" in its treatment of Negroes, and only 53 firms out of the 170 that employed Negroes for the first time during the war represented new occupations for Negro women. The writer then said that charges that the Negro woman was "less efficient" than others originated with prejudiced foreladies; he contended that Negroes were more efficient than whites and "more intelligent than foreign girls."[77]

The expansion during the war lasted only a little over a year. Peace brought with it the concern for jobs being lost and the awareness that men and women were going to be competing for positions formerly held by men only. Van Kleeck noted that part of the danger of firing women after the war was that this practice "would inject into the labor movement a new alignment of men workers against women workers.[78] One solution was to claim that "men and women alike have the right to work," as the Washington, D.C., Central Labor Union stated. After the war, they said, employment should be redistributed "so as to deprive no man or woman of employment, but to redistribute workers, male and female, according to the new industrial needs."[79]

The WTUL was cognizant of the hardship for women who were about to be laid off, such as those in munitions factories, who were described as strong women, doing heavy work, but also thinking of their children. Making good money on the night shift, these women met the demands of both home and work and, according to the writer who had visited such women in one plant, took pride in their skilled work. But the question was, now what? Their men probably couldn't find work yet, and "they still [needed] to earn war wages." But the ads for women workers read: "Want supply of women—$6-8 per week" or "Wanted—Women. At prewar wages."[80]

In analyzing these shifts, it was hard to say how many women actually entered the labor force for the first time as a result of the war. A survey of one plant indicated that most women had changed from other trades: 65 percent were from other factories, 25 percent were from domestic service, and 5 percent were from laundries, while only 5 percent had not been employed previously.[81] The unemployment problem after the war, then, was "that the men [were] out and the women [were] in," but the writer asserted, "Just because tradition holds that the situation should be reversed, we now recognize the problem as acute." The writer commented, "A reserve of unemployed is not only a waste of potential energy, it is a direct menace to the maintenance of a high standard for labor," and will serve to dilute union labor. We need a policy of "reconstruction," not "adjustment" for the women workers.[82]

The war was followed by a period of reaction which was felt in both the political and economic spheres. Red baiting became strong, and the WTUL—which, especially in New York, had cooperated from time to time with socialists—now resisted attempts to red-bait them. In 1920, at the height of the repression, the United States Chamber of Commerce and the National Association of Manufacturers, with the War Department's cooperation, distributed what became known as the "spiderweb chart." This chart "purported to show communistic connections and influences exerted through members of the Women's Joint Congressional Committee upon all the national organizations affiliated to that Committee,"[83] of which the WTUL was an important member. The WTUL forced the repudiation of the document by the secretary of war, but it continued to be circulated (see chapter 8.)

The WTUL continued to run articles generally favorable or informational in tone about conditions in the Soviet Union following the revolution.[84] Quite a few of the active WTUL members, like Helen Marot, were connected with the Socialists at one time or another, but the league seems to have emerged from the attacks successfully.

The antilabor legislation forces used the loyalty issue in their campaigns, however, and opposition to various "welfare" bills in Albany up through the early 1920s came from groups with patriotic titles. In 1919 and 1920 the eight-hour day and minimum wage bills were defeated in the New York legislature by organized opposition from the New York League for Americanism and the Joint Legislative Committee to Investigate Seditious Activities, headed by Senator Clayton Lusk.[85] The Americanism organization was said to be the name for the Associated Manufacturers and Merchants in New York State.[86]

THE EQUAL RIGHTS AMENDMENT: THE WTUL DEFENDS PROTECTIVE LAWS

In contrast to the National Woman's Party, which ultimately opted for equal rights for women and opposed protective labor laws for women, the WTUL did not reevaluate their position in favor of protective labor legislation, and denied that these laws harmed the situation of working women. This denial brought them into direct confrontation with their former allies, the NWP.

In February 1921, the National WTUL's Secretary was able to write to Maud Swartz that their "apprehensions" about the upcoming Woman's Party Convention and Alice Paul were unfounded, and she doubted that the NWP would adopt a program antagonistic to them on this.[87] When finally confronted with the new position of the NWP and others who argued for equal treatment of women and for judging job qualifications on an individual, not a sex-determined basis, the WTUL waved their credentials as representatives of working women and claimed that the opposition was not in a position to know working women's needs.

When the International Woman Suffrage Alliance introduced a resolution opposing protective labor laws, the WTUL stated:

There appears to be among middle-class and professional women a lot of mis-information on the strictly wage-earning and industrial groups. This form of legislation, far from restricting the opportunities of factory workers, has been of great benefit to them by preventing the employers from exploiting beyond certain limits.[88]

When the suffragist Anna Howard Shaw took a position which the New York league disapproved of, they noted that she hadn't "very much knowledge of industrial conditions," and that she had simply echoed the position of the hated League for Equal Opportunity in opposing the laws. They countered, "We are all seeking protective legislation. We have not come to the point where we believe that women should be free to work in any industry or in all industries, regardless of the conditions thereof."[89]

One of the few letters the league printed which opposed protective legislation for women, accused the laws, and the WTUL for supporting them, of taking "the typical anti-suffragist, anti-feminist attitude—i.e., that women must 'be protected' and that they must 'shrink' from meeting men on the level ground of equality." The writer mentioned in particular the nine-hour bill for office work and the night work ban on morning papers. She stated:

I found that such work in no way impaired my health, either physical or mental . . . It is with a sense of ironic despair that women like myself, who had hoped with the ballot to end the paternal legislation of the past, contemplate the spectacle of the women's trade unions, the consumers leagues, and *Life and Labor* all altruistically and determinedly beginning the *maternal* legislation of the future!

She also noted that equal pay for equal work was impossible when "the hours and conditions of [women's] work [were] hedged about by taboos and thou-shalt-nots which [did] not apply to the young men with whom [they were] competing."[90]

The above writer was easy to rebut because of her obviously non-working-class character. Margaret Robins responded that the writer was a professional woman and an "individualist," and pointed out the nineteenth-century laissez-faire nature of some of her arguments, which stemmed from a time when "it was believed that government had no right to determine conditions of work."[91] Rose Schneiderman added, "competition among workers is a disastrous thing and only helps the employer," and said that if she were a laundry worker she would not think nine hours was so short a day: "The whole mistake [the writer] makes is in the idea that there is a career in industry or in the department store."[92]

When the WTUL were forced to justify their position against the argument that the legislation assumed the inferiority of women, they sometimes asserted that it tended to improve conditions for *all* workers in the industry. Mrs. Robins stated in her address to the First International Congress of Working Women: "A great advance has been made since the days when it was felt necessary to plead for the eight-hour day for women only. The call is now for the shorter day and the human life for everybody, man or woman . . . Protection for men as well as woman."[93] They denied that the equal rights amendment (or the "blanket amendment," as they preferred to call it) would lead to real, economic equality for women. Ethel Smith (secretary of the WTUL) argued that, although everyone believes in justice, we know we cannot achieve it by decrees, and similarly with equal rights. She referred to the National Woman's Party as the "extreme left" of the women's movement, a minority with "millionaire backing" which played into the hands of wealthy men. She contrasted "the active lobbying of well-to-do women of the NWP" with the opposition: "an equality active, but by no means well-to-do" group protesting against it, which included the WTUL and the American Federation of Labor.[94] She said that women must not seek equality by "taking away what one sex has gained merely because the other sex has it not." She mentioned that the equal rights amendment assumed that social and economic rights were "the same as legal rights, or [could] be secured by legislative enactment," and she argued: "As a matter of fact, legal rights may actually defeat economic or social rights. This had been labor's most bitter experience."[95] Besides labor legislation, the equal rights amendment would affect a host of other laws, such as a wife's right to her husband's support: would it take that right away, or extend it to the husband also? What about the father's liability for an illegitimate child? The amendment's potential effect on these laws could not be known in advance, Smith concluded.

CONCLUSION

The early militant activities of the league, their willingness to join with working women in strikes and to offer their resources when needed in a very direct, personal way, gradually gave way to an emphasis on legislation and lobbying activities. This change happened despite the fact that while they were hardening their support of legislation for women workers only, labor laws for *all* workers were becoming increasingly acceptable, and some harmful effects of laws for women were becoming evident.

Women printers were one group of skilled, organized women who were harmed by the laws. The WTUL never considered their plight a serious problem. They were called atypical of women workers and were criticized for kicking up a fuss about a few jobs lost when the vast majority of working women benefit from the laws. When women streetcar workers were also adversely affected, the WTUL contended that it was not the laws that did them out of their jobs but the men returning from the war who claimed their old jobs back.

The WTUL also rejected the feminist arguments of the Woman's Party for equality before the law, saying that it was better to correct inequities piecemeal as they arose than to undo protections that were vitally needed by women workers. Although they frequently emphasized the strengths of women, women's dedication to the trade union movement, and women's ability to do jobs beyond those to which they were confined, the WTUL denied the problematic nature of laws which placed specific restrictions on working women. In fact, the league increasingly defined the benefits of those laws in terms of women's importance as "mothers of the future generation": the domestic function of women had primacy over their position in the labor force.

When forced to choose between better-paid skilled jobs for women and protective laws which preserved women's status as reproducers of the future work force, the WTUL opted for the legislation. They saw themselves as advocates of the interests of working women, but the improvements they sought were always those which would serve to maintain the existing system, including the family structure, not to destroy it. And the chief role of women in that system lay in their domestic functions as *reproducers* of the labor force, not primarily as wage workers.

When these two positions conflicted, the WTUL chose the course which reinforced women's secondary status in the work force. The most striking illustration of this is Rose Schneiderman's complete about-face. Her unequivocal declaration in 1914 that women, as members of the working class, had the same vested rights to their jobs as men did gave way to her assertion ten years later than women were guilty of "taking" men's jobs.

The WTUL, as a labor-oriented social reform organization, recognized the problems of trying to organize women into male trade unions that did not want them. Their support for the AFL sometimes placed them in awkward situations, but they consistently avoided the radical alternative, that is, the IWW. They also did not try to organize women outside the AFL unions. The role of the AFL itself will be considered next.

These, Our Lamented Dead.

Chapter Seven
The Role of Organized Labor

Should the Wife Help to Support the Family? I have no hesitancy in answering, positively and absolutely, "No."

Nor do I wish to be understood to be opposed to the full and free opportunity of women to work whenever and wherever necessity requires.

Samuel Gompers,
January, 1906

INTRODUCTION

The welcoming handshake with which organized labor greeted women in industry had been lukewarm at best. Ambivalence or outright hostility toward women workers permeated the early statements of many of the early male craft unions. By the turn of the century, however, women were a permanent and growing part of the industrial work force, and organized labor's statements, if not their underlying attitude, had softened somewhat to allow that women perhaps could be granted admission to the fraternity of labor if their place were carefully circumscribed. Men worked for a living as a matter of course; women worked out of "necessity" or "misfortune."

In fact, this position had a side of truth to it—young girls worked until they married (or had children) and then quit, whenever possible, to take care of the children, husband, and house. If they returned to work, their household responsibilities did not cease but were added to their wage labor, a combination which made for long days of work. This fact was taken for granted. Small children might help with housework; the husband, never. The demands of the present-day women's movement to spread the joy around when it comes to housework were completely outside the realm of discussion throughout the period under consideration here.

The actions of male unions indicated their commitment to uphold the prevailing situation, in which women were responsible for the reproduction of the labor force within the home; their treatment of women workers indicates how peripheral to the wage labor force they considered women workers. Male-dominated unions accepted differential wage scales for women on the one hand, and on the other made little serious attempt to organize women into unions. Their goal was to make *men's* wages adequate to support the family, and although they recognized that women worked out of necessity and sometimes were the sole support of a family, this recognition did not cause them to change their views.

Although women represented at best about 20 percent of the work force during this period, they were either completely absent from most major industries, like mining and steel, or were majorities or sizable minorities in a few, like the ladies' garment industry and the printing trades. For the vast majority of men, women were not likely to be co-workers or potential competition for jobs, and were therefore a negligible factor in industrial life. Only where women were a major part of the trade, or becoming so, was there likely to be any discussion at all of their "proper place."

For the most part, labor unions had far more pressing problems than deciding what to do about women workers. The opening of this century saw the beginnings of a frontal attack on organized labor by the National Association of Manufacturers, the forceable breakup of craft unions in the growing steel industry, and a decline in union membership after 1904 from which the AFL did not fully recover until about 1911. In addition, the growing strength of socialist movements and the Industrial Workers of the World (IWW) posed another threat to conservative leadership within the AFL. Politically, there was pressure from the left to form an independent labor party as in Britain, which meant that the AFL needed to formulate an alternative strategy which would demonstrate their power while remaining within the existing two-party structure.

Faced with all these issues of survival, the AFL was concerned with other issues than with organizing women workers or with lobbying for legislation on their behalf. It was probably not until the beginnings of the war effort, when women were going to be used in place of male labor in many industries, that there was real concern for their status.

The labor organizations which will be examined here include those that were the most influential, such as the AFL, and those which are of interest because of their unique situation with regard to women workers, namely the International Ladies Garment Workers' Union (ILGWU) and the International Typographical Union. The special situation of a group of women printers who were thrown out of their jobs as a result of the no-night-work law in New York State will also be considered. The relative involvement of each of these organizations in the passage of labor legislation, at either the state or national level, will be assessed to evaluate whether they were instrumental in working for protective legislation for women workers. Of particular concern will be the attitude of these unions toward women as workers and as union members of the trade. Both the ILGWU and the printing trade unions were members of the AFL; the differences between their approaches and the AFL will also be considered.

The American Federation of Labor

The AFL emerged as a craft-based organization in opposition to the declining Knights of Labor in the 1880s, and Samuel Gompers was its head by the turn of the century. Throughout this period, he remained its leader until his death in 1924, and its policies are virtually inseparable from his own views and pronouncements. Gompers was vehemently anti-Socialist, he was opposed to the establishment of a labor party or independent political power for the union (although this opposition did not preclude lobbying for labor objectives at both state and national levels), and he concentrated on economic gains for a limited sector of skilled craft workers. He viewed the large mass of unskilled workers as a threat to be neutralized in whatever way possible, and favored exclusion of Chinese immigrants.

On the other hand, Gompers worked closely with top corporate leaders, through his membership in the National Civic Federation, to develop procedures of accommodation and conciliation with the growing power of monopoly capital. For this effort he gained their approval of unionism, provided it was the "right" sort that opposed "unauthorized" strikes or socialist rhetoric. His relations with the National Association of Manufacturers (NAM), by contrast, were implacably hostile. They were The Enemy. They were the ones that had him convicted of sponsoring an illegal boycott against Bucks Stove & Range Co. (owned by the NAM head, Van Cleave), and who successfully opposed all his anti-injunction efforts in Congress in the prewar period.

The position of the AFL was important because it represented organized labor to the public and to political leaders, and Gompers was the AFL personified. During the early part of the period, the extent of labor's power was unclear. It was not known whether there was a "labor vote" despite the absence of a labor party, or whether the lobbying power of the AFL was strong enough to gain its objectives. By the beginning of

World War I, Gompers was established enough to be included as a member of the war policy board (Council of National Defense) representing labor.

The AFL's views regarding women workers and the desirability of protective labor legislation for women are important because these laws were ostensibly designed for the protection of working women. Some unions viewed the laws mainly as a way of eliminating women from trades in which women competed with men, and their rationale for promoting the laws will be discussed. How much of the impetus for these laws came from organized labor, and how did labor unions justify their position? Their thoughts about women's commitment to the trade compared with women's obligations in the home will be examined in this chapter.

LEGISLATION AND THE AFL

In the United States, unlike England and other European countries, the dominant part of the labor movement was generally suspicious of using legislation to improve wages and working conditions.[1] By contrast, in England, it was axiomatic that trade unions should seek to use parliamentary measures as one means toward their ends, according to the Webbs and others. Although laissez-faire doctrines were also used there to prevent labor legislation, their effect was of short duration. With the emergence of the factory system in the nineteenth century in England, the demand for statutory limitation of the working day grew.[2] The Webbs pointed out the difficulties of legislative strategies: after endless commissions were appointed to study an issue, bills were drafted and reworked, and so forth, the outcome was the minimum possible concession to public opinion and workers' demands. It was, however, a relatively permanent form of agreement, uniform for all districts, and "once any regulation has been adopted, it becomes practically impossible altogether to rescind it," so that the rule slid more likely "up" than "down" from the workers' point of view.[3] This is the other side of the legitimation problem (discussed in chapter 1) which these reforms generated.

In the United States, the AFL, with its craft-union base, perferred to gain hours limitations primarily by collective bargaining. In each case in which hours were legislated for a limited sector (for example, for public employees, or women and children), the result was less of an improvement than some of the highly organized crafts had been able to secure by contract. In almost classical laissez-faire logic, the AFL and Gompers disclaimed interest in legal regulations or invasion by the political sphere into the economic realm, which was the province of the trade union. (This issue will be discussed more fully below.) But Gompers was very much concerned with those aspects of the political arena which were vital to the existence of unions and which provided the milieu within which collective bargaining could take place. If labor were to have its hands tied by anti-injunction laws, antitrust indictments, yellow-dog contracts, and "iron-clad" oaths (for example, that the worker will not join a union), then the very means by which unions function would be destroyed.

Until the beginning of the war, this was the major concern of the AFL. Their major lobbying efforts, the prime targets for attack, centered around these issues. Although protective legislation for women workers was being passed by the states and being tested in the courts (for instance, Muller v. Oregon was being appealed through the courts in 1907), there is little or no mention of these cases in the union's official writings.

The two most pressing legal problems for the AFL from the turn of the century until about 1914 centered on employers' prosecution of unions for being a conspiracy in restraint of trade (illegal under the Sherman Anti-Trust Act) and the use of court injunctions aimed at preventing picketing and striking. This legislation is qualitatively different from protective labor legislation (whether for women or men) because it is aimed at unions per se, rather than conditions of works for individuals. In this country, a labor union has always been a legal organization (unlike in England, where the nineteenth-century Anti-Combination Acts made them unlawful). But the *activities* of unions came under strong attack, and the law, which was ostensibly framed for the purpose of limiting the formation of corporations and trusts, was first used against labor. According to the meaning given to the "conspiracy" doctrine, acts which one person could legally do could be harmful and illegal when done in combination with others. Strikes (quitting work) easily came under the provisions of the Sherman Anti-Trust Act according to this interpretation, and so did boycotts.[4] This use of law again demonstrates the futility of analyzing legal doctrines as abstract principles in isolation from the social context.

Gompers denied that the union was being un-American by using the boycott, noting that American revolutionary patriots also used it. The trust itself, he stated, was "a logical development of the present economic era," and it was futile to try to oppose it. The union, however, "while not a trust [was] just as inevitable and logical a development as the trust itself," that is, it came out of the same economic conditions.[5] But unions were to be distinguished from trusts, he contended, in reasoning that he repeated intermittently until the Clayton Act of 1914 exempted unions from most Sherman Act provisions.[6] The court held differently, however, and in December, 1908, three AFL officers were found guilty of contempt and sentenced to jail. (Litigation continued until 1914, when the decision was ultimately overturned by the U.S. Supreme Court on a technicality.)

In addition, the Adair case, decided by the Supreme Court in January of 1908, held that an act which had made it unlawful to discharge a worker because he joined a union interfered with the employer's liberty of contract. These legal decisions, combined with an aggressive open shop campaign by National Association of Manufacturers' employers and others, meant that belonging to a union was legal, but that the worker could be blacklisted or fired for joining up, and could not strike, boycott products, or try to get others to join the union. The anti-union campaign of 1902-1904 had borne results.

These adverse decisions by the courts meant that the AFL had to act quickly to get favorable legislation exempting them from these penalties, or face an uncertain future. At the same time, there was growing pressure from the Socialists and others within the AFL who were dissatisfied with the results of the nonpolitical, "nonpartisan" policy of the AFL to find an alternative strategy. But Gompers's antagonism towards the employers was fully equaled by his sarcastic denunciations of Socialists Eugene Debs, Hillquit, and others, and he frequently lumped them together.[7]

By 1908 the AFL had assessed the two major parties and had concluded that the Democrat Bryan was more favorable to labor than the Republican Taft, and advised the labor vote to support the Democrats fully. (Debs, who also ran as a Socialist, of course, was not considered.) Taft's victory showed the inability of the AFL to deliver the vote even where it had sizable membership.

These were the pressing concerns of Gompers and the AFL during the period before 1912. Open hostility to organized labor by the courts and the federal government dominated their attention. It was during this period that the case of Muller v. Oregon was appealed and won. The Supreme Court, which upheld the validity of the Oregon ten-hour law for women, was the same court that was busily finding all activities of labor unions subject to injunction or sanctions under the Sherman Act. Clearly, the Court did not view an hours law which infringed upon the right of employers' and female employees' freedom of contract as a serious threat, but organized labor's use of the strike and boycott was severely dealt with. During this period (before the coming of a Democratic administration in Washington), it appears that even conservative craft unionism was viewed as an unnecessary and possibly dangerous development.

THE AFL AND WOMEN WORKERS

Prior to World War I, the AFL barely gave lip service to the need to organize women workers. Almost nothing appeared in the official AFL journal about them until the shirtwaist strike of 1909-10. In 1906 there appeared a "Women in Unions" series, which discussed women's participation in different trades. For example, the Cloth Hat and Cap Makers' Union was described, and the gains made through unionization were stressed. Each process in the trade had a union, with separation of jobs by sex. Unionization, initiated by women themselves, achieved a decrease in hours from twelve-hour days at home and more at night, to eight- or nine-hour days and no homework, and the pay went from $5.00 to $7.00 per week, the author claimed.[8]

Another article, by Professor John Commons, described women in the meat packing industry. Women entered the trade around 1876 along with fathers and brothers, but were not then "competition" for men workers. But these Irish-, German-, and English-speaking girls were replaced by newer immigrants, and by 1894 and 1904 they evidently *were* considered competition. Women worked soldering cans for lower pay, and in April 1905 the girls formed a women's local. Commons noted that they did not fight speedup like the men did. Women worked by piecework (which encourages self-induced speedup), and they also expected to work "only a short time in the industry . . . their chief object [being] to earn as much money as possible and then leave the industry for homes of their own."[9] Another article noted the lower dues and lower benefits for women, who were organized into separate locals of the Bakery and Confectionary Workers' Union.[10]

Typical of the AFL approach to women workers in this period was the discussion by Eva McDonald Valesh of the New York Federation of Women's Clubs. Valesh argued that the AFL had been the only force in society to help the working women and that unions were even more necessary for women than for men, since women were "physically weaker and temperamentally less fitted than men to combat the strain and tension of modern industrialism." The opinion which both the writer and the union shared was stated as follows: "The AFL realizes that the normal place for women is in the home. Much of the most valuable work done by the Federation is in the direction of gaining such conditions for men workers that it will be possible for their wives and daughters to remain at home."[11] Since women would continue to be wage earners, Valesh also stated:

> It is criminal negligence to permit [them] to sacrifice health, mentality, and life itself to the shortsighted policy of the employer who does not realize that kindly and just treatment of employees brings

its rewards in dollars and cents, as well as in the consciousness of contributing to the welfare of humanity.[12]

The editor of the *American Federationist* never permitted so patronizing an analysis of the condition of men wage earners to appear in its pages. *Welfare work*—the employers' term for installing clean rest rooms, cafeterias, and sanitary provisions—was usually scorned by unions as a paternalistic substitute for unionizing, but it was favorably described by Valesh.[13]

During this period, the Women's Trade Union League was beginning to take an active part in the women's labor movement, and one notice of their convention by Mary McDowell, WTUL vice-president, did appear in the *American Federationist*. She discussed the question of separate unions for women, and agreed that women "must pay equal dues to receive equal benefits" (most women members paid lower dues and received fewer benefits). She suggested the possibility of a "marriage dower" for women to offset their temporary status and to insure that they would also get some benefits from the union.[14] It is not surprising that in his end-of-the-year report to the twenty-seventh annual convention of the AFL (1907) Gompers stated, regarding organization of women workers, "Some progress has been made . . . but it has not been of such a character as to be gratifying or satisfactory."[15]

THE AFL AND UNIONIZING WOMEN

Until about 1909 there was little mention of protective legislation for women workers. The only legislation of working conditions (distinguished from legislation concerning unions) which concerned the AFL was the passage of an eight-hour law for workers in federal employments, where the wage contract was in essence a contract with the government and hence could be differentiated from other types of hours legislation for workers. This bill was successfully opposed by employers during the prewar period.

In 1909, however, after the AFL convention, which made the usual resolution favoring women's suffrage, the union also called in a general way for organizing women workers, noting that there were 600,000 textile workers, of whom 60 percent were women and children. This was a situation which made it very difficult to rely on organization. An article in the AFL journal mentioned that since the union realized that women and children were "largely dependent upon legislative action for an amelioration of their present condition," uniform laws were to be recommended.[16]

The union dutifully mentioned the need to organize women, and one writer stated (in a speech to the Women Bookbinders' Union) that the only way for women to better their conditions was through unions: "The right to vote is not half so important as the will to organize." Women were to be found in virtually all trades, the writer noted, and asked: "How, therefore, can we longer talk of 'a woman's sphere'? Who can fix its boundary?"[17] She said that women sometimes hesitated to pay dues to a union because they figured they would quit and get married, but the writer cautioned that this view was very selfish, and that such a woman would not be a good wife or mother either. Furthermore, in marriage, they thought they would be on "easy street," with an electric clothes washer and convenience foods, but she warned them that these foods were not wholesome fare, and that even though the labor-saving devices might give us leisure, women should continue to be productive after marriage. She concluded:

> My last word to you is—go on with work of some kind. Go on being helpful. Go on being producers. Go on being breadwinners, whether you are single or married. Work, work, work! . . . Support your unions! . . . Don't wait for better legislation. Don't wait for philanthropic friends. Don't depend upon outside effort to alter your condition. Get together among yourselves and hustle and win out as self-supporting independent women.[18]

One wonders how this polemic on the dangers of leisure was greeted by the bookbinders, who were at the time working twelve-and fourteen-hour days or longer during the busy season.

The official AFL view of women was that, properly speaking, they ought not to have to work at all. In 1906, Gompers had stated:

> At least in our country, generally speaking, there is no necessity for the wife contributing to the support of the family by working . . . In our country, rich and fertile as any in the world, producing wealth in such prodigious proportions, the wife as a wage-earner is a disadvantage economically considered, and socially is unnecessary.[19]

Gompers was voicing the generally held view that, although many women did have to work, this situation was only temporary, and that they were only hired in the first place because they were cheap labor. Although it would be nice if they joined unions, this hope was not realistic, and perhaps the best thing for them would be some kind of legislation, as for children.

This kind of thinking was temporarily shaken by the events in New York during the winter of 1909. The striking shirtwaist workers, most of whom were young and foreign-born women, showed such steadfastness and courage that even the AFL had to take notice. The strike of twenty thousand shirtwaist workers was not union led and did not arise from a union initiative. The ILGWU only had about five thousand members at the start of the strike and gained in membership as the strike gained force as a consequence, not as a cause, of the militant actions.[20] The *American Federationist* commented that it was the better workers who were the best strikers, not the most downtrodden, and added that the women received help from the upper class and "prominent people" as well. No mention was made of the role of the WTUL in organizing strike support or in joining up members for the union.

Ida Tarbell called the shirtwaist strike an important achievement;[21] Elisabeth Marbury called it a cry to women still without unity. Marbury continued, this kind of action, with thousands of girls coming together gradually and forming unions to gain shorter hours, more pay, and more sanitary conditions, was valuable because "these girl workers of today [would] become mothers tomorrow," and hence the union was protecting the life of future generations.[22] The AFL had recognized the militancy of women workers only when it could no longer be ignored. But its basic analysis remained unaltered.[23]

The first real recognition by the AFL of a campaign for legislation affecting women workers was a discussion by Alice Henry of the passage of the Illinois ten-hour law. Illinois had passed an eight-hour law in 1893 which was declared unconstitutional two years later; the ten-hour bill was subsequently passed and upheld in 1910. Several accounts state that it was supported by all organized women, who lobbied effectively on behalf of an eight-hour bill in Springfield but were forced to accept a compromise bill calling for a ten-hour limit. Henry gave credit to the efforts of the WTUL.[24]

By 1911, the AFL began to carry reports of organizing activities among women workers in department stores and other occupations, stating that the organizing was proceeding rapidly and that working women were gaining a new spirit of self-reliance which had a natural outlet in organization. Rose Schniederman and a new American organizer had a promising future, the *American Federationist* predicted.[25] Then, in the wake of the Triangle Shirtwaist Company fire, both women trade unionists and the WTUL relief committee organized the protest demonstration and also the relief work. This activity was heralded as "the most remarkable of its kind" by any workers in this country.[26]

AFL ATTITUDE TOWARDS LABOR LEGISLATION

Following the Triangle fire in 1911, public outcry (which included strong support from the Socialists) led to the formation of the New York State Factory Investigating Commission, which included Gompers as a member. The purpose of the investigation was to propose "remedial legislation" in the areas of factory safety and sanitary conditions, and to secure the health and welfare of the workers. The investigation considered both the physical plant (fire hazards, ventilation, and other factors) and the conditions of employment of the workers, and it succeeded in pushing a number of regulatory measures through the New York Legislature.

The *American Federationist* continued to downplay the importance of legislative remedies for adverse working conditions and emphasized the need to confine efforts to the economic sphere. In a discussion covering a convention of the WTUL, which noted the increasing attention given to trade unionism among educated, intelligent women, an article added: "But in the haste to remedy wrongs quickly, it is a temptation to work along the line of least resistance rather than wait upon slower and better methods." The proper course would be to *organize* for industrial betterment and freedom.[27] The above statement of position appeared while Gompers was a member of the Factory Investigating Commission.

As the war in Europe was slowly leading to American involvement, by 1914-15 its effect was being felt in industry. A special assessment of the AFL membership was ordered in January 1914 and was to be used to organize women workers in recognition that they were becoming a permanent part of industrial life.[28] The AFL remained ambivalent about whether legislation for women was desirable, however.[29] A new issue (for the United States), minimum wage legislation, raised questions which remained unresolved throughout the period. The 1914 AFL convention showed "great diversion of views" but remained uncommitted; while Gompers opposed minimum wage legislation. In July and August, in testimony before a U.S. commission, he stated the following AFL position:

> The AF of L is in favor of fixing the maximum number of hours of work for children, minors, and women. It does not favor a legal limitation of the workday for adult men workers. The unions have very largely established the shorter workday by their own initiative

... The AF of L has apprehensions as to the wisdom of placing in the hands of the government additional powers which may be used to the detriment of the working people. It particularly opposes this policy when the things can be done by the workmen themselves.[30]

Throughout the next year or so, as the war drew closer, Gompers continued to emphasize that relying on legislation was a sign of weakness both moral and otherwise, and that "the history of all attempts to fix hours of labor or wages by laws, maximum or minimum, for the workers generally, shows that they resulted in shackling the workers with bonds that had to be broken before further progress could be made."[31]

Gompers argued that legislation could lead to a false security that could damage the union, and he cited the fate of the New York bakers, who had succeeded in getting a ten-hour law passed around the turn of the century. The bakers agitated for the law and thought when they got it that the bakers would realize the value of organization and join up. "But," they said, "we had to find out very soon that we had made the mistake of our lives, as from that day on the members dropped from the organization." Only through organization did bakers get the shorter workday, said a Bakers' Union official.[32]

Finally, Gompers argued that legislative methods were indicative of a deeper, underlying weakness which was dangerously close to socialism. In a moralistic editorial entitled "Self-help is the Best Help," he deplored the tendency for people to seek a law to correct every evil:

Whither are we drifting? There is a strange spirit abroad in these times ... Whether as a result of laziness or incompetency there is a steadily growing disposition to shift responsibility for personal progress and welfare to outside agencies.

What can be the result of this tendency but the softening of the moral fibre of the people? When there is unwillingness to accept responsibility for one's life and for making the most of it there is a loss of strong, red-blooded, rugged independence and will power to grapple with the wrong of the world and to establish justice through the volition of those concerned.[33]

Undoubtedly, part of the reason for Gompers' intense antipathy to legislative methods came from his fear that such methods would become linked with the formation of a labor party with socialist objectives. A British M.P. was given space in the January 1915 issue of the *American Federationist* to state the following opinion of the textile industry in his country: "The greatest activity for the Labor Party prevails among the workers in those districts, trade union organization is weakest, wages are lowest, and general conditions of employment are poorest." The conclusion was inescapable: "The workers cannot be saved; they must save themselves. The shorter workday for the unorganized and for women is a problem of organization. Let us not be beguiled into short-cut methods that lead into the quicksands of lethargy imposed by legislation."[34]

Gompers was attacked directly by the Socialist party for the view that the eight-hour day should be gained only through economic efforts and not through legislation. He in turn attacked the Socialist Party for being "the instigator back of propositions to secure the eight-hour workday in private industries by legislation" and for trying to get the unions to support them in this.[35] Gompers cited a list of trades that had an eight-hour day and argued that in state and federal employment it was union power that got the legislation.

Gompers was willing to go along with labor legislation for women and children, as noted (and willing to take credit for its passage).[36] The kind of law which this barrage of propaganda was directed against was the industrial boards' power to regulate wages which existed in Australia and New Zealand. These boards sometimes were empowered to arbitrate and mediate labor disputes, included antistrike provisions, and had broad powers to regulate labor conditions. They came under severe attack over a period of months by the *American Federationist* and were seen as a kind of precursor to socialism by Gompers. An article on the working of the industrial boards in New South Wales began the first sentence with the quotation: "Socialism makes provisions for everything except liberty."[37]

These attacks on the wage board system (which was currently being passed by several legislatures in the United States but with powers to set wage rates only for women workers) were accompanied by scathing polemics against the Socialist newspaper the *New York Call* and American socialists like Robert Hunter. Gompers refused to support an unemployment demonstration they sponsored.[38] During this period also, the U.S. Commission on Industrial Relations was formed to investigate the causes of industrial unrest, in particular, the McNamara bombings of the *Los Angeles Times*. Gompers testified before the commission as a representative of labor and was forced to defend his brand of unionism under direct cross-examination by the Socialist Morris Hillquit.

In this period, which was a high point for the passage of protective labor legislation for women, the main thrust of the official AFL line was that women were workers and should be organized. AFL coverage of the WTUL convention in the July 1915 issue stressed that "Industrial freedom is not a sex problem—it is a human problem. The same principles apply to men and women alike." It noted approvingly that the function of the WTUL was to organize women into trade unions, and warned that it must not let itself be diverted by

> frivolities and pink-tea imitations that have so long kept women from healthy, sane living. Those who profit by the exploitation of women will offer substitutes for the trade union movement—welfare work, vocational associations and other charitable or semi-charitable institutions. The fight of women for industrial freedom is made doubly difficult . . . by those who would protect woman in order to keep her from exercising her own will power and becoming a member of society upon equality with all.[39]

During the period just before the American entry into the war, in 1916 and 1917, an increasingly patriotic spirit came to dominate the *American Federationist*. The Adamson Act (for an eight-hour day in railways) was attacked as industrial slavery by Gompers, although it was upheld by the Supreme Court. The union campaigned for an eight-hour day through collective bargaining, not government regulation.[40] At the 1916 AFL convention, several resolutions in favor of the eight-hour day were introduced, for example, resolutions calling for "the securing of the eight-hour day throughout all industry, both by industrial and legislative action," or "to be secured through and by the National Government" "by legislative enactment." The resolution adopted was to "strongly urge all workers, organized and unorganized, to concentrate their efforts to secure the eight-hour workday at the earliest possible time," and to wait and see the outcome of the eight-hour law in transportation.[41] Again, Gompers emphasized that the passage of a law was no solution to the workers' problems; rather, it was necessry for workers to have "economic" strength. An article entitled "Regulation by Law! law!! law!!!" stated: "The mere enactment of eight-hour legislation would not decrease one iota the necessity for economic organization and the economic struggle. Indeed, instead of helping, it only adds another obstacle to the achievement of a real, general eight-hour day."[42] Other forms of government social welfare plans were also attacked in the paper; health insurance was virtually called unpatriotic because the Germans had it and because the American "spirit of the people and the institutions of the country [were] so totally different" from the Germans'. Americans would find compulsory authority and regulation uncongenial.[43]

Aware that the war was also affecting the position of women in industry, the report of the executive committee to the convention in 1916, noting the possibility of increasing numbers of working women, stated: "The AFL throughout its history has realized that women in industry would become a continuing economic problem and has endeavored to the best of its ability to extend organization among women." Equal pay for equal work was especially important now, it added, wherever "women in industry becomes necessary because of shortage of manpower."[44]

In 1918, the AFL executive council's declaration of principles to govern worker-employer relations during the war included the following statement: "Women in Industry. If it shall become necessary to employ women on work ordinarily performed by men, they must be allowed equal pay for equal work and must not be allotted tasks disproportionate to their strength."[45] Note was taken of the proposed minimum wage bill for women and minors in Washington, D.C., that it had the support of local labor organizations, and also the Merchant and Manufacturers' Association of Washington, D.C., whose president appeared at the hearings for the bill.

Considerable concern over the effects of women in war industries was expressed by a number of speakers at the AFL convention. One speaker stated: "Women are replacing and often displacing men in industry at this time, and these women are recruited from the families of the working man." She said that since women had to be taught "the fundamental principles of organization and it [was] impossible to teach them after their entrance into industry," ladies' auxiliaries ought to be formed.[46] A resolution from a delegate of the International Brotherhood of Electrical Workers, noting the increase of women workers as men were going off to war, stated:

> Many unfair and unscrupulous employers are taking advantage of this condition to lower the wage standards and to pay women less wages than they paid the men whose places these women are taking ... [The AFL should] make every effort to bring these women into the organizations ... to which the men whose places they have taken, are members.[47]

Melinda Scott, fraternal delegate (having no vote) to the convention from the WTUL, said that women taking men's places during the war must be taught not to take less money for the job: "We have got to save those jobs for those men when they come back, and we have got to see that the women do not underbid the men while they are away." She continued, "We must remember that women are the potential mothers of the future race and we have got to take care of the future generation."[48] Again in

1919, the executive council of the union repeated its support for equal pay for equal work and its concern that women "not be permitted to perform tasks disproportionate to their physical strength," and added, "or which tend to impair their potential motherhood and prevent the continuation of a nation of strong, healthy, sturdy, and intelligent men and women."[49]

As late as 1921, the legislative report to the AFL convention made it clear that the AFL opposed fixing wages and prices by law and claimed that bills to establish "industrial courts" were successfully defeated by opposition from labor and farmers and the people. In New York, despite an antilabor legislature, a number of "vicious measures" were killed, including the repeal of the fifty-four-hour law for women and a bill permitting restaurant waitresses to work until 1:00 A.M. (night work restrictions came under specific attack by women printers opposed to protective legislation for women, as will be discussed below).[50]

However, when the Supreme Court struck down the minimum wage law for women in Washington, D.C., in 1923, the wrath of the AFL came down in force. The union was as much outraged at the veto power of the court over the legislature as it was about the legislation itself, and an editorial by Gompers asking "to take away its usurped power," called the decision another "reactionary" decision, along with the demise of the child labor law. Had the composition of the court been slightly different, the law might have been sustained, he said, and he continued:

> The brutality of the majority decision can beget nothing but wrath. It went so far as to unblushingly liken the purchase of labor power of women and girls to the purchase of provisions in a grocery store, or meat in a butcher shop. Perhaps, in the minds of some of the justices the butcher shop parallel is the most apt.[51]

A cartoon appearing in the same issue showed the fat, smirking representatives of Big Biz standing among the tombstones of the Women's Minimum Wage Law, Child Labor Law, Human Rights, etc., and was captioned "These, Our Lamented Dead."[52]

In summary, the predominating theme in the AFL was that women workers were to be treated as only temporarily in the work force because their primary place was the home. Women were hard to organize because they did not take their jobs seriously, and that situation was inevitable; therefore legislation might be the best way to improve their working conditions. However, the AFL had to recognize that women had on occasion proven their militancy and their ability to sustain a strike, and during the period before the war, the AFL began to give lip service to the need for women to organize and not to rely on the benevolence of legislatures. Although Gompers was a member of the New York Factory Investigating Commission, which participated in efforts to pass labor legislation, he remained ambivalent about its merits and considered these laws to be socialistic, an employers' plot to weaken workers' initiative or both.

The AFL went from generally ignoring the Women's Trade Union League and its major role in strike support for women workers to accepting their offer to organize women into unions within the AFL. But the basic concern of the AFL remained the protection of *men* workers; they supported equal pay for equal work because, as women entered industry prior to the war, *men's* pay scales had to be protected. When the emphasis was on organizing women, they stressed that "industrial freedom" was necessary for all workers regardless of sex, but they continued to support legislation like no-night-work laws, which applied to women only, and explicitly referred to their role in the preservation of the race as justification. This dilemma—whether to treat women workers as primarily workers or as women who were responsible for reproduction of the labor force *within* the home—remained unresolved throughout this period.

Protecting Women Workers: Male Unions

The AFL is a national organization. But protective laws for women are passed at the state level (except for Washington, D.C., which is under congressional jurisdiction). One of the more important male-dominated unions in the AFL, the Iron Molders, which also had representation on the AFL executive board, was actively interested in getting certain kinds of legislation for women passed. Members of the Molders' Union appeared before the New York State Factory Investigating Commission (FIC) and reported on the dangers of women working in core rooms of foundries. Although the main purpose of the investigation was to recommend fire and other health and safety regulations in factories, women in core rooms received a great deal of attention. At that time, there were three hundred women working in core rooms in New York State, and these women had generally been hired to replace boys under eighteen.[53] Although seats were provided, the nature of the work meant that they could not use them, and core makers were exposed to dust, noxious fumes, and heat from the ovens. The report noted that women did not usually remain in the industry for more than four or five years, a fact which they felt might lessen the long-term harmful effects of the work.

A number of witnesses appeared before the commission to testify to the harmful effects of women working in the core rooms of foundries. In addition to social reformers like Florence Kelley, the main witnesses were representatives of the Iron Molders' Union. One member from Rochester stated that there were no women employed in Rochester foundries because the women did not work steadily. He was asked by WTUL member Mary Dreier, a member of the commission: "Is this proper work for women?" He answered: "It is heavy work for a woman; I do not think it is fit work for them." Dreier then asked him, "Women really ought to be prohibited from working in foundries?" He answered, "Yes."[54]

At hearings in Syracuse, another Molders' Union member said he believed that "no women should be employed," and that the work was "of an awful gasy nature" and made their eyes run all the time. When asked why women were employed, he answered that employers claimed it was "impossible to get boys." He said: "In my opinion, the women, of course, may be more steady workers and it may be a little handier on small core work. That may be so, but as a matter of fact they employ them for a lesser wage, and that is a fact."[55] In Syracuse, men earned $3.15 a day, while women earned $7.00 to 8.00 per week in the three foundries in the city which employed women. Women were not included in the union, the witness said: "It is the same class of work but we cannot recognize them for one reason, because we know they are out of place." He then described a situation in which a woman eight months pregnant was working under a crane, and considered the increasing number of women in foundries: "That is why we would like to prohibit it, because women that are becoming mothers, and girls who are to have children and who are to make up the next generation will be [entering the industry] if this thing is carried much further."[56]

Another witness from the Molders' Union submitted a written report of the dangers of the trade in Utica and a statement in support of a bill "having for its object the prohibiting of the employment of women in the core rooms of foundries."[57] A Buffalo molder suggested that if the legislature did pass a law forbidding women to work in core rooms, it would not cause them any hardship, and the women ought to check out some of the want ads for "girls in housework where they belong." He continued: "I don't think they should be employed in factories. I think men should be left to make living wages to support the girls and their families."[58]

The principal objection to women working in core rooms came from the union itself, with support from the members of the commission and doctors' testimony. The report of the commission came to this conclusion: "The foundry is no place for women. The work is arduous and the surroundings are bad. We believe that it would have been far better if women had never been originally allowed to enter this employment." The few women who did work in foundries were dependent upon this work for support, however, and the report continued: "Many of these have appealed to the Commission not to deprive them of what they, in small country towns, consider their only means of earning a living."[59] The report stopped short of recommending "an entire prohibition of work that would result in throwing the three hundred women . . . in the industry out of employment." But it said that hiring women for such work "should be discouraged and ultimately suppressed. Every obstacle should be thrown in the way of its increase and expansion."[60]

It is significant that the commission did not choose to use the presence of women, however few, as an additional reason to insure the safety of all workers in core rooms. Instead it chose to work for the elimination of women altogether from this skilled, better-paid work, and did so principally at the behest of the Iron Molders' Union. The thrust of the investigation was toward defining the *limitations* of women's industrial participation.[61] A woman working in a dirty, rough place like a core room was a ready symbol of the evils of unregulated work for women.

On the other hand, the work of women (and children) in canneries in the state was also characterized by intense overwork during the seson ("The Lord ripens the crops," the cannery owners said), but the New York State fifty-four-hour law was amended to exempt canneries and sheds from its provisions. Women worked as long as 119 hours in a week, standing on wet floors, and were subject to intense speedup. Although canneries and food-processing sheds were pictured by the canners as nice, pleasant places for women and children to work snipping beans or husking corn, they were really factories, the FIC report claimed, and ought to come under the factory law. The report stated: "No words of ours can express too strongly our condemnation of the inhuman greed and avarice that permit women to be thus exploited. We do not believe, however, that the 54-hour law should apply to the canneries during the canning season." The report suggested that a ten-hour limit, with a twelve-hour limit at peak periods, would "stimulate the canners to more scientific management so that the necessity for overtime [could] be largely eliminated."[62] The existing regulations were notoriously unenforced in canneries, although canneries had a more lenient hours limit than industrial factories.

The no-night-work law recommended by the FIC eliminated another small group of skilled women workers—the printers—but there had been no comparable effort on the part of the printers' union to get women out on "health" grounds. The attitude of the printers' union towards women in the trade and the women printers who were "protected out of a job" will be considered next.

THE PRINTING TRADES' UNIONS AND WOMEN

The printing trade is an old one, and the International Typographical Union (ITU) is probably the oldest craft union in the country. In the mid-1800s a number of women were to be found in the trade. Some had entered through their family business, and others had become compositors as a result of a strike in 1853 in New York City, where an employer stated: "We advertised for girls to learn to set type, determining to teach them the art rather than submit to the tyranny of any trade union in the universe . . . We see no reason why they will not make good compositors and earn their eight or ten dollars a week, which will be to them good wages."[63]

Therefore, as early as the 1850s and 1860s, the Typographical Union had been forced to face the issue of women in the printers' trade. Several conflicting resolutions were proposed, for example:

That the National Typographical Union recognizes none but male compositors;

That this union, taking into consideration the present organization of society, are of the opinion that the practice of employing females in the composing department . . . is calculated to operate detrimentally upon the morals of those so employed, especially on account of the execution of many medical and other scientific works . . . which contain matter eminently unfitted and highly improper for the perusal of modest young women. Also that it is injurious to the interests of the trade . . . ;

That we recognize the right of females to any employment for which they may be fitted and that we . . . leave all legislation in this matter in the hands of subordinate unions.

It ultimately passed a resolution "that this union will not encourage by its acts, the employment of females as compositors . . ."[64] Horace Greeley felt that women would be able to do certain kinds of compositing work but that men need not fear their competition:

The girls who marry and have families to look after will stop setting type—never doubt that—unless they are so luckless as to get drunken, loafing, good-for-nothing husbands, who will do nothing to keep the pot boiling, and then they must work, and you ought not be mean enough to stop them, or drive them back to making shirts at 3 or 4 shillings per day. If you find yourselves troubled with too strong a competition from female workers just prove yourselves worthy to be their husbands; marry them.

To those who argued that women would be exposed to "immorality and vice" by setting type alongside the men, he told them, "Did it never occur to you that this is her lookout rather than yours?"[65]

In 1867 a report was submitted to the National Convention (by a committee whose membership was largely from Local No. 6, New York) which stated:

We are clearly of the opinion that no hindrance should be placed in the way of females who have been unfortunate enough to have learned the art or profession of a compositor . . . Female labor will never cease injuring male labor . . . as long as female labor is ostracized and place beyond the pale of our union organizations. The men of our local unions . . . should throw around their sisters the protecting power of their organizations and tell unscrupulous capitalists who thus use the female to degrade the male, that it can be so no longer, that the female laborer is as equally worthy of her hire as the male.[66]

Women in the trade had been admitted into the ITU since 1869 and had organized into separate female locals. The woman founder of New York Local No. 1, Augusta Lewis, was an active member of the union and was on the National Board during the period under study here. But that did not mean that the "problem" of women entering the printing trade had disappeared, that women received equal pay with men, or that women were consequently no longer competing with men for the same jobs at lower pay.[67] Edith Abbott remarked upon the "organized hostility of the men" and said that although women were admitted to the union on the same terms as men, this was done "to protect the wage scale, not to encourage women to enter the trade." She continued: "In the unions, the women form an insignificant minority; they seldom hold an office, and they have little influence in directing union policies."[68]

Despite their aversion to female co-workers, the ITU seems to have relied mainly on craft-union exclusionism, not legislation, to keep them out. Apprenticeships were supposedly open to girls and boys, but in fact no employer hired girl apprentices. Instead, she "steals the trade," that is, learned it outside the apprenticeship system, and, Abbott felt, were thereby also not as versatile or expert as the men."[69] The union also counted on the cooperation of the union shop employer to keep out women.

Some kinds of protective labor legislation for women did not affect printers at all (for example, hours limits) because the union already had conditions equal to or better than the laws provided. But one kind of law—prohibiting night work for women—did directly affect a small group of women. It does not appear that the New York printers' unions were especially concerned with protecting women printers' health or morality or with eliminating women as competition through the passage of a no-night-work law. The law was passed by recommendation of the FIC report in 1913, and, judging by the evidence, the women printers only belatedly realized they were affected by it. They do not appear to have opposed it before its passage. These women were a maverick group. They maintained that, ever since the law's passage, they had contributed their time and money to the struggle to get the law amended to exempt them, but there is scant evidence that they appeared as a vocal force before about 1916, and they continued their opposition to labor legislation for a number of years after their particular grievance was won (in 1919 they were specifically exempted from the no-night-work law). They were a constant source of embarrassment for social reform groups, especially the WTUL. They organized under the League for Equal Opportunity, and their arguments in opposition to protective labor laws for women will be considered next.

THE WOMEN PRINTERS: WORKING WOMEN OPPOSED TO PROTECTIVE LABOR LAWS FOR WOMEN

In the period after World War I, opposition to protective labor legislation for women developed in another quarter—with a group of women workers who called themselves the League for Equal Opportunity (LEO). Their more vocal spokespersons were women printers, although others also joined, such as the women streetcar conductors, who were temporarily employed during the war and were then let go after the men returned.

This group's arguments against protective legislation stemmed from several different sources. Some took their cue from the arguments for women's equality expressed by the National Woman's Party, while others appear to have derived from the National Association of Manufacturer's (NAM) more conservative position that labor legislation was an infringement upon freedom of contract. The League for Equal Opportunity condemned male-dominated unions for collaborating with legislators and social workers to eliminate women from their trades.

These women were generally considered a nuisance or downright dangerous by the established women's organizations which lobbied for protective laws with the backing of the newly created U.S. Women's Bureau after the war. Whenever possible, they were excluded from government deliberations regarding women in industry. This exclusion infuriated them. When Mary Anderson of the Women's Bureau called a conference to determine "a policy of special industrial legislation for women and children" in 1923, they were excluded allegedly because they were not a national organization. They responded:

> BUT WE ARE WAGE-EARNING WOMEN, ALL OF US; we have been fighting this type of legislation for years and proving that it is a handicap instead of a protection; we are citizens about to be exploited by the recommendations of organizations whose members know nothing of economic conditions, the law of supply and demand, etc., and by the sentimental, insincere mouthing of a group of non-working workingmen whose unions refuse to take women in as members yet presume to demand their "protection" through the medium of restrictive laws that the men, wisely refuse to be saddled with.[70]

This group therefore opposed women's bureaus, whether federal or state, and especially the federal bureau head, Mary Anderson.

But although these women could be effectively excluded from a policy-making conference in Washington, there was no way to silence them at public hearings, and they appeared in New York, Rhode Island, and other states where women's "welfare" bills were before the legislatures. When New Jersey passed a law prohibiting night work for women, the LEO ran a picture of the governor signing the "wicked bill" under the caption "New Jersey's Greatest Crime," and noted: "The smiling women in the picture are POLITICANS, they are NOT WAGE-EARNING WOMEN."[71] The year 1923 was not good for welfare bills in New York, however, and by the end of the legislative session, when none of the bills had passed, the LEO gloated: "The rich women who lobbied for these 'welfare' bills (the same women, year after year) have now gone to their country homes, where they will keep their domestic servants working more than eight-hour shifts to entertain their friends . . . 'Marie, did you give Fido his bawth?'" [72]

Besides using a generally snide tone toward the women reformers and making ad hominem attacks on the motives and credentials of proponents of protective labor laws,[73] the LEO used arguments which derived from two conflicting sources. On the one hand, these women were apparently from the Republican, conservative end of the working class (their journal had a long eulogy for Harding), and some arguments coincided with the NAM old-line notions of laissez-faire capitalism; but from 1923 on they also used the consciously feminist Woman's Party position.

Both these tendencies are reflected in their attack on a Rhode Island bill which would restrict minors under sixteen and women to forty-eight hours per week:

> Besides insulting every woman of the State in classifying their sex with children under sixteen, these bills will have the same effect that child labor bills are frankly intended to have: Make the employment of women so difficult and expensive that employers will hire them only in emergencies and at a lower rate of pay than that of men.
>
> WOMEN WAGE EARNERS OF RHODE ISLAND, YOUR LIVE-LIHOOD, YOUR SELF-RESPECT, YOUR RIGHT OF CONTRACT, YOUR RIGHT TO DECENT LIVING CONDITIONS OF YOUR OWN CHOOSING, ARE IN GRAVE DANGER.[74]

These women contended that such laws treated women like "Peter Pans who will never advance beyond a 16-year-old child's mental and physical development," and would "void the most important legal right a person can possess, the right of contract."[75] They also claimed that this kind of regulation (a New York eight-hour, no-night-work bill) did not regulate health or morality because of the exemptions contained in it and therefore was "CLASS LEGISLATION and not a legitimate exercise of the police power."[76] The league generally did not favor such laws even if they were extended to men "because it did not believe in placing in the hands of politicians matters that should be settled in agreements between employer and employees, and because it believed working men agreed with this view."[77]

These women also opposed a minimum wage for women, although they favored it for minors under twenty-one, and also favored an eight-hour shift for all workers (but not an eight-hour law for women only). They stated: "There is no minimum wage for men, and a man is able to earn as much as he is worth. If there were a minimum wage for women, we know that the wages of women workers would remain at the minimum, and it would establish a precedent for paying low wages to all classes of women workers."[78] The true intent of these restrictions, they said, was "TO THROW 10,000 WOMEN out of work, with the object of creating an artificial labor scarcity in the industries concerned and thus raising slightly the wage scales of the boys over sixteen and men who take the women's places."[79] The argument that the legislation was simply a "stepping-stone" to better conditions for all workers was also denounced:

> Statistics proving that such legislation reacts on the women by lowering their wages and taking away their jobs does not alter the enthusiasm of the women's welfare propagandists.

> Rather, they assume the attitude that women should be proud to serve as stepping-stones, as they have done since cavemen times, no matter how they themselves may have to suffer . . . Labor men will sooner or later learn that their problems of higher pay and shorter hours are not to be solved by making the wage earning women stepping-stones for the men's advancement.

And they maintained that women would also have to learn that they could solve their labor problems only by "determined, conscious and persistent action." "When they arise from the posture which allows others to use them as stepping-stones to their full height of erect human beings, then and then only can they 'play the women'! . . . side by side with the men they love—comrades, not stepping-stones!"[80]

But this group saved their sharpest attacks for the no-night-work provisions, using the inconsistencies in the law to point out that its real effect was to deny women jobs they preferred to daywork. For instance, the league's Providence, Rhode Island, branch was led, according to one article, by "a charming young woman; not an agitator or a feminist, but devoted to her seven children." For this reason she was "demanding that her right to work on a night shift shall not be denied." Like all good mothers, this woman preferred to be home with her children after school hours, and so she worked at night. The article continued:

> Her health is the best, her home is a happy one, and her youthful apperance, which has doubtless annoyed some of the elderly spinsters of consumers' leagues, etc., belies the claim of the self-appointed guardians of adult wage-earning women that "night work is deadly."

> Strange, isn't it, that dancing, card-playing, autoing, etc., in the deadly night hours is harmless, but earning a good wage by honest work is dangerous to the future generation if performed in the same night hours?[81]

The laws also applied only to certain kinds of employment of women. The league illustrated this fact by contrasting two women, "Sue" and "Lou." "Sue," a "pretty waitress," supported an "invalid mother, with whom she would like to spend the afternoon in the park"; but Sue was forbidden to work on a night shift and so could not be with her mother. "Lou," on the other hand, was "the carefree and clothes-free young person on her toes." As can be seen from the two pictures illustrating the point, Lou was "very pretty, very desirable in male eyes, before which she aim[ed] to display as much of herself and as often as possible," but she was herself a widow and was supporting her two children by "displaying the talents Nature gave her—pretty much as Nature gave them—in an expensive cabaret revue, both before and AFTER 10 P.M." The writers added: "Don't mistake us. Lou is a good girl, though appearances be against her," but one would suppose that the law would "protect" her, "who twice nightly court[ed] pneumonia," as well as the well-clad "Sue." What the law did do, they pointed out, was to prevent "Sue," the ordinary waitress, from working when the tips were the best, while it specifically excluded from its provisions women working as singers and performers in restaurants.[82]

One article argued that the laws affected all women, not just the weaker ones, but said: "The way for us to get power . . . is to organize, and rely on ourselves, cooperating, of course, with those men who have the same needs as ourselves." However, the crux of the matter was that the legislation

> enable[d] women to keep on working and being moral, living at a minimum and having children at a maximum . . . [The State] persist[ed] in regarding women as a means to an end—that end being the production of children—rather than as individuals responsible for their own acts and choosing their own careers.[83]

And in fact they were not so far wrong. Their own union, the International Typographical Union, saw women in just that way. With over two million married women working, the union had stated: "Such a condition is a menace to our nation's home life, for children cannot receive proper care while their mothers are away at work." Their remedy for the "crime wave" being discussed was to "pay a living wage to their men workers so that women folk could remain where they rightly belong—in the home."[84]

It is difficult to tell just what the attitude of the Typographical Union was towards these women printers. It never became an issue at the national level. Official histories of the union stress the fact that although comparatively few women did enter the trade after they were admitted in 1869, the official union position was that the "benefits and advantages of the ITU have been available to women on the same basis as to men."[85] No mention was made of legislative restrictions on women during the period, or of any friction over the restrictions.

An exchange at the Albany hearings in 1919 over the "welfare bills" gives some indication that the union was not supportive of the women's efforts. The two most active women printers, Mrs. Ada Wolfe and Ella Sherwin, both appeared in opposition to the bills, and the president of the State Federation of Labor charged them with trying "to make it appear here today that this bill would affect 4,000 women throughout the state," when it would not affect even twenty-five women.[86] Joseph Lynch, former president of the ITU, also testified in favor of the "welfare bills" in his capacity as member of the New York Industrial Commission. He referred directly to the women printers, calling them a highly organized and skilled group of women workers who were selfishly denying all the other women of the state needed protection. In Philadelphia the relations between the ITU and the Women's Trade Union League suffered as a result of the women printers' stand (see chapter 6), but in New York it appears that "Big Six" (the New York local) and the WTUL continued on friendly terms.[87]

The ITU was favorably disposed towards government regulation of public utilities and also went on record favoring a health insurance plan. Lynch addressed the New York local on the subject when it was before the Albany legislature. In the context of this kind of overall support for "welfare bills," it appears unlikely that the women printers who opposed it would receive much encouragement from the union. Since Big Six was friendly with the WTUL, which was itself at loggerheads with the women printers, it is unlikely (but not impossible) that the New York local could remain on good terms with the women printers. The women printers scrupulously avoided attacking their union, however.

Thus the one group of working women which came out in organized opposition to protective labor legislation for women came from a highly unionized craft, the printers, in which women had been admitted to the union long ago as a small minority within the trade. These women printers pointed out many of the inconsistencies in the legislation, which applied only to women in the industrial work force and not to professional women or domestics (who worked for middle-class families). They saw clearly that these laws served to define women in terms of their function as reproducers of the labor force and tended to eliminate women as competition in male trades like their own, an aspect which the middle-class social reformers did not consider important.

They also recognized that government agencies like the Women's Bureau shared the reformers' perspective, and that the government policies reinforced the secondary position of women workers. However, the women printers also claimed that they needed their jobs, and in some cases preferred night work, *because* they were mothers and supporting families, and that the legislation was preventing them from doing so effectively. They contrasted their situation with that of the middle-class reform women, who either were "spinsters" or could hire domestic help in the home and did not need to work for a living.

Their union, the ITU, did not support them and did not oppose protective laws like the no-night-work laws, which would eliminate female printers from the trade. On the contrary, the ITU established friendly relations with the Women's Trade Union League, which on occasion they supported even against their own (female) union members. (In Philadelphia the ITU broke with the WTUL over the issue of women printers, as is described in the previous chapter.)

In the bookbinding trade, by contrast, women were a bare majority and were treated better by the Bookbinders' Union.[88] In the garment industry, however, women were the majority of unskilled workers (men were cutters), and this union drew its strength from the militancy of the women and their efforts at organizing at least as much as through the men's efforts. The attitudes of the International Ladies Garment Workers' Union (ILGWU) toward women as workers, and their position regrding protective labor legislation for women, will be considered next.

The International Ladies Garment Workers' Union

Workers of the world unite! You have nothing to lose but your chains.
Masthead, *Justice*

It is impossible to discuss the ILGWU without also emphasizing the deep commitment to socialism shared by a large part of its membership and its leaders. In the catechism of the AFL, to call something "socialistic" was understood to be damning it; in the ILGWU it was a compliment.[89]

The early years of the union were filled with struggles and factions that derived from the different strands of radical and socialist organizations—DeLeonists, Wobblies, Debbsian socialists, and after the Russian Revolution, Communists. Several locals in New York abandoned their affiliation with the AFL for a short period and joined the IWW.[90] This union always had close ties with the Socialist party. The *New York Call*, the daily newspaper of the Socialist party, carried detailed news of events in the ILGWU, and toward its end in 1923, when the Palmer raids and the postwar reaction had taken their toll on the newspaper, the ILGWU contributed heavily to it in an attempt to get it back on its feet.[91]

Both the Socialists and the ILGWU were in favor of getting anything they could out of a hostile capitalist state, but considered it proof of the states' class bias when they lost. A speaker at one ILGWU convention who mentioned protective labor laws gave credit for their passage to the unions, which, she said, "with the strength that comes by cooperation . . . have been able to force from unwilling hands the concessions that now plaster the statute books."[92] Although the union favored protective laws as ameliorative under an unjust system, their support usually included a more basic criticism of the capitalist system. In a report entitled "Legislative Appeals at Albany and Elsewhere," they noted that the union had "occasionally seen fit to exert its influence" on behalf of laws in New York, but added: "Not that we believe, or ever believed, in the policy of lobbying for or against legislative measures, but these were occasions when the voice of the International had to be heard on behalf of the tens of thousands of our workers."[93]

But the problem was always the capitalist system, nothing less. The ILGWU, after printing a generally liberal and reformist article on the human costs of production, tacked an editorial comment after it saying, "Our view of the entire matter of labor and wages is that profits from production are unjust and should be entirely eliminated."[94] They duly noted the Karl Marx Centenary in May 1918. Although the McNamara bombings of the *Los Angeles Times* building shocked organized labor, few unions condemned it outright (although deploring the violence); but the ILGWU went further than most in blaming capitalism. When the capitalists, they said, who "by the aid of dynamite . . . kill and maim people" have been dealt with, "then there would be no McNamaras." Although they "utterly repudiate[d] violence in any shape or form," they said it should be remembered that the "root causes" of it were the "legalized barbarity of the steel magnates."[95] And in the postwar period, they declared that the recession was evidence of capitalism's weakness, and showed the "inevitable nature of the social revolution which [was] coming to pass."[96]

The ILGWU, which belonged to the AFL, usually muted their criticism of official AFL policies. But they differed with the AFL on almost every major policy issue. The AFL favored limiting immigration to the United States; the ILGWU favored an open-door policy.[97] They took this stand because the majority of their members were Jewish immigrants from Russia and Poland and a fair number were Italians as well as other

nationalities, but also because their socialism inclined them to an inter-
nationalist view of working-class solidarity.[98] The AFL also devoted much
of its energy to avoiding forming a labor party; the ILGWU favored a
socialist (labor) party and supported Victor Berger, Meyer London, and
other socialists who ran, occasionally successfully, for political office in
New York.[99]

The Socialists, although they believed in the long-run abolition of
the system, nonetheless worked very hard to win elections within it, and
also favored protective labor legislation. They joined with other more
reform-oriented groups to work for the passage of "welfare bills," including minimum wage laws and health insurance, which, as previously
mentioned, the AFL did not approve of. The antipathy of the AFL to
using legislative means to help workers was not shared by the ILGWU (or
the Socialists).

The AFL did little or no educational work with its members; the
ILGWU was passionately involved in sponsoring or publicizing lectures,
courses, and books. The workers' classes the ILGWU set up in New York
City at Washington Irving High School were outstanding, although they
ran into some difficulty with the New York Board of Education because
they conducted their classes in a language other than English.[100] A committee from the AFL which was set up to investigate educational systems
of unions had high praise for the ILGWU's efforts. While noting that the
need for such courses showed that the public schools were not meeting
this need, the committee concluded: "One of the things that impressed
the committee in the classes of the Ladies Garment Workers' Union in
N.Y.C. was the feeling of the students that the classes belonged to them,
that they were at home in them, and took a collective pride in them."[101] A
well-known lecturer or a cultural event could draw overflow crowds of
hundreds. The ILGWU also ran health articles and notices of sex education lectures—some for men, some for women.[102]

Although the AFL was on record as favoring women's suffrage, some
of its constituent unions were not so sure. Despite their political radicalism, for example, the Brewery Workers did not favor votes for women,
fearing that the Prohibition Amendment was one of the issues women
would support as a block. The ILGWU and the Socialists supported wom-
en's suffrage as a necessary step towards sex equality and as a matter of
conscience for good socialists. Aside from straight labor issues like strikes
or negotiations, the *New York Call* probably devoted the most coverage
in its pages to the growing suffragist movement, urged its readers to participate in rallies and demonstrations, and noted, "Suffrage Parade to Have
Red Wave," that is, a socialist section of marchers.[103] In 1919, when the

suffrage campaign was growing increasingly militant—when women were being jailed for picketing the White House and traveling across the country publicizing jail conditions and the fight for suffrage—the *New York Call* had almost daily coverage of their activities.[104]

The ILGWU itself was somewhat less enthusiastic about the suffrage campaign, although they favored votes for women. Jane Addams had said that working women needed the ballot in order to pass "anti-sweatshop laws, prohibition of tenement house work, minimum wage, limitation of hours of work, prohibiting night work, protection of child-bearing women . . . [and] liquor legislation."[105] But an editorial entitled "Working Women and Suffrage" stated:

> Trade union women, as a rule, attach more importance to the trade union ballot than to the political vote, much as they care about the latter, their argument being that without economic independence it is next to impossible for them to be politically or socially independent . . . Therefore, while we do not find union girls nibbling "angel food" at every suffrage pink tea, whenever they mount a suffrage platform they distribute substantial food for thought.[106]

The ILGWU were also not so sure that the effects of the vote would be as beneficial as supposed. While applauding the suffrage victories in other states, they said that, as voters, women might in the beginning be "politically petty, narrow, sentimentally hysterical," but that they were like this because they were "half-educated," and these traits would "disappear" with "experience."[107] However, women's right to vote should not be questioned: "Here and there pathetic appeals have appeared in the Labor press—appeals to men—to give women the right to vote." Such appeals to good unionists and Socialists should be entirely unnecessary, because only the employing classes need fear the women's vote. By contrast, "anyone advocating the least restriction in women members in the Union" (that is, a voice and vote in union affairs, and also equal pay for equal work) "on the ground of sex would be considered antiquated."[108] And in the period after women gained the vote, the ILGWU reported, somewhat naively:

> Within the last three years politics have become cleaner due to the influence of women . . .
> The legislature is harkening to the voice of women, regardless of party politics . . . The cause of this peculiarity of women voters to flock together even though their men folk may be as varied a political

hue as Joseph's coat, is the kindlier outlook that they have on life. "Competition," "the life of the trade" . . . "labor cost" . . . are meaningless phrases to them.

Wealthy "club women" take the lead, often, in deciding on politics, and the others follow.[109] Here, the writer seems to have concluded that class interests are irrelevant when *women* are concerned.

Almost from the beginning, the ILGWU had a majority of women members. When the union was struggling to become established, around the turn of the century, it was the more skilled men workers, like cutters, who formed the skeleton of the unon. (In 1903, 5,527 members were men and 3,338 were women.)[110] The women organized themselves during the great strikes a few years later, as previously noted. They did not organize into separate female locals, as the bookbinders did, although job segregation within the trade tended to separate them. Wage scales in the trade reflected the sex-segregated nature of the job. This union consciously downplayed aspects of competition between men and women—either for the same jobs, or for maintaining wage rates. Although they sometimes discussed the difficulties of organizing women workers, they preferred to emphasize class unity rather than sex differences. But one organizer commented on the problem of getting women to attend union meetings when they were generally held in saloons, which were very unpleasant for the women members; and asked, why not have a ladies garment workers' building?[111]

A few years earlier, an organizer had commented on the attitude of some male unionists towards women:

> It is amusing to see how many of our men still cling to the old-fashioned attitude of men towards women. When women first came to work in the factory the men thought the only way to deal with them was to force them out of the industrial field, but they soon learned that the same economic pressure that kept the men at the machines was also keeping the women at work.

However, instead of joining forces with the women, "the men looked with contempt at every effort to get women to view things from the social standpoint." But women did succeed in organizing and in winning the men's respect, although a few men still refused to take the women seriously. In the writer's own city, the Joint Board did not even send the girls' local the reports of their meetings. The writer asked, "When will our men learn that the time has gone by when there was any chance of getting the women out of the trade?"[112]

Another article criticized the "men domination in the big locals" and suggested that possibly locals should be separated by sex instead of by language, as they then were:

> Apart from the fact that men necessarily bring into the meetings too much of a distasteful masculinity . . . the women in their own branch would have a better chance to assert themselves, learn their own strength and the ways and means to govern themselves. Of course, this idea is only in its infancy.[113]

The writer added that it would help to have the "enthusiastic temperamental Jewish girls" in with the American branch. Pauline Newman, organizer for the union, was very proud of the fact that she had been able to organize an "AMERICAN BRANCH," because "that they [were] always the last ones to realize the benefit of organization [was] an old story." Because they were "so totally different" from Jewish girls, whose meetings were not in English, they needed a different branch.[114] There was also mention of the difficulty of organizing Italian embroidery workers, but their nationality rather than their sex was considered the problem.[115]

One of the problems specific to organizing women workers in Local No. 25 (New York Waist and Dress Workers) was that this local was composed mainly of girls and women—84 percent women compared to 16 percent men:

> Thus the working population changes every few years.
>
> After working 3 or 4 seasons some of them may leave the industry to get married. Others, owing to its seasonal character, may go into other trades and occupations. These are replaced by newcomers who do not always realize their obligations to the Union or to their sister workers—at any rate, not until the Union has gone to considerable expense of money and energy to impress union truths on them and get them into line. In the meantime, employers see their best chance to exploit them under one pretext or another.[116]

Elsewhere, the *Ladies Garment Worker* noted the large number of young girls in their teens working in the children's dressmakers branch of the trade, who, "owing to their youth and inexperience . . . had proved the easiest and most unresisting human material whose labor could be exploited at leisure, without protest from themselves." This situation posed a danger for the more organized trades, and they felt the union shop was the best defense.[117] Another reference, this time to the difficulty of organizing a group of women in the white goods and waist industry in Baltimore, blamed the problem not on their sex, but on the fact that "most of the women in the trade [were] those who [were] entirely uninformed about the union, their parents not having worked at any organized trades."[118]

Wherever possible, the strength and unity of women workers was stressed. One strike in Bridgeport, Connecticut, was duly reported with the comment, "We have seen numerous sights and scenes in which girls on strike were able to give points to their more sturdy brothers," and there were many other "episodes of heroism and endurance which encouraged and urged on the men to similar efforts."[119]

Working women were considered as vital a part of the trade union movement as men were, and like men, this meant that their class interests were paramount. The possibility of working-class women having interests as women which conflicted with the "true" interests of working-class men was never considered. A somewhat naive discussion entitled "The Problems of Life of the Working Girl," written by an obviously middle-class woman, included the following statements:

> The interests of the women of the working classes are diametrically opposed to those of the middle classes, although each is struggling for her own conception of freedom. The working woman has troubles of her own. She is not only a woman but a worker in the shop. She belongs to the female sex but she is also a proletarian. Womanhood, motherhood, machine [illegible], this is the trinity which patrols the fate of the working girl.[120]

Fannia Cohn, organizer for the ILGWU and one of the mainstays of the Women's Trade Union League (and who also had her share of difficulties with recalcitrant male unionists), proclaimed:

> Our women in our organization were ever ready to carry the brunt of the economic and industrial struggle side by side with their fellow-workers, the man. They never were willing to accept better conditions unless their brothers who were working with them were also included. Our women workers realized long ago, as well as did our International Union, that there must be no such thing as sex division in the trade unions, and from the inception of our union, women enjoyed the same rights as men. And in the time of strike, more than at any other time, they lived up to their responsibility.[121]

Women workers gave "a demonstration of the power of unity" in a strike of waist- and dressmakers, and showed "enthusiasm and militant spirit" in their strikes.[122] The same point was brought home in stories appearing in the paper. In one story, entitled "The Apple," a girl worker in a shop is insulted by the boss and has the apple she is eating at work thrown away. The next day, all the girls appear with apples in their hands, and the end result is a freer shop in which they can eat apples, sing, etc.[123]

Consistent with their position that women were independent, capable unionists was their view that women were (or ought to be) independent, thinking people who did not depend upon someone else (men) to tell them what to do, and who did not serve men either. This theme was stressed in the short stories and apocryphal tales that the paper ran from time to time.[124]

During and after the war period, discussions of the "modern woman" and her "new role" in society were more common. One story, called "Winning 'A Woman's Place'," described the success (with boys) of the girl who wants to go out in the world, work, and be independent, despite the warning of her old-fashioned mother who fears she will never attract a man. But, lo and behold, she becomes more popular with men than her stay-at-home sister, much to her mother's horror, and the story concludes, tongue-in-cheek, that "woman's place is in the home, but a girl's got to get out in the world looking for one."[125]

The paper ran stories translated from the Yiddish. One, entitled "Equal Rights," by Abraham Reisin, tells of a young couple, sweethearts, who like to go out together; when the man "treats" the woman, she occasionally protests. When she gets a job that pays her better, she announces her intention to treat him for a change, which leaves him "as if paralyzed." She calls the waiter, pays the two checks, and as they leave he declares that she has insulted him by "treating" him like that. She responds: "Then why have you insulted me so many times?"[126]

The real problems faced by women who must work and also take care of children, like the lack of public facilities for child care, was discussed by one writer, who was herself in the situation of needing child care. Although the difficulties of working and coming home to cook and clean had been mentioned in the paper before, this (1923) was the first time child care was seen as a social issue.[127] There was usually little or no discussion in the ILGWU of conflict of interest between men and women workers, but one instance of competition for the same jobs was discussed in the vice-president's report of 1912. He stated that in the West women were rapidly taking over men's jobs, and added: "Not that I have an objection against women workers in the suit and skirt trade, but it tends to the reduction of wages, as the employers look upon women workers as a sort of cheap material and in many instances they receive about 25% less for the same labor than men do." He therefore recommended "at least three women organizers, [since] the workers alluded to [were] all English-speaking and with the assistance of the WTUL organizing work [could] be carried on successfully."[128] Fannia Cohn also pleaded for an end to the destructive competition between men and women on the job:

> The working man does not benefit from the exploitation by the employers of the women workers in the industry. On the contrary, the employers use them as a means of defeating the men in their efforts to improve conditions.
>
> This competition between men and women must be abolished once and for all ... in a world where an unnatural difference is made between the sexes, even if this difference is in favor of one sex or the other, men and women cannot be realy happy.[129]

The direct threat of lowering men's wages was discussed on another occasion regarding the cloak industry in Cleveland. This industry had always had two wage scales, one for men and a lower one for women. The writer described the situation:

> We demanded that the women receive the same wages for the same amount of work, but the manufacturers countered our position with a suggestion that the men's wages come down to the level of the women's wage scale or that we eliminate men entirely from the factories. Of course, the absurdity of this idea in an organized industry is self-evident.[130]

With the greater employment of women in formerly all-male jobs during the war, the union warned that employers wanted "cheap women's labor" and were using women to replace men as car-men and conductors. They added that "organized labor [was] strongly opposed to the employment of women at lower wages on men's jobs," and that if women were hired they should receive equal pay for equal work.[131] However, a few months later the union reported on the employment of women as street railway workers and also in shipyards with the following comment: "It is plain that there is in reality no shortage of men, but rather a short-sightedness and lack of principle on the part of the employers" (that is, by using the women to keep wages down). The article continued: "There is no reason why women should take the place of men in work for which they are unfitted. The workers should stand together, whether they belong to a union or not, as long as capital is so firmly and formidably arrayed against them."[132]

THE ILGWU AND PROTECTIVE LABOR LEGISLATION FOR WOMEN

During the earlier part of this period (from 1905 until about 1912), there was little or no mention of the desirability of protective labor legislation for women as a means of improving their working lives. When the Brandeis Brief material was published as a book following the court victory in Muller v. Oregon, the recommendation of the ILGWU newspaper was that "this book should help in the agitation for the eight-hour day for both men and women."[133]

When the fifty-four-hour bill in New York for women and children was passed, the union applauded it, although there had been no previous mention of its having been proposed: "Nothing more important in industrial history has been accomplished this year than the passing of that bill . . . The ILGWU is justly proud of its important share in the passage of the law." Although the law unfortunately did not include canneries, it still was a victory, the governor having signed it only reluctantly after meeting with a delegation of trade unionists, they stated. Their only objection to it would be that it was "sex legislation" and therefore might create "complications in industries where both men and women" were employed. The article continued:

> some may hold for this reason that it is undemocratic; and there is some truth in the claim. Still, as long as the State withholds the ballot from woman and thus deprives her of the power to protect herself she must look to the male legislatures as her "natural protector" to see that she is not utterly destroyed physically and morally in the handicapped race in the industrial field. Therefore let us celebrate with enthusiasm an event in the industrial history of our State which indicated a marked advance in civilization.[134]

Although in this instance they hailed the law as unreservedly beneficial, a few months later an editorial warned that political parties in the upcoming elections were making all kinds of promises to do things for the "poor working girl," and commented sarcastically:

> Why do women always have to have things done for them? What's the matter with the working woman getting busy and doing a few things for themselves? Why should they always be spoken of in the same tone as we speak of imbeciles and infants, as though someone had to charitably do things for them, as though they were incapable of attending to their own affairs?

The writer stated that women had the same rights as men to organize into unions, and that they should go on and demand their right to the ballot as well: "Through your trade union and your political ballot you can make yourselves equals of men, and shake off the stigma of dependence upon benevolent and special legislation."[135] In the legislative session the following spring, the ILGWU did take note of labor bill hearings in Albany, and specifically mentioned that a representative of the ILGWU was included.[136]

This was the era of the protocol agreements in the garment industry, and the union placed far more emphasis on administering and setting guidelines by collective bargaining with the representatives of the employers than they did on legislative methods. Since the Protocol contained an elaborately worked-out means of setting wage scales (which were, of course, lower in women's trades) and working conditions, as well as of adjudicating grievances with a mediator, this was the logical forum for correcting abuses in the industry. The employers were not always averse to having unionized workers in their shops if the workers would also agree to abide by top-level union-management decisions and not to go out on "unauthorized" strikes or exceed union demands. Therefore, the ILGWU's interest in protective laws for women generally took a back seat; negotiations and potential strike situations were far more important to them.

This did not mean that the ILGWU were indifferent to protective legislation, but rather that they viewed it as only one front on which to fight the battle for workers' rights under an exploitative system. They were openly critical of Gompers at the AFL convention for his stand against night work legislation, stating that although they had "high regard" for President Gompers, it was "therefore all the more surprising that he should so stubbornly stick to a view which in all industrial countries [had] been consigned to the scrap heap long ago." They added: "President Gompers' position on this and legislative efforts in other directions is glaringly contradictory."[137]

As minimum wage legislation began to be passed in one state after another, the ILGWU reported on it informationally, and by 1919, when the Washington, D.C., minimum wage law was passed by Congress, they commented: "The most striking feature of the hearing was the lack of opposition to the bills or to the principle of minimum wage determination for women and children employees."[138]

By 1922, this unquestioned support of anything that appeared to benefit workers, especially if it applied only to women and children, was beginning to come under attack by feminists. The newly proposed equal rights amendment challenged the basis for labor laws for women. In 1923, notice appeared in the *New York Call* of a debate in the Debs Auditorium on the subject "Is Special Legislation for Women Workers Desirable?"[139] In February 1923, the union newspaper reported at length on a "Women's Blanket Bills" symposium held at the ILGWU building, at which representatives of the National Woman's Party debated the issue with the Women's Trade Union League. The position of each side was stated in detail. The NWP wanted to remove discrimination against women and favored "the elimination of laws protecting the interests of women in industry" because these laws caused "a great many women to lose their positions and deprive[d] them of occupation, because men [were] employed in their stead." The NWP was not opposed to labor legislation per se, but objected "to having laws passed for women as women. They wish[ed] these laws to protect all persons regardless of sex."

The WTUL's position was then summarized by stating that the court had said that women were physiologically different from men, and medical experts said they needed special safeguards. Women workers were young, 80 percent of them were of childbearing age, and only one-eighth of them were organized. The WTUL did not want to restrict women in industry, they argued: "We know better. Women are more numerous in industry today than they have ever been and in more trades." Regarding the eight-hour bill for women, they continued, that men had not asked for such a bill was no reason to deny it to women if they wanted it. A spirited discussion followed the debate.[140]

Although both sides were fairly presented in the report of that debate, the union's position was clearly on the side of increased labor legislation for women workers. As the Washington, D.C., minimum wage law was working its way upward through the courts to its demise in 1923, they attacked the courts' antilabor stand, saying that such actions went far toward "explaining the widespread hostility of labor to the courts."[141] The decision "thereby deliver[ed] another blow at the vitals of labor," and when the final decision at the Supreme Court level was handed down, they commented bitterly:

> What concerns us primarily is the seeming futility of all labor legislation. Consider only how much time, labor and money every piece of leglation is costing American labor . . . It took twenty years of effort to make pass its enactment in some states and today the women workers of the country, thanks to the fiat of the Supreme Court, are practically in the same position legally in work they were two decades ago, just as helpless against the greed and avarice of their employers. Today the fight has to begin all over again. Isn't it a devastating process?

The Supreme Court decision was unequivocally condemned by the union, as it was by the AFL.[142] The Washington D.C. minimum wage law was also described as having been passed because of the efforts of working women and labor over a long period of time—despite the fact that there had been no significant opposition to the Washington, D.C., bill, according to their own account of it.

WHERE WERE THE WOMEN WORKERS?

As the above discussion indicates, support for protective legislation for women did not arise out of the demands of working women, organized or not, and neither was the primary impetus for it from (male) organized labor, although unions offered varying degrees of support for such bills, depending upon the bill and the state. In fact, in one instance (the women printers in New York), women workers did act in response to proposed labor legislation, but in opposition to it, not in support of it.

Yet some accounts of legislative lobbying and hearings stress the large numbers of working women who came to support the bills. An account in the *New York Call* describes one such hearing under the heading "Measures to Guard New York Women Workers Favored at Hearing":

> Hundreds of women workers from all parts of the state, representing numerous women's organizations, carrying banners and displaying pennants, marched upon the Capital today, and laid the case of the women workers of the state, at a hearing on the five bills of the woman's program, before the Joint Committee of Labor and Industry of the Legislature.

This hearing included delegates from the WTUL, the state women's suffrage party, the Consumers' League, and other organizations. The following day, the *New York Call* reported on the opposition in a column headed "N.Y. Women Back Bills for Labor." Women speaking in opposition to the bills were listed; they included "Miss Amy Wren, a prominent Brooklyn woman lawyer; Nora Stanton Blatch, a prominent engineer of New York; Stella Benson, the first woman to operate a high-speed elevator; and Ella Sherwin, president of the Women's League of Equal Opportunity." This report was given without comment.[143] At an earlier session of the legislature reported in the *New York Call* under the headline "State Legislators Hear of Horrors in N.Y. Factories," six hundred people were said to be at the hearing. They included representatives of business opposed to the

bills, like the cannery owner who spoke against the child labor bill, saying that working in a cannery was nice outdoor work and without it
the children would just be running wild. Women representing the various social reform groups (WTUL, Consumers' League, etc.) were also
present.[144] No specific mention was made of the presence of working
women among the crowd. Another hearing in the New York legislature
was described under the heading "Workers in N.Y. State Make Fight for
Minimum Wage and 48 Hour Week"; this fight was supported by the
Women's Christian Temperance Union by over 100,000 working women
represented by the Joint Legislative Conference.[145]

It is difficult to determine where the "hundreds of women workers"
described in the *New York Call* on March 5th, 1919 had come from.
Certainly they were not recruited from the pages of the ILGWU newspaper or from the *New York Call*. When it was a question of getting workers
out to support a strike or picket line, or people to attend a demonstration
or parade on suffrage, announcements appered in the *New York Call* for
days and weeks before the event. Calls to demonstrate in support of one
or another group of striking workers in the trade were frequently made in
the pages of *Justice*.[146] But no calls for mass support for labor legislation
appeared in its pages.

Therefore, it seems clear that, whatever the union's political support
for these laws may have been, the ILGWU did not actively participate in
campaigns for mass support of protective labor legislation for women.
They included it with their support for other "welfare bills," which were
usually presented as a "package" deal to labor-minded legislators. They
did not oppose these laws on principle for being discriminatory or for
hindering women, even when such arguments were being made in a coher-
ent, logically consistent fashion by supporters of equal rights for women.
If women workers appeared in numbers at hearings, they were recruited
from other sources than labor unions, and social reform organizations,
especially the WTUL, appear to have bridged that gap.

CONCLUSION

Women were never considered an integral part of the work force by
organized labor. The AFL, especially before World War I, considered
women unorganizable, in part because they were unskilled workers and
in part because they were women for whom wage work was only a temporary condition pending their assumption of family responsibilities in
the home. Politically, the AFL leadership was conservative, antisocialist,

and opposed to either a labor party or legislation regarding working conditions for men. They did support hours limitations and no-night-work laws for women (and child) workers, with the rationale that women were unorganized and therefore helpless to achieve improvement on their own, and also that women needed special protection as future mothers. The AFL was on record in favor of equal pay for equal work; however, since sex-segregated jobs were the norm, this position meant that they accepted the prevailing practice by which women's jobs were paid on a different wage structure from men's. Even in the printing trades, which had a relatively strong craft-union tradition, working conditions for women were not considered important unless they affected men's jobs. (That shops could use the union label when women were not in the union is an example of their disregard for women in the trade.)

In all-male trades like the iron molders, exclusion of women was the norm, and these trades successfully enlisted the aid of social reformers to remove women from their ranks. They justified their position on the grounds that the work was unhealthy, but regardless of that, they felt that women belonged at home—either as wives and mothers or, if necessary, as domestic workers, but not in core rooms of foundries.

The only concerted, vocal opposition by women workers to protective laws for women came from a small group of women printers. They argued that the laws restricted women who were in skilled trades while leaving untouched other women's jobs like domestic workers or cleaners, and that the impetus for the laws came from middle-class women who, either in ignorance or malice, were driving women out of skilled crafts. Although this group, the League for Equal Opportunity, recognized that working women were also wives and mothers, they contended that protective legislation was intended to limit women to this function or else to hamper them when they tried to support a family effectively. They also argued, as did the employers, that women's freedom of contract was being abridged by these laws. These women printers were union members but do not seem to have received much support from their union; in some instances, just the opposite.

The ILGWU, on the other hand, downplayed the aspect of competition between men and women workers for jobs during this period (1905-25), although they did not challenge the sex-based job segregation within the garment trades. Women garment workers were among the most militant, as the shirtwaist strikes showed. Perhaps because of their political radicalism, the ILGWU tended to consciously define women as a basic part of the working class, and they viewed protective labor legislation as a concession to workers by the (capitalist) state.

Thus, organized labor of whatever political stripe accepted the sex-segregated division of labor within a given trade and resisted attempts to change it, whether from employers or from women themselves. The unions also defined women almost universally in terms of their functions within the home as wives and mothers, and saw their work force participation as temporary or as an interference with their primary place within the home. When unions supported protective labor legislation for women, it was often with the explicit aim of restoring them to their "rightful" place, the home.

PROTECTION

Legislator: Women are not strong enough for night work.

Woman-in-the-Home: Oh, you must mean night work with wages.

Chapter Eight
Employers' Associations

INTRODUCTION

Support for protective labor legislation for women is relatively easy to document. The WTUL, the National Consumers' Leagues, and government committees filled volumes with their evidence demonstrating the need for legislation. Court battles and lobbying efforts on behalf of the laws were supplemented by attempts to convince the public by means of articles in popular and scholarly journals, by speeches and lectures, and by investigations of working conditions. How could anyone oppose those who worked to improve the lot of the poor toiling working women? How could any group be so crass as to assert its own self-interest by maintaining that it needed the labor of women (and children) more than ten hours a day in order to fill its own pocket?

Laws opposing unions and the right of workers to organize and strike were easy to justify by appealing to individualism and the laissez-faire principles which dominated American political and economic thought through the early 1900s. But those who defined their interests as antithetical to a limitation on the hours of work, or to no night work for women, did not usually wish to justify their stand publicly in the same way that the laws' supporters did. There is therefore a qualitative difference in the kind of evidence which is available to demonstrate support of protective labor laws and that which indicates opposition. (The exception is the opposition which developed in the 1920s as a consequence of support for an equal rights amendment which was based on a principled position in favor of equal rights for women and men.)

The same problem of documenting the opposition is addressed by Eleanor Flexner in her discussion of women's suffrage. In contrast to the open, concerted efforts of the prosuffragists, the opposition appeared much harder to pin down. Some of it was a result of the anti-Negro sentiment in the South and the Southern whites' fear of any changes in the voting system and the Jim Crow restrictions, and some of the opposition was from "women of irreproachable social position" who led organizations opposed to suffrage. But Flexner also found other forces at work which were harder to document. Liquor interests opposed women's suffrage but preferred to do so in relative anonymity, by their own account.[1] Other difficult-to-uncover sources of opposition to suffrage included political machines and the Catholic church. But, Flexner stated:

> Most difficult of all to link with the opposition to woman suffrage were the business interests. The proceedings of the annual conventions of the National Association of Manufacturers and the U.S. Chamber of Commerce, or the pages of the *Wall Street Journal*, do not contain a word of protest against granting women the vote . . . Yet some business groups fought suffrage tenaciously and bitterly, albeit with the greatest circumspection. One suffrage organizer after another reported the presence and activity of the railroad, oil, and general manufacturing lobbies, wherever suffrage was up for legislative action or referendum.[2]

Opposition by business interests grew out of their general stance against "communistic" legislation like the federal income tax, antitrust legislation, and popular election of senators—but especially their fear "that women would use the vote to improve the working conditions of women."[3] That was precisely one of the reasons that women suffragists demanded the vote—to pass laws which would help women. Opponents of women's suffrage in the U.S. Senate were also supporters of business interests in states like New York, Massachusetts, and Delaware, judging by their voting record on other issues. Although the existence of a body of women opposed to suffrage served as an "excuse" for legislators disposed to vote against it, the suffragist Carrie Chapman Catt stated, "A trail led from the women's organizations into the liquor camp and it was travelled by the men the women antis employed . . . These men were observed in counsel with the liquor political managers too often" to doubt the connection.[4] This activity was covert, and neither minutes nor other records were usually kept to document it.

Many of the same business interests which opposed women's suffrage also opposed protective labor legislation for women. In both instances their opposition appears plausible in the light of their own interests as they defined them. Although this opposition was usually hidden, the very open and determined stand these businesses took on other kinds of labor legislation makes it plausible that they also opposed women's suffrage and protective labor laws. Furthermore, challenges to the laws were invariably made by those businesses that were directly affected, such as Muller the laundry owner, or Schweinler Press.

The problem is how to uncover the means by which this opposition made itself felt in legislatures and courts, and the arguments that were used when it became necessary to go publicly on record against the laws. Principle opposition to the laws seems to have come from the sector of business most affected, that is, by manufacturing interests and retail businesses. Large corporate interests of the kind represented in the National Civic Federation, such as steel, railroads, and mining, frequently did not employ women in large numbers and seem to have had little or no involvement in protective legislation for women, as will be discussed below.

EMPLOYERS' ORGANIZATIONS:
THE NATIONAL ASSOCIATION OF MANUFACTURERS

The first national organization of manufacturers that was concerned with more than specific trade interests developed out of a suggestion by a Southern trade journal in 1894 that there was a need for a general organization which would consider matters of interest to manufacturing and marketing. In 1895 and 1896, the National Association of Manufacturers (NAM) was formed, and quickly became open to individual members as well as trade organizations. It focused primarily on the issue of foreign trade.[5]

The concerns of the organization before 1903 reflected the development of a strong American merchant marine to prevent dependence upon foreign shipping, the construction of a canal in Nicaragua or Panama, and the reform of the American consular system so that foreign influence would be minimized.[6] The NAM's interest in stimulating home markets led to their advocacy of a Cabinet-level department of commerce, rate regulation of railroads (since, as shippers, they suffered from the differential freight rates of the railroads), and a number of other domestic reforms.

Then, according to Robert Wiebe, this "relatively quiet organization," which until then had had little or not interest in the "labor problem," came under the direction of a minority whose primary interest lay in promoting the open shop, and with the accession to the presidency of David Parry in an upset election in 1903, the organization declared war on organized labor.[7] Although a sector of the membership was displeased with this shift, the organization grew rapidly from 1902, when it had about one thousand members, to almost two thousand within a year, and to almost three thousand by 1904, which indicates support for Parry's strong challenge to organized labor.

At the same time, procedural changes made it more difficult to amend the NAM's constitution, and from 1903 the officers carefully controlled the annual meetings, presumably to prevent themselves from being over-ruled (as they had done to the previous leadership), or, more charitably, "to secure greater administrative centralization and efficiency."[8] Although attendance at annual meetings declined, the influence of the organization grew with the greatly increased income from the growth in membership.

Although the NAM undertook many activities in its own right, includ-ing congressional lobbying activities, a number of other organizations, nominally independent but closely connected with the NAM, were formed to promote specific aspects of its drive against labor. One such group, the Citizens' Industrial Organization, was formed in 1903 with Parry as its president. Parry shortly turned over the leadership to C.W. Post, another staunch anti-unionist, but the Citizens' Industrial Organization did not remain an effective organization for more than a few years. According to Wiebe, it was always a financial appendage of the NAM, but with broader membership. It appears that infighting and the interest of the new NAM president in establishing another organization, the National Council for Industrial Defense (NCID), may have had something to do with its demise.[9] The NCID was also financed primarily by the NAM, with Van Cleave as the head and James Emery the general council of both groups. It was the "legislative and political department of the National Association of Manu-facturers."[10] State and local associations also made up the membership of the NCID.

The American Anti-Boycott Association was another organization which, thought nominally independent, was closely connected with and endorsed by the NAM. This group jointly undertook legal challenges to boycotts with other organizations (for example, it underwrote the NAM prosecution of Gompers and the AFL in the Bucks Stove and the Danbury Hatters cases).[11] It then became the League for Industrial Rights.

These organizations were more or less direct subsidiaries to the NAM. They were formed to promote one facet or another of the NAM's cam-paign against organized labor through lobbying, legal battles, propaganda, and educational work. Employers also were organized by states or by trades. The National Founders' Association and the New York Associated Manufacturers and Merchants are some examples. These organizations were usually either members of the NAM or closely affiliated with it. Because the NAM was a national organization, its main efforts were directed at influencing national policy and congressional activities, while the statewide groups were more concerned with local legislative measures, including protective labor legislation for women.

At the national level, manufacturers' associations constituted the chief opposition to unions' efforts to insure a legitimate right to strike, boycott, and organize effectively. The manufacturers openly opposed efforts to amend the Sherman Anti-Trust Act to exclude unions from prosecution under it, and they also openly fought anti-injunction legislation supported by unions, as well as eight-hour bills for federal employees. These were the main forms of labor legislation at the national level which affected the relationship between employers and unions. (See chapter 7.)

At the state level, the issue was legislation affecting working conditions per se, and here the employers' position was much more guarded. They granted the need to protect workers from abuses to which *some* employers were unfortunately prone, but they usually opposed legislation which was sympathetic to workers or which regulated some aspects of business. This kind of opposition was usually much more covert than opposition to, for instance, boycotts. Employers usually voiced the same concern to protect women and children that other observers did, but opposed legislation which was intended to regulate their working conditions. This section will first discuss the NAM's position regarding labor unions in general and will then examine what the NAM said, compared with what they actually did, regarding legislation for women workers and working conditions in general. Although they tended to express support of protective legislation—at least, once it was on the way to becoming more acceptable to the courts—in practice they attempted to vitiate its effects. One of their methods was changing the wording of bills when passage of some kind of legislation appeared inevitable. Another was admitting the problem but denying the employers' responsibility for it or denying that it could be "regulated" away.

THE NAM AND THE OPEN SHOP DRIVE

Just before the beginning of the period under consideration here, the NAM, faced with a growth in union membership and a potentially radical labor movement in a number of sectors, responded with a concerted attack on organized labor. In 1903, their newly elected president, David M. Parry, launched the open shop campaign among manufacturers. Their opposition to organized labor was carefully couched in terms which emphasized their concern for all workers' welfare but which claimed that labor unions were tyrannical, despotic organizations which worked against the best interest of all honest workers. The principle of the open shop was that nonunion and union labor should both be permitted in a given shop at the employers' discretion.

The code of the NAM was based on that set forth by the National Metal Trades Association in 1901. It stated the NAM's "unalterable antagonism to the closed shop and insist[ed] that the doors of no industry be closed against American workmen because of their membership or nonmembership in any labor organization."[12] The NAM was also on record against the employer blacklist (used against union members), and an editorial note by Van Cleave stated: "For this practise no defense, no apology, has ever been offered which is worth a moment's consideration."[13] Nothing in theory prevented an open shop from including both union and nonunion workers, but employers knew that if the "closed shop" meant that they were to hire only union members, the open shop meant that they would hire no one who belonged to a union.

Standing on the principle of individual rights and individual freedom of contract, employers' associations contended that their opposition to unions was necessary for self-defense. Organized opposition by labor could only be met by organized opposition on the part of employers, and the employers' organizations were developed as a defensive measure, they contended. One sympathetic writer described several examples in which one business standing alone was powerless to withstand labor pressure, but when helped by the employers' association, "made a fight against the tyranny of labor organizations." The writer stated that as a result of the open shop fight in Chicago in 1903, the sympathetic strike was practically abolished and the effectiveness of the lockout was proven. For instance, when the laundry workers in the city had struck nine of the plants in an attempt to pit one employer against another, "on the same day every laundry owner in the organization locked his shop—locked out his workers."[14]

The development of employers' organizations was considered a natural response to the "mass advance" of the labor movement during the period. It was "but a logical step in, and the natural complement of, the trade-union movement."[15] This writer viewed the development cautiously, since it could lead to the formation of two powerful organizations, representing labor on the one side and the employers on the other, which could "establish a modus vivendi [whereby] . . . these two associations, acting in accord, [would] be able to dictate almost absolutely the conditions that [should] prevail in trade."[16] This possibility was not usually considered by the employers during the early open shop campaigns. Their aim was to destroy the "labor trust" entirely, not to reach an accommodation with it.

This point is brought home by the National Founders' Association in its fight to break control of the craft unions in the trade. When faced with union demands in a number of different cities during the period around 1905-1908, their position was

> that the real issue at this time was nothing more nor less than union restrictions, and that any difference in wages could be settled in short order. In many towns, they said: "We are ready to pay the wages you demand. We do not blame you for asking an advance, but we are not going to stand this radical unionism any more. We are sick of it."[17]

According to this view, the danger lay in union recognition per se, regardless of the content of the agreement, and that was why it was so important for the employers to resist. There could be no middle ground — either the unions would dictate terms to the employers, or they would have to be eliminated. Firms were urged to co-operate to withstand the unions' onslaught, and also make plans for taking care of fellow employers' needs in the event of strikes. What they meant by having plans to take care of its members was a system of spies, detectives, and nonunion molders who were to be a floating force available to members engaged in anti-union strikes. For the lack of "trust" leading to this state of affairs they blamed the unions:

> After years of individual effort to find a way of living and doing business with their men on a fair basis, the employers have been fairly driven by the union tactics to organize in associations, and adopt in some degree the methods of the unions themselves . . . Spies? The history of labor unionism fairly reeks with them.[18]

The use of spies was also supported by the Citizens' Industrial Association of America (one of the NAM offshoots, run by C.W. Post), which carried ads by agencies offering their services. For example, the Joy Detective Service (Incorporated) of Cleveland, Ohio, ran the following advertisement:

> *Quick and Effective.* The handling of labor troubles in all their phases a specialty. We guard the property during strikes, provide necessary men to keep the plants in operation, arrange board and lodging, etc. Branches in all parts of the country. Write us for references and terms.[19]

It is not surprising that the open shop turned out to mean an anti-union shop.

THE USES OF LAISSEZ-FAIRE AND INDIVIDUALISM

The employers took their stand upon their right to freedom of contract and a defense of "individual rights." In a case in New York, an employer had been "charged with coercing [an employee] to enter into a written agreement . . . not to become a member of any labor organization as a condition of securing employment." The employer's right to require workers not to join a union was upheld by the court, and the decision was commented upon at length by the NAM journal. The journal maintained that although labor unions were in themselves "looked upon with favor by the law and by the courts," and so were strikes, if lawfully conducted, "it [did] not follow . . . that it is competent for the Legislature to force individuals against their will to become members of labor organizations as a condition of obtaining employment, or to compel employers under penalty of fine and imprisonment to employ union men only."[20]

C.W. Post, president of the Citizens' Industrial Association, stated, speaking of his firm, "We have discouraged Labor Unions, and, in fact, do not permit a union man to have employment in our works."[21] The consequence of "no more closed shops in the National Cash Register" was that the women workers there were told "that from them as well as from the men the company expected an honest day's work for an honest day's pay." They were warned that in the past, "they were to some extent spoiled by the consideration the company had had for their comfort and welfare." The company warned: "Some of you have threatened to boycott the Dayton businessman . . . we won't stand for this boycott a minute. And any of you who make such threats will be discharged."[22]

One of the sources of opposition to unions was, of course, that they encouraged limitation of output and attempted to control the work process. Employers argued that unions achieved these ends by exercising tight control over the workers, discouraging individual initiative and terrorizing the rest into submission. As James Emery put it, it would be slavery if a man were compelled to work when he wished to quit, or under conditions that did not suit him, but "it is equally slavery when a man may not sell his labor without securing a license from another to do so, and when he is to be annoyed or intimidated" if he seeks to work.[23] Therefore, the "labor trust" was guilty of violating fundamental rights by seeking to extend its power over independent workmen (*independent* was a synonym for *nonunion*). This behavior was a violation of basic rights. "The inalienable right of man to work, as God gave him hands to work with, must not be abridged by any man or by any set of men who set themselves above the power and authority of the law and above the authority and will of the Almighty."[24] A Dayton employer stated, "Scratch an anarchist and you will find a socialist; scratch a socialist and you will find a trades unionist . . . trade unionism is the kindergarten of socialism."[25] The social Darwinism expressed here, with its emphasis on the natural laws of capitalism and individual enterprise, was a frequent theme of the NAM, and was usually combined with a discussion of how unions throttled the individual initiative and independence of the better workmen.

Thus unions were opposed because they presumably enforced collective regulations and restricted individual opportunity. Their aim of regulating the supply of skilled labor by limiting apprenticeships was a particular target of the Founders' Association. The association's lead article of one of its journal's issues demanded: "OPEN THE DOOR of opportunity for the American Boy."[26] Strikes were described as good opportunities for hiring nonunion men, training them, and keeping them on after the strike. One foundry was mentioned approvingly because "they had not in their employ a single molder or coremaker whom they had not educated since the strike."[27] With the changing technology in the trade, moreover, the time needed to train a molder had decreased from four years to between six months and two years. The association claimed that the "right of the foundryman to introduce molding machines and appliances of any kind, and to have the same operated by whomsoever he [found] to his best advantage," had to be defended against unions' attempts to prevent it. The Founders' Assocoation also commented on the workers' tendency to restrict production, even when on piecework.[28] They then described a plant in which workers were guaranteed that increased output would not lead to rate cutting; instead, a bonus system (Taylor's plan) was instituted, but more importantly, a permanent record of each worker's output was kept. This record had the effect of "restoring at one bound the individuality which the wage earner [had] been losing since the establishment of the factory systems."[29] These records revealed the good man, they said, and also pointed out, "indubitably, the listless, the shirker, the dull, unintelligent man," who soon found himself "without the gates."[30] The article emphasized that although wages increased under this plan, production and profits increased even more.

Thus the "individualism" which was in principle so important to the employers had a practical side also, and unions, which worked against individual ability, were said to harm the most capable worker as much as the employer. The closed shop, employers said, "throttle[d] initiative [and destroyed] the ambition to surpass in skill and productiveness, thereby barricading the road to progress and development." They also charged that the closed shop sought to maintain control over the process of production and would give the labor trust "full power to control industrial conditions and enforce its policies with respect to how, and by whom, work [would] be performed, the productiveness of the workman, and the compensation that [should] be paid."[31] The open shop, on the other hand, had shown "its ability both to improve and increase production," and also reduced antagonisms and intimidation.[32]

In their campaign against the "tyranny" of unionism, employers appealed for support to the public as well as to the workers, saying that the unions were responsible for violence and intimidation against independent workers and were instituting a reign of terror. According to Parry: "Organized labor knows but one law, and that is the law of physical force—the laws of the Huns and Vandals, the law of the savage . . . It is, in all essential features, a mob-power, knowing no master except its own power."[33] Although Unions claimed to be opposed to trusts, they themselves were the worst trust of all: "It is the *muscle trust*, the trust of men who make their living by manual labor."[34] The consequences of this power were, employers argued, truly devastating to honest people. Strike violence, injuries to "independent" workmen, and harm to other innocent victims of the unions' power were frequently cited. C.W. Post, one of the more flowery speakers of behalf of the open shop, pleaded for an end to this abuse:

> I plead for the children of the public schools who sickened from cold and exposure because the Teamsters Union refused to permit anyone whatsoever to furnish them fuel . . . I plead the cause of women whose modesty and virtue have been assaulted, clothing torn from their bodies, insults heaped upon them and their unborn babes, malformed and branded with the terror of attack by demons of the labor union . . . I plead for the mother and children trembling in the agony of terror through the long nights alone, while the husband and father was away bravely asserting his right and liberty to earn bread to keep life in their bodies.[35]

The NAM contended that the blame lay squarely with union leaders, not with the average American worker, who, they said, deplored the actions of unions in fomenting strife. "The American laborer is a patriot and not a buccaneer . . . He adores law and order, not crime and disorder.

But in order to live, Gompers needs war," they argued, and the anti-injunction legislation could be blamed on him, not American labor.[36] Picketing per se was also condemned, and employers frequently brought court cases challenging the right of workers to picket even where violence was not the outcome. *The Review* devoted a full page to one sentence in an antipicketing decision: "There can be no such thing as peaceful picketing any more than there can be chaste vulgarity, or peaceful mobbing, or lawful lynching."[37]

By 1908, Kirby expressed the cautious belief that the "tide of unionism [had] been stayed."[38] With the decline in union membership following the open shop campaign and the economic slowdown, the NAM was able to report the "acceptance of reduction of wages by employees of Republic Iron and Steel." This acceptance indicated that "labor [was] at last realizing that its interests [were] inseparable from those of capital," and was "a sign of the much needed entente cordiale between labor and capital and an indication that the labor demagogue's reign of terror [was] coming to an end."[39]

This theme, that the interests of labor and capital are one, was repeated frequently by manufacturers' interests. The Founders' Association pointed out the social benefits of increased productivity, despite workers' inclinations to believe the contrary. Workers, they said, had the mistaken view that "because a man with a machine produces more castings than a man without a machine, other workingmen are deprived of an opportunity to earn a living."[40] What workers neglected to consider was that, historically, even though the introduction of machinery was opposed by workers, for example, in spinning and weaving 150 years ago, the result had been beneficial to all: "By reason of the introduction of this same machinery, the price of the commodity was reduced to such an extent as to be placed within the reach of all the working people . . . [and] the consumption increased to such an extent as to increase the number of persons engaged at this trade many times."[41]

THE NAM AND UNION LEGISLATION

As is indicated in chapter 7, the main issues which were being fought out in the period before World War I were the right of labor to unionize, to strike, and to boycott. As part of the open shop campaign, manufacturers sought to have the boycott declared a conspiracy in restraint of trade. The NAM charged that the unions were in favor of the Sherman Anti-Trust Act until it got *them* — it all depended upon whose ox was being gored.[42]

The Anti-Boycott Association (later the League for Industrial Rights) was organized in 1901, when a different conception of industrial rights prevailed and "the law was undeveloped." According to the historian for the league, "legal relief from union abuses was comparatively unknown" at this time.[43] In 1902 there was a meeting of "champions of the open shop in the hatting industry" to get other members on the AFL "We Don't Patronize" list to join together in a "defense organization." The organization membership was a carefully guarded secret and "had to be confidential because men were afraid that the union machinery would be turned against them if their membership were disclosed."[44] Some members did not even appear on a membership list and sent their contributions through an attorney.[45]

They must have collected a fair amount of money, however, because they handled a number of court cases for employers opposing closed shop agreements, and then took the case of Loewe the Hatter. His company was the target of a nationwide boycott by the AFL, following long-standing grievances and a strike against the company in 1902 by the United Hatters of North America. According to the Anti-Boycott Association's account, Loewe was an ideal person to bring suit: "He had an untarnished record. He shunned publicity, bravado, and invectives and could not be pictured as a harsh or rabid employer . . . His assailants, on the other hand, were bold and ruthless; their power and resources were great." When the case was finally taken before a court in Connecticut, the jury awarded Loewe the full amount of damages sought, and then "rose to sing the Doxology at the close of its deliberations."[46] The verdict was finally upheld by the Supreme Court in 1915, and was unique in that individual members of the union were held responsible for the acts of the union's officers. Only 2 of the 197 defendants were union activists.[47] The Anti-Boycott Association was then faced with the task of collecting the judgment awarded by the court, and when it was necessary to have a foreclosure sale "on the various pieces of real estate in Danbury, Bethel and Norwalk," that is, the homes of the workers involved, they were annoyed by publicity with "pictures of old men being ejected and thrown with beds and bedding into slushy streets"; but at the last moment a settlement was reached, they stated.[48]

Similarly, the association underwrote the court expenses for Van Cleave, when in 1906 he "made application to the American Anti-Boycott Association for legal protection."[49] Although the NAM, and its $500,000 "war chest" to be used against organized labor, was the main target of attack by the AFL, "the taciturn American Anti-Boycott Association, which in fact shouldered the entire responsibility, remained in the background."[50]

As can be seen from the preceding discussion, manufacturing interests were openly involved in anti-union activities, in their stand against amending the Sherman Act, and also covertly through their support of the Anti-Boycott Association. Although it may have been difficult to connect any given manufacturer with the organization, the court challenges are, of course, a matter of record. The NAM justified their position by appeals to laissez-faire individualism, and basic principles of freedom of contract in the wage bargain. However, their stand in opposition to labor legislation for women (and children) was much more covert. No lengthy defenses of women's equality with men appear in the NAM literature; nor is mention made of suit being brought in the case of Muller v. Oregon or his attack on the ten-hour law for women. Yet Muller's lawyer was a prominent member of the bar who took corporate cases.

THE NAM AND PROTECTIVE LABOR LEGISLATION

These manufacturers opposed labor laws for women. But their opposition was guarded and was usually justified by implications and indirection rather than by open arguments. They agreed that employers who overworked or abused their employees were acting unjustly, but maintained that most employers were fair, decent men and that overall conditions were good for workers. Where they could, they showed instances where workers themselves opposed protective laws. Since protective labor legislation for women was becoming a fait accompli, they also accepted what could not be undone, but fought further incursions into their private agreements with their workers. Then, following World War I, they again resumed the campaign against unions and radicalism and against protective labor laws.

As early as 1903, even Parry had cautiously agreed that child labor laws might serve a useful social purpose. He said: "I see no objection to reasonable legislation . . . in order to protect health and insure the safety of workmen as well also to prevent an imposition and hardship upon helpless children . . . The great majority of men, manufacturers as well as others, do not care to see our young folks stunted in growth."[51] C.W. Post's journal, *Square Deal* (which also carried little "fillers" attesting to the health-giving properties of Postum), commented very favorably on the Muller decision, calling it "a victory of vast importance for men and women workers throughout the country." An adverse decision in the case would have invalidated hours for women. He continued:

> It would have left the women wage-earners in factories and every other kind of arduous manual labor at the mercy of unscrupulous employers, who could have worked them 12 and 14 hours a day if they saw fit . . . The consensus of public opinion the world over is that such regulation protects the public health, safety and welfare.[52]

Employers' associations much preferred to stress the good working conditions and health of the workers and to describe model factories rather than to dwell on the unpleasant side.[53] One writer's investigation of a cotton mill for poor whites in the South concluded that her "sympathy was with the employers . . . the children learned to be industrious, to be on time, a thing unknown in the families from which the mills take their employees." She "never knew of a girl or boy broken in health by work in the cotton mills." In addition, hookworm disease was being eliminated through the "sanitary conditions enforced by the mills."[54] Another testimonial was to the value of having children in textile mills, which employed "far more women than men, and a few children between 14 and 16"; implementation of a minimum wage here, this writer said, would be a disaster: "In every case where we have employed children in our plant, they were not going to school, had no chance to go to school, and were running around the streets in idleness and mischief. In some cases they are the sole support of widowed mothers or crippled fathers."[55]

Manufacturers opposed a proposed federal child labor bill which would have prohibited shipment in interstate commerce of articles produced by child labor in excess of eight hours per day, not because they opposed all regulation of child labor, but because the means was impermissible:

> not because there should or can be justifiable opposition to the rational regulation of child labor, but because the subject matter naturally excites a sympathy which may blind the mind to the revolutionary principle of control suggested. A bad principle is never so alluring as when offered in support of a cause of having popular sympathy and approval. Under the pathetic appeal of protection for the child, Congress is urged to regulate "production" under the guise of regulating "commerce."[56]

As late as 1925, a study done by the National Industrial Conference Board (an educational agency of the employers) on the effects of child labor was unable to conclude that this labor was actually harmful to health. So much depended upon the individual person's situation—the family environment, habits, maturity, kinds of work, and so forth—that it was difficult to come to general conclusions. However, it said: "There is practically no body of authoritative information relating to the specific effects of industrial or other regular employment on children."[57] The board felt that for a child's proper mental development and character some education and work were necessary, but "just how much and what kind of work, schooling and play [were] best depend[ed] upon the individual child and his age."[58] Moreover, the existing conditions must be taken as the point of comparison:

> It must be remembered that for the child the choice is not between pleasant and injurious labor and the proper education, play and wholesome work, but between the available schooling, play, work or idleness . . . Literacy and school attendance are not in themselves measures of educational progress of children or of the effect of work upon it.[59]

Therefore, their considered conclusion was that "few, if any, valid generalizations [were] possible in regard to any aspect of the child labor problem at the present time."[60]

Thus child labor legislation was not opposed outright. It was often connected with unnecessary limitation of apprenticeships or with the natural desire of a boy to help support his family. In the context of a general attack on John Mitchell, the AFL, and the proposed eight-hour-day laws, Kirby, then president of the NAM, stated his position as follows:

> I am a firm believer in rational regulation of child labor, but I can see neither policy nor wisdom in compelling, by law, a strong, husky boy, out of school at 14, willing and better able to work than many grown men and whose help is needed by a hard-working father, or perhaps a widowed mother, to spend the most important two years of his life in idleness, acquiring the initial habit of indolence, and of vice and crime, and unfitting himself for a life of thrift and usefulness, simply because the law says . . . he shall not be employed more than 8 hours a day until after he is 16.[61]

Square Deal also carried stories describing how well off the American working woman was compared to her European counterpart. When Mary MacArthur of the Women's Trade Union League in Great Britain visited this country, *Square Deal* reported her comment that here even the poorest class of women workers were "well dressed, as contented looking as . . . our best paid working women. Why, they actually had on both hats and gloves." She favored organizing them, but added, "I doubt if such a move will meet with great success in this country so long as the present standard of high wages prevails."[62] The journal also mentioned a report issued by the National Civic Federation, "Department Stores Pay Highest Wages," which stated that few salesgirls "lapse[d] from the moral code," that there was "no basis for the assertion that white slavery" resulted from the low wage scale, and that "employees [were] treated with much consideration."[63] This article described "welfare work" in retail stores.

Since one facet of the reformers' fight to secure protective legislation for women workers was the claim that low wages were in part a cause of immorality and vice, employers were always glad to find evidence that the working girl was moral and virtuous, or to defend her against charges that she was more prone than others to succumb to temptation. The foundrymen's journal printed a lengthy discussion of a Scranton newspaper story which had described the "disgrace befalling a girl coremaker employed in a Scranton foundry." It stated, "The story in all its horrible and disgusting details has been reprinted and sent broadcast by the iron molders' union in an attempt to stir up a contrasentiment to the employment of female coremakers." Assuming the story to be true, it asked: "Why tramp further in the mire a young girl merely because she chanced to work in a coreroom? What had the occupation of the girl to do with the case, except to furnish the opportunity of acquaintance with the author of her ruin?"[64] It then pointed out that the conduct of the union men themselves left much to be desired, and that "parading the shame of an unfortunate girl for union aggrandizement [was] poor business and poorer argument for any labor journal."[65]

Employers maintained that wages were sufficient, that working conditions were good, and that proposed "remedies" by law or otherwise were doomed to fail. In their testimony before investigating commissions, at state legislative hearings, and in legislation-oriented newsletters like *Monitor* (New York Associated Industries) and *Law and Labor* (League for Industrial Rights), they stated their position against protective legislation more openly. For example, although during the prewar period employers were growing more safety conscious (*American Industries* ran a series of articles demonstrating different types of safety devices), they were reluctant to give up the view that accidents were inevitable or that the worker was liable. One expert from the Institute of Mining Engineers made the following report to the New York Factory Investigating Commission: "A very heavy percentage of the accidents which happen are the inherent risks of that industry; a very heavy percentage of our accidents in industrial pursuits cannot be very well avoided." Among those which were preventable, he continued, were "the ones that [were] due, first of all, to the negligence of the employers," whose plant lacked necessary safety equipment, but he added: "Of course, a pretty heavy percentage of accidents

is due to negligence and recklessness on the part of workmen themselves
. . . also his fellow worker."[66]

The inspection procedures were a frequent source of complaint by
employers. The secretary of the Manufacturers' Association of New York
complained to the Factory Investigating Commission that some fifteen
different departments were responsible for safety inspections, and made
the following suggestions to remedy the problem:

> A. Wipe about 90% of it out . . . Q. Are you in favor of any inspec-
> tion at all? A. Certainly, absolutely . . . Q. What kind of inspection?
> A. Proper inspection. I wouldn't send a girl into a factory, as they
> have been sending them in Brooklyn lately, to go around among
> machinery, and tell men what should be done. I would put a man
> there to tell what should be done.[67]

When questioned further, he couldn't say which department had told him
about the "girl" inspectors.

Employers also felt unjustly blamed when fires broke out; they felt
that the ensuing uproar and clamor for legislation was misdirected and
worked an undue hardship on business. Although the impetus for the
New York Factory Investigating Commission had originally been the Triangle Shirtwaist Company fire in 1911, there was also a lesser-known fire
at the Diamond Candy Company four years later. The *Monitor* commented that the labor laws of 1913 were a result of an "outcropping of
hysteria" and added that the cause of the fire was not a deficiency of law,
since "the law [was] ample if it [was] enforced"; rather, the fire was a
result of the "personal equation . . . the miscalculation, the errors of judgment, the criminal negligence or whatever you want to call it."[68] The
writers commented on the possible consequences of these fires to manufacturers in an article entitled, "The Permanent Sufferer":

> Because someone locked a door in the Triangle Shirtwaist Company,
> some one out of 55,000, the other 54,999 were paralyzed by an
> avalanche of so-called remedial laws.
> Now history is making a lusty attempt to repeat. Because someone
> locked a door in the Diamond Candy Company building in Brooklyn
> all the self-appointed protectors of unwilling humanity are rolling
> up their sleeves preparatory to taking a wallop at industry's jaw.

But this time, they said, "industry [had] mastered the manly art of self-
defense."[69] They advised those preparing to testify that glittering general-
ities "didn't count with the State Industrial Board. But solid, concrete,

constructive criticism such as we gave them brought forth specific promise of relief."[70] A few months later, they were able to report the following: "The final rules give the manufacturer considerably more leeway than the original draft of the rules. *American Industries*, upon receipt of a copy of the proposed rules some months ago, submitted a brief to the Committee on Fire Hazards asking for modifications so that the rules would be practical."[71]

Manufacturers either sought to prevent passage of protective legislation or, when passage appeared inevitable, to make it as benign as possible. This goal was pursued at both national and state levels. At the national level, the NAM succeeded in blocking labor bills through its allies in the Speaker of the House and the chairmanships of key committees. The legislative and political department of the NAM, the National Council for Industrial Defense, issued periodic bulletins directed at congressional representatives and their own membership stating their position regarding various pieces of federal legislation and recommending the action to be taken. Strategies included recommending defeat or passage of a measure, or proposing amendments which would make it less offensive.

In 1913, the legislative lobbying methods of the NAM came under investigation by separate House and Senate inquiries following charges by a former lobbyist for the NAM, Martin Mulhall. The NAM was accused of improper activities aimed at influencing elections, of conducting anti-union activities and of strikebreaking, and also of influencing tariff policy. Mulhall had worked as a field agent organizing "Workingmen's Protective Associations" just before elections to recruit labor men who could be convinced to vote for candidates sympathetic to the NAM's economic programs.[72] The minority report, submitted by the House Select Committee making the investigation, concluded that Mulhall, Emery (NAM counsel), and others

> did influence legislation; did prevent the enactment of laws . . . by the expenditure of exorbitant sums of money, aid and attempt to aid in the election of those whom they believed would readily serve their interests . . . And, as is shown by literally hundreds of items in the Mulhall expense accounts, by the purchase of organization labor men to betray their fellows in election campaigns and strikebreaking activities, they instituted a new and complete system of commercialized treachery.[73]

According to Albert Steigerwalt, this scandal resulted in "the end of direct political activities by the National Association of Manufacturers; no evidence is available which shows any continuance of such activities after 1913."[74]

Albion Taylor contended that "the fundamental attitude of the National Association of Manufacturers toward organized labor [had] not materially changed since the pronouncements of 1903 and 1904," although the "style [was] more pleasing than before, less bold, with a veil of satire covering but thinly the old antagonism."[75] Steigerwalt, who is sympathetic to the aims of the NAM, also agrees that the basic orientation of the organization remain unchanged, but says that in early 1913 this orientation gave way to the realization "that its program of opposition to unionism had failed." He continues, "The question at this time was not whether to revise the association's principles with respect to organized labor, but to discover tactics that would best counteract the continued growth of the union movement."[76] The Industrial Betterment Program was one result of this shift, and meant that employers were now to pay more attention to safety, educational activities, and other amenities. What this change meant in practise is illustrated by the following exchange before the New York Factory Investigating Commission, when a paper box manufacturer was interviewed:

Q. Are you opposed to the organization of your workers?
A. Not at all, we encourage them to organize. In fact under the welfare management they do organize. We see that peace and harmony prevails and we have a dance every second and fourth Tuesday.

The employer might have to deprive them of these welfare benefits if the workers asked for higher wages, he continued, but when asked, "You don't think that the welfare work takes the place of wages, do you?" he answered that it did not.[77] An indication of this shift by 1914, and a recognition of possible benefits from protective legislation, was voiced by Walter Merritt: "Let the legislature protect them against the worst abuses rather than arming them with the weapons of militancy to defend themselves. Let state narrow the field of industrial warfare."[78]

The organization was undergoing a corresponding shift in tactics, if not in its underlying opposition to protective legislation for women workers. As noted, this opposition was not expressed as openly as with other kinds of labor laws. Nonetheless, employers lobbied against protective legislation when necessary, and continued to do so throughout the postwar period. The attitudes of employers toward women workers and toward protective legislation for women will be examined next.

The NAM and Protective Labor Legislation for Women

As early as 1904, *American Industries* had printed a small "filler" item entitled "Women in Men's Field of Work," which asked: "Do you know that 130 women have been found in this country who are expert woodchoppers, and make their living with the ax? There are 100 lumber women, as tough and strong as oxen."[79] The journal offered no editorial comment on this blurb. A few months later it ran an article entitled "Women in Industry Here and In England, making cores and chains and working at the lathe." In addition to the customary "lighter" work, the article stated, women were now found in the more "exacting occupations" like working in a brass foundry in Detroit. The article said that "their regularity of attendance as compared with that of the young men formerly engaged in the same work [had] led to their receiving in some cases higher wages." In an English bicycle plant, women [had] been used when "price cutting in the manufactured article [had] necessitated economies in the cost of production."[80]

In 1906, the no-night-work law affecting women was contested in New York state court by David L. Williams, who ran a printing company and who had been arrested for violations of the law. He admitted the act and was discharged by the judge, whose decision was printed in part in *American Industries* under the headline "Without Reference to the Position of the Hands Upon the Dial of the Clock; How Women May Work." The decision touched upon two major points, the right of freedom of contract and work, and the need to protect women because they are "mothers of future citizens." The article quoted the judge's opinion in part:

> Does the state look merely to the children of the factory woman for its future good citizens? Why should the housewife, the woman who toils at home ... the society woman—be exempt from legislative interference ...? Some of them may be mothers of future citizens, and it should be of as great interest to the state that their progeny should have proper birth and breeding to conserve its welfare.

And if healthy progeny were the "only excuse" for the law, the judge continued, "what becomes of the rights of the non-childbearing woman, a considerable class? What of the woman beyond the age of childbearing" who might have considerable technical knowledge? No argument was made in defense of the law to show that the factory conditions were unsanitary. The judge commented, "The employer, even though she be a woman, may work when and so long as it pleases her. The single employee, on the contrary, if she be a woman, may not."[81] Although the NAM clearly approved of the decision (which was subsequently upheld by the U.S. Supreme Court), it refrained from undue comment on the case. The Judge's words seem to have been comment enough.

The NAM's position appears to have alternated between claiming that women and motherhood are to be held in especially high regard and protected, and that women are independent, contractually free workers and do not want any special legislation for themselves. Both views of women were combined in an address by Van Cleave in 1909. He said: "In these days of the militant and ubiquitous suffragette, woman is far from being as voiceless as many persons imagine." Except for a few occupations like soldier, he said that women in America worked at all the jobs which men did, and that "in all of them, and very properly, she [was] treated with the consideration and deference which [had] always and in every walk of life, been extended to her by Americans." For women workers, children, and men also, he continued, we ought to "make the surroundings as sanitary as practicable." He warned:

> But we must guard against cumbering our statute books with too many laws for them. Some of the special legislation which is urged for them . . . would if enacted, be exceedingly likely to prove unconstitutional and unenforceable, and therefore to arouse distrust for all laws in this general field. Thus the women and children would be harmed instead of helped.[82]

As previously noted, *Square Deal* commented favorably on the Muller decision upholding a ten-hour law for women in Oregon. It felt that women should have the right to choose their own working conditions, but it added:

> The progress of civilization demands that they be saved from overexertion or from unsanitary and unhealthful conditions that tend to wear them out or incapacitate them for family life. Here, again, an abstract question of personal liberty has had to give way before considerations of national welfare and progress.

The Muller decision was considered a sound one, "not only just in morals, but . . . from the economic point of view" also, since output was not the less for the shortened hours, and physically exhausted workers would not lead to industrial progress.[83] Again, commenting on labor's support of the eight-hour law in public works, which was intended to be an opening wedge for other laws, the writer claimed that some protective legislation was valid under the police power where public safety or health was at issue: "Such cases would be the hours of employment for children, for men working in mines or other unhealthful places," and so forth.[84] No specific mention was made of women here, although it would appear that they would be included in the list of "acceptable" legislation along with mine workers. Later, one writer explicitly stated that laws forbidding "unconscionable and oppressive practises . . . protecting the mothers and children . . . [did] not seriously infringe upon industrial liberty."[85]

Employers maintained that they were reasonable men and did not wish to exploit women or to violate the law, and in Oregon, where a new series of laws had gone into effect, they proclaimed, "The employers of the state are desirous of reaching equitable and practicable methods of dealing with girl and women workers." The spirit as well as the letter of the law was being adhered to; the important thing, they said, was willingness to work things out.

> [The employers' willingness] to recognize the special claims upon consideration of girls and women, carries with it greater assurance than could be guaranteed by the law or by the courts were employers inclined toward antagonism and unfairness. When consciences are swept of cob-webs and people of all classes are bent upon doing right for its own sake, the employer and the employee will experience no difficulty in adjusting their differences.[86]

They noted a short time later that the Oregon law, because of its hours limitation, had automatically eliminated Saturday night shopping as well as the traditional late Christmas holiday shopping, while "some department store proprietors protested vigorously, but in vain. One department store owner helped to frame the ruling and defended it warmly."[87] As the minimum wage provisions in the Oregon law were about to be put into effect, the employers commented: "We are inclined to believe that such legislation will not work out as many of its advocates seem to think it will. Workers are always entitled to proper wage consideration, but we question if the adjustment of wages can be brought about in this way." One possible beneficial effect of a minimum wage scale might be to compel greater efficiency. Regarding the wage scale itself, and the hours provision, they cautiously stated:

> The wage scale adopted does not seem to be excessive from our knowledge of living conditions in the State of Oregon. The hours for women are in keeping with advanced legislation in many other states. While questioning the advisability of the legislation, we wish it well and hope for its success.[88]

Employers also defended a nine-hour law in Nebraska, ostensibly against the women workers themselves, saying "Western Working Women Dislike 9 Hour Law." They said that the women workers objected "on the ground that it [would] force them out of employment and replace them with men." The women were inclined to sign agreements waiving the provisions of the law, which, the writer noted, was of course not legal, but the real issue was the long-term readjustments that would occur. The next effect which could be expected to follow was "that women [would not be] displaced but that the shortening of hours [would have] the effect beyond what the law provide[d]," that is, two shifts would give way to three: "And when the process is completed there is found not a loss to any member but a gain to the whole body that justifies the change. There is no record of turning back from regulations that shorten woman's working day."[89] The New York contingent, however, attributed the eight-hour day to "pressure-constant, unrelenting, continual pressure," and made it clear what they thought of it. "The 8 hour day is undeniably with us," they agreed, but added, "The lessons that the years have taught point no moral to most of you. Oh, you ostriches."[90] By 1920, in its opposition to the proposed eight-hour bills, the *Monitor* claimed:

> Associated Industries has never, until this year, recorded formally an objection to the enforcement of a law limiting the hours of labor for women to 48 per week. Its objection at this time is not an objection to the principle which it is desired by the proponents of the bills to have established, and under any other conditions than those which obtain at present, Associated Industries might not offer any objection and might support the bills.

However, it did object to the bill on the grounds that "there is no need to undertake to establish by law that which is practically here. Nearly all the industries are operating today on the 48 hour week basis." It then cited the figures for the average number of hours for females in 144 establishments, which included 37½ percent of the women working less than and 37½ percent working more than the forty-eight-hour standard.[91]

There may have been less concerted employer opposition to protective laws for women in some states than in others. As previously noted, the Illinois ten-hour law was passed only after a long legislative fight. But in other places (such as Oregon and Washington, D.C.), it appears that there was less of a struggle against such laws. However, in New York State, manufacturers formed an active and organized opposition to "welfare bills," including those affecting women. They maintained a lobbyist in Albany, Mark Daly, who kept his constituents informed of the legislature's activities via the *Monitor,* a monthly bulletin. The *Monitor* offered information on bills pending in the New York legislature and possible amendments that manufacturers might suggest to existing laws that would make them more "acceptable." For example, the manufacturers' recommendation for recodification of the state laws requiring one day's rest in seven would be to add the following:

> ... except in an establishment where it can be proved to the satisfaction of the State Industrial Board that the work is necessarily continuous and where two-thirds of those regularly employed in such establishments voluntarily sign and present a petition to the ... Board requesting permission to work seven consecutive days.

They also recommended the inclusion of the following clause, which would extend working hours: "Males and females over the age of 18 years may be employed not more than 12 hours in any day nor more than 60 hours in any week for a limited period."[92] The *Monitor* reported: "Force of [Factory] Inspectors is Not Too Large ... Multifarious Duties Keep Labor Department Men on Jump."[93] The manufacturers drafted their own group of labor laws amendments to counter the ones offered by labor.[94]

One consequence of these efforts was that the Foundry Code affecting the employment of women in core rooms was ready for passage. The *Monitor* reported that a "sub-committee of employers and employees which worked on this set of rules had done its work so well that in the final analysis the rules were as perfect as possible."[95] By July, it was able to report that a review of the labor legislation showed "an entire absence of adverse laws."[96] The following year, in its coverage of the 1916 legislative hearings, the manufacturers included a list of witnesses appearing in favor of and in opposition to their bills. Social reformers and labor representatives appeared on both sides (for example, Rose Schneiderman of the ILGWU and Mrs. Frederick Nathan of the New York Consumers' League opposed the bill, while Henry Seager of the State Industrial Commission, and labor representatives, favored them).

The *Monitor* had more thorough coverage of hearings in Albany than any other source. It provided a full transcript (assuming it to be an accurate reporter) of the 1919 hearings at which the women printers opposed the representatives of women social reform groups and organized labor, and which also afforded evidence of the employers' position. Employers who testified at the hearings all expressed their concern for the welfare of women workers and their gratitude towards those who worked to safeguard it, but stated their opposition to the specific bill in question on the grounds that it would work irreparable harm to their business.

In the Albany hearings, a representative of the New York State Hotel Association spoke for, in his words, the "big hotels to which we naturally refer when we speak of hotels, but also the smaller hotels and also these little hotels in the summer places through the state." He pointed out that hotels have to be open twenty-four hours a day, seven days a week, to serve travelers as a temporary home, just as "in your private home making it is a 24 hour a day proposition." The proposed legislation affected hotels as well as factories or mercantile establishments, but conditions in hotels, he said, were very different from those in factories; therefore, he said, "If you adapt those hours to us you will make it impossible for us to take care of our trade." Women were employed in hotels in increasing numbers as waitresses and elevator operators, where they had been very satisfactory; he added,

> We hope we shall be able to continue them in our employ and we shall . . . unless these misguided but well-intentioned sisters press upon you legislation which you may pass which will surround the conditions of their employment with so many regulations and restrictions as to make it impossible or impracticable for us to continue them.[97]

The next speaker, president of an upstate New York textile mill, made the following statement:

> Even if we desired (and perhaps some won't admit that we do have these good intentions, but I think we do)—even if we desired to benefit the health of our employees in every way we possibly can, we are limited by the necessity of doing business, and to do business under present conditions, at all events, you have to do it at least at cost.

The problem, he argued, was that lowering the working day from fifty-four to forty-eight hours per week would increase cost "out of all proportion" because the manufacturing establishments had hundreds of millions of dollars invested in capital. The "people interested in this legislation" did not care about this problem but the manufacturers had to, he continued, and they also had to compete with other states (such as Georgia and South Carolina) that lacked the regulations that most other states had. Most of these laws he "cordially approve[d] of," and, he said, "I wouldn't go back to the old days even though it would help us to compete" with states lacking the laws because "I wouldn't want to see the little, pale-faced, anemic kids coming into the mill and have them on my conscience"; all the same it was true, he said, that the yarn cost less to produce in such places than in New York. He then showed that it would be utterly impossible for his mill to cut his profit down by one-ninth and that if the law were passed it would force his company to try to reduce the cost of its goods back down again:

> We may be decent-minded people. We may feel that in these serious times in which we are living that it isn't wise to cut down our pay-rolls, that it isn't wise to screw out of labor any more profits. We may feel that seriously, as I do myself, but what are we going to do? Where is the cost going to be saved?

It was impossible to increase the rate of production any more than it already was, he argued, in his kind of industry, "which is governed by the speed at which the wheels go around, and where the wheels go round as fast as they can with safety to the lives of the employees and property of the employers."[98]

Another employer spoke out against the effect of a proposed bill to require twenty-four hours of continuous rest in one calendar week. He spoke for Western Union telegraph offices (although, as Rose Schneiderman got him to admit, the government itself stood for one day's rest in seven, and the telegraph company was under government control). Telegraph offices had a standard eight-hour day in the larger offices, he said, "but owing to the emergency conditions with which the telegraph company is frequently confronted, it is necessary to work our force over the eight hours and also work seven days a week, in order that we may give service." Storms and other emergencies affecting the lines required these long hours.

Another speaker for the telegraph comnpany called attention to the fact that there were over one hundred telegraph offices in the state with only one operator, and these offices served wide surrounding areas which had no offices; therefore the Sunday closing in those areas would do "a very serious injury to the public." The telegraph company would gain from the closing, but messages transmitted on Sundays were likely to be emergencies, and therefore closing would be to "deprive the community entirely" of this necessary service.[99] The telegraph company was asking for an exemption to the provisions of the hours bill for telegraph operators, and one telegraph operator was also present to speak in opposition to the bill. He spoke as a representative of the Western Telegraph Workers (not a union), and said, "We feel that we ought to be able to work out our own salvation without paternalism." He added that he was speaking purely from "the viewpoint of the worker," not the company, and said that it was simply a question of money for the operators. He also took a dig at the social reform women: "It is a strange thing that the folks who have household workers in their employ never think of giving them a day off, yet they would come here and ask that the telegraph worker, the worker who must cover his situation in all times, be forced to take a day off."[100]

The *Monitor* also took note of the "unexpected opposition of women" to the proposed bills. The first speaker in opposition to the bills was Nora Stanton Blatch. The chairman had asked for the names of "prominent women" speaking in opposition. Blatch responded that there weren't any because the women opposed to the bills were "women directly affected," and added, "of whom probably none of you know the names." She said these women were now asking not to be classified with minors industrially, as in the past they had asked not to be politically. She attacked the legislation for affecting primarily those women who were making relatively good wages—$17.00 per week or more as ticket choppers, ticket sellers, and so forth, and who worked nights. She said, "But the woman who sweeps the platform can work all night, so that if you claim that this legislation is on the ground of the health of the workers, it is not so." If it were, it would apply to scrubwomen, nurses, and others.

> The whole effect of this legislation is to interfere in a mischievous way with the rights of women who are receiving fairly good salaries, and with the exceptional women who have climbed up the industrial scale. You crush them down into the ground for whom you are not legislating at all, namely, the absolutely unorganized group of scrub women and women like that.

Blatch emphasized that the vast majority of women affected by the proposed laws were unaware of what was going on and did not have paid representatives at the hearing. She observed, "I suppose of 50 elevator workers none of them have heard of legislative committee, and the first thing we know they will lose their jobs and then you will begin to hear from the women."[101] When Rose Schneiderman challenged her to state who she was representing, she answered that she spoke for a number of office workers and also the League for Equal Opportunity.

A representative of that organization charged that it was because women had been successfully competing with men for their jobs that the legislation, especially the no-night-work provisions, was being proposed. When, during the war, women were permitted to enter machine shops, given special training, rest rooms and lunch rooms, and two fifteen-minute breaks, the employer found that it paid off: "He found what was sauce for the goose was sauce for the gander, and he is extending that to the men." She added that the women were paid exactly what the men were:

> Now, men resent the fact that women can do work just as well as they can and get just as much money. He has had that superior position for so long that he looks upon her as his physical, social and mental inferior. It hurts him to realize that she is his equal, and at the same time it would hurt him a lot more if that woman would come in and work for less. He would feel it in his pocketbook then. His pride would be hurt in the first instance; his pocketbook in the second.

She described an informal survey she had done in the subway, asking women ticket sellers and others their opinion of night work, and reported that only one woman had preferred day work, while several said they had tried day work and had asked to be changed back again to the night shift. The opposition to women working at night was not based upon health grounds (she cited two doctors as proof), but came rather from the union:

> Take all of this agitation against the street-car women and it comes from the Central Federated Union. They were interested not one whit in the women, but they were interested in keeping the jobs for the men, and it is possible this legislative program was decided upon early last summer before the armistice was signed.

She told the assembly not to worry about whether a certain line of work was "fit for a woman," since the woman herself would choose what she was physically and mentally fitted for. Women were not "dragged into the industry," but went voluntarily, "knowing the conditions they [would] meet." She added, "The minute they find it is not to their liking they can step out of it, but do not force them out by state legislation." She commented on the fact that the president of the State Federation of Labor (James Holland) was present at the hearing and was speaking in favor of the bills limiting hours, etc., for women, while the AFL itself had turned down resolutions at its previous conventions to limit hours, the length of the working day, and other conditions:

> That was turned down because men refused to be bound by the State. They wanted to be free and act between themselves and their employer. Now, doesn't it look rather sinister that these men while refusing this for themselves are perfectly willing to bind women? It places women at a greater disadvantage.

She said that the only time that legislation for women was proposed was when they were in competition with men for jobs and received decent pay, not, for instance, in domestic work, which would force their employers to hire two sets of domestics instead of one, and would make domestic workers "too independent and it would be more difficult to get domestic help."[102]

Although the *Monitor* expressed surprise at the presence of working women opposed to the bills, it made use of it thereafter, and subsequent issues reported other instances of women who spoke against "welfare legislation." It said that limiting women to ever-shorter hours of work, which "chain them with the threat of the future of the race," would result in lower pay "and hobble them with the alternative of such trades only as they [could] dominate." This would mean that "out of all the wartorn world, the women who work, who made victory possible, alone [would be] denied the right of self-determination."[103]

The manufacturers also proclaimed that the attitude of labor unions "hound[ed] them out" because equal pay for equal work would become impossible if women could not work at night:

> Again, it is openly hinted that certain labor groups advocate welfare legislation as the means of ousting women from the well-paid jobs they covet for men, whereas, it is well known that bodies of women who believe that woman's place is in the home and that the social order will never be restored until she is safely caged therein, approve any move to legislate women out of industry.[104]

They quoted Ella Sherwin, who said, "It is an open secret that the labor fakers are not in favor of women in industry at any fair or decent wage." Sherwin predicted that manufacturers would use legislation to force women out, and that women would then be confined to an ever-smaller number of trades with ever-shorter hours and still would not be secure, "unless in a trade they dominate[d], as they [did] in the needle trades."[105] (Sherwin was a printer herself, as noted.)

A few months later, manufacturers reported: "Prominent Woman Opposes Special Laws for Women Because of Injury Done. Miss Mary Newton Declares That Class Legislation Does Not Benefit Those For Whom It is Passed—Insults, She Avers." The woman, who was described as the daughter of Major General John Newton, assembly Republican leader from the 7th Assembly District in New York City, was a member of the Women's League for Equal Opportunity, and was asking the legislature to defeat the office workers' eight-hour bill and the minimum wage bill, as well as to repeal the elevator law and other laws. She was described as being known as a leader in the suffrage movement and was opposing the laws because they were "opportunist legislation which would attempt to create a pampered people," and which, under the guise of protecting women, would "drive practically all women out of work—starving into the streets." She concluded:

> Grown up women should not be insulted by parlor socialists who have never worked and do not know the needs of working women . . . It is absurd and suicidal for America to ape Europe. These very laws have been the undoing of Europe and have helped surrender its separate governments to Bolsheviki.[106]

Whether this woman was an "active suffragist" is uncertain, but Harriot Stanton Blatch (mother of Nora Stanton Blatch and also an opponent of "special treatment" for women), was surely known as a long-standing militant suffragist from before the war and was a well-known member of the National Woman's Party. (The NWP did not come out in favor of an equal rights amendment and against protective labor legislation for women until about 1922.) But another opponent of the legislation who spoke at the 1919 hearing was from the Women Voters' Anti-Suffrage Party and wished "to go on record against this radical legislation that [was] being put upon the working women of this State." She observed: "Isn't it queer, gentlemen, that a woman could work in 1918 for 54 [hours] and in 1919 she is only able to work 48. At that rate of increase in about 1925 she will only be able to call around once a week in a limosine to collect her salary."[107]

Opposition to the bills described by the employers came from the employers themselves, from a small group of women workers who used some feminist and some laissez-faire arguments, and, as the previous examples illustrate, from what was evidently a conservative core of women who linked the bills with socialist, radical causes. Opposition was also expressed by nonunion workers who accepted the view that limitation on the hours of work would be reflected in their paychecks. Organized labor, including the State and local Federations of Labor, generally favored the bills to limit hours, and other conditions for women (although they generally opposed minimum wage legislation, as indicated).

ANTI-RADICAL ACTIVITY AND THE NAM

During the postwar period, the growing political reaction and anti-radicalism grew stronger at both state and national levels. The employers' associations' attacks on social welfare laws also relied increasingly on "red scare" tactics, as well as attempts to connect the laws with German propaganda. The New York State League of Women Voters charged that the "Daly Lobby" (Mark Daly was editor of the *Monitor* and an Albany lobbyist), under the cover of the "so-called League for Americanism," had "sought to create the impression that such legislation [was] of pro-German and Bolshevik origin." The Lusk Committee (the Joint Legislative Committee to Investigate Seditious Activities) called the Health Bill then before the legislature bolshevism, and also attacked the eight-hour and minimum wage bills for women. Speaker of the Assembly Tad Sweet, a notorious opponent of labor legislation, also took part in the anti-red attacks. A pamphlet circulated by the League of Women Voters (and reprinted by the American Association for Labor Legislation) stated:

> A deliberate, undisguised and widespread effort has been made to create the impression that well-considered and temperate legislative proposals for human welfare are "symbolic" of and in some way connected with Bolshevism . . . the speakers, the pamphlets, and the press propaganda of the so-called League for Americanism, backed by the Daly Lobby and an inner group of the Associated Manufacturers and Merchants, has widely and generally availed itself of this method of misrepresentation.[108]

For its part, the *Monitor* took note of the charges levied against it by the League of Women Voters' pamphlet, which charged "the Daly lobby" with "interfering with open and orderly legislative action," with coercion in getting petitions from workers, and with having a fund of between one and two hundred thousand dollars for propaganda used to support the League for Americanism, whose "real object" was to "kill off health insurance and other fool legislation," according to one manufacturer cited in the pamphlet. The *Monitor* countered with Daly's rebuttal. He agreed that part of the work of Associated Industries was "attendance on the legislative sessions," but that its actions had "been honorable and legitimate." He denied that there was a lobbying fund or that there was any connection between Associated Industries and the League for Americanism, beyond "friendliness."[109]

This attack by the New York Manufacturers and Merchants Association coincided with a national campaign against other groups supporting "welfare" legislation. The Women's Joint Congressional Committee (which included the National Women's Trade Union League, the National Consumers' League, the National League of Women Voters, and the National Board of Young Women's Christian Associations) was the target of a campaign directed particularly against their work for a federal education bill and a child labor amendment. Boone's history of the WTUL had stated: "The spear-head of the opposition was the United States Chamber of Commerce and the National Association of Manufacturers, but they had as allies employees of the War Department." The War Department had distributed a photostatic chart of "communistic connections"; although the secretary of war was subsequently forced to withdraw the document, it continued to be disseminated by employers' associations, including the Associated Industries of New York.[110] (See chapter 6.)

The American Anti-Boycott Association's monthly newsletter, *Law and Labor,* a nonsubscription, free newsletter which advised "employers and employers' associations concerning legal phases of the labor problem," contained summaries of legislation "affecting labor controversies and all new kinds of contracts with employees," and also of antisedition bills, arrests of IWW Wobblies, and anarchists. This periodical informed employers of court suits and judges' decisions in state courts across the country, frequently citing at length from the case record with little or no additional editorial comment. The earlier, prewar campaigns against the open shop had abated somewhat during the war years, but following the war were again resumed, along with an interest in "shop committees" as a substitute for unionization.[111] The association stated: "Our stand for the real Open Shop as a principle of human liberty, condemning discrimination against union men as well as against non-union men, and looking with disfavor upon contracts which curtail that freedom, receives hearty support."[112]

From its inception in 1919, this periodical devoted considerable attention to anti-leftist activities. An article on a deportation case was headed "Forfeiting Citizenship for Membership in the IWW."[113] Again, in February 1920, the periodical presented the provisions of the Sterling Anti-Sedition Bill, the House version of which included the following: "The use of a red flag or banner is forbidden at parades and meetings; the fact of use is made prima facie evidence of use for an unlawful purpose." The House sponsor of the bill explained that "the whole bill [was] drawn along the line of punishing the use of force and violence exclusively." In its comment on it, *Law and Order* stopped short of unqualified approval of the bill, since the definition of sedition, which applied to those who defended others who were seditious, went too far: "Every man who is morally courageous knows that he may sooner or later become an apologist for some such person."[114] The same issue reported on a case in Washington State in which fifty-nine members of the IWW, named and unnamed, were "permanently enjoined and restrained from continuing as members of said Industrial Workers of the World."[115] The National Industrial Council (national lobbying and political group of the NAM) reported approvingly on a bill before Congress in 1919 to exclude or expel anarchists and other seditious aliens:

> The measure, while preserving every legitimate right of free speech, of free press and lawful assembly . . . appropriately punishes those who incite such acts [i.e., to violence] in accordance with the consequences of their indictment, even to the death penalty if the jury recommend it.[116]

Law and Order's close continuing coverage of political events included a detailed description of the nationwide Palmer raids, which took place on January 2, 1920. The periodical described the arrests and detentions in Boston of over six hundred people. The article gave what was apparently the decision of the Massachusetts court, with evidence of civil rights violations, detentions, and confiscation of personal books and papers, described and criticized.[117] These were usually reported in a factual tone without much additional comment.

Similarly, the issue of protective legislation for women and children was usually presented in a neutral tone, with a simple statement included in a summary of legislation, that "the tendency [had] been to favor protective standards for labor," and that "further advances were made in raising the legal minimum age of employment for children."[118] In April 1915, when *Law and Order* reported on the "program of the AFL—destroying the Constitution," it commented on many of the AFL provisions, but in the section on Women and Children, in which the AFL proclaimed that "women should receive equal pay for equal work and the physical welfare of both women and children should be safeguarded and protected against exploitation," the periodical gave no additional comment.[119]

Throughout this period, the manufacturing interests represented by the NAM, as well as the state-level trade and business associations, opposed the passage of protective labor legislation for women and a variety of other social and labor legislation. As they began to recognize that this kind of legislation was here to stay, their opposition took different forms, but their basic stand remained unchanged. When the political climate was right, anti-radical attacks were combined with other legal arguments against the laws. Whatever the measure, the economic consequences were held to be detrimental to the interests of both workers and business.

By contrast, the organization which was representative of the largest corporate and banking interests, the National Civic Federation, played little part either in opposing this legislation or in helping to shape it along lines that would be acceptable to business interests, although they were actively involved in other aspects of labor-employer relations, including industrial "mediation" and the drafting of workmen's compensation bills. Their role in relation to organized labor will be considered next.

THE ROLE OF THE NATIONAL CIVIC FEDERATION

The National Civic Federation (NCF) did not play a part in either proposing or supporting protective labor legislation for women workers. They were actively involved in numerous other kinds of labor relations and legislative programs, but not in shaping legislation for women (or child) workers.[120]

The NCF was supported by business interests but included representatives of labor, business, and "the public" for the purpose of "industrial conciliation," and was in direct opposition to militant or socialist labor action. Gompers frequently came under strong criticism from labor for his membership in the organization, but he remained an active member of it and defended it against its critics. By contrast, the National Association of Manufacturers and Gompers were traditional enemies (although this position softened somewhat during the war period). Lorwin, in his history of the AFL, concluded:

> Indeed, allowing for differences in composition, geographic distribution, and ideas, a certain similarity can be detected between the National Civic Federation and the anti-union employers' associations. Both were protests against militant unionism, and against corrupt business unionism. The Civic Federation proceeded with more sophisticated or enlightened methods; but it was bent on pulling the teeth of aggressive unionism.[121]

Where the NCF differed from the open shop employers of the NAM was in method, not in purpose.

Over a period of decades, spanning the time period under examination here, Gompers maintained close connections with the NCF through his personal friendship with Ralph Easley, with whom he shared views on a whole range of issues. The two men exchanged personal visits, inquired about each other's families, vacations, and health, and maintained an ongoing working relationship between their respective organizations despite differences of opinion which cropped up from time to time. Perhaps the most striking aspect of their shared outlook is the vehemence of the antisocialist views which they both espoused. Their different "class" interests invariably took a back seat when it was a question of fighting against the IWW or other socialistic organizations. For example, Easley sent Gompers a clipping on an NCF speaker at a Women's Club meeting. The speaker had stated that woman is part of industrial life through the family, if not herself, and that clubwomen could help by "personally looking after the degree of enforcement of laws and endeavors for improving factory and shop conditions." She continued, "There will be found no greater antidote to the dangerous encroachments of socialism than such welfare work." The speaker made special mention of Gompers for his antisocialism.[122]

In 1915, Easley informed Gompers that they "were able to get the legislature to deter action on the Sage Bill at Albany, the purpose of which [was] to provide for direct payments" in a workmen's compensation plan which they evidently did not favor.[123] And when Gompers was faced with his own internal political problems, Easley assured him, "The American Federation of Labor could not tear you down without repudiating all the officials, and as officialdom usually runs a convention there was no worry about that proposition."[124]

The NCF did not advocate labor legislation to improve working conditions. However, they had a Women's Department (which was composed of women in the NCF, that is, female relatives of men members), and a Welfare Department. Welfare work included "sanitary workplaces, recreation halls, educational classes, model homes and provident funds, including sick, accident, death and pension funds," which were to be advocated by example and educational means.[125] From the beginning, organized labor was suspicious of the motives behind this benevolence, and considered welfare work an anti-union, paternalistic scheme. Even conservative trade unionists refused to identify themselves with these efforts. Philip Foner points out that it is significant that the Welfare Department of the NCF was the only committee which did not have labor membership.[126]

The Women's Department expressed their desire to use their influence in favor of welfare work but noted that it was difficult to organize support for their efforts, "due to a distrust that exist[ed] on the part of some persons in regard to the NCF, and a feeling among others that [they were] duplicating the work of other organizations." Therefore, they said, "It is necessary to prove the need of welfare work by showing conditions as they exist, good and bad—proving that good conditions are financially profitable as well as right."[127] Mrs. J. Borden Harriman, chairwoman of the Women's Committee, stated its object as follows:

> To use its influence in securing needed improvements in working and living conditions of women and men wage earners . . . Should not the woman who spends the money which the employees help to provide take a special interest in their welfare, especially in the woman wage-earners? A decent, wholesome environment for the worker has come in this progressive age to be a part of the social and civic obligation of the modern employer.

Change was to be effected by education and example, with "friendly conferences and conciliatory methods." She continued, "Our visits to cigar factories, hotels and other business concerns are from the standpoint of invited guests, for our policy is to carefully refrain from invoking any official aid."[128]

The NCF's concern for the condition of women workers and possible protective measures which ought to be undertaken were described at an early date at a Conference on Welfare Work in 1904. Under the heading "Protection for Women Workers," they specified the following:

> In applying these primary beginnings of any system of welfare work, several moral questions are encountered. In factories where both men and women are employed, it is desirable, though unfortunately not always possible, to separate by a period of 3 or 5 minutes their times for leaving and quitting work. This simple precaution for the protection of the feminine element among the employees of any large establishment has the effect of preserving respect for womanhood.

They also recommended the employment of a matron who would also be a "confidential advisor and render temporary relief in case of illness."[129] They then reported on various employers and how they implemented various measures, including lunchrooms for women employees, and free overalls and laundry. One employer described his "Motives of Welfare Work" as follows: "We became interested in welfare some 20 years ago. The expectation of profiting thereby was never in our minds . . . As we are passing through this world just once, and shall never pass this way again, we should like to do what good we can as we pass along!"[130] As another example of the way in which the NCF conceived of its role, the Welfare Committee reported the following of one of its members:

> [He] recently became the head of one of our great public utilities [and] found the working conditions of the employees unfit for animals, to say nothing of human beings. The women were driven at such a pace that one department became known as the "Whited Sepulcher." This member, who was quick to recognize his responsibility

as a Christian employer, sought suggestions, and one of the first moves on his part was to install a rest room—unheard of there ... The transformation which has been made in conditions is such that many old sores are gradually being healed.[131]

Opposition to the NCF's efforts came from "the socialists [who had] been trying to keep welfare work from being presented to the General Federation of Women's Clubs," they noted. Florence Kelley and Jane Addams came in for special criticism, as well as Mrs. Rheta Child Dorr (who chaired the Industrial and Child Labor Committee), who had announced that she was a socialist and who had criticized the Women's Department of the NCF for not taking up the issue of child labor. The writer noted, "We shall always have to fight the Socialists on Welfare Work and for it."[132] The NCF had a running battle with other more liberal women's organizations and did what they could to lead the women's clubs in a more conservative direction.[133] They wrote thanking Gompers's secretary, Miss R. Lee Guard, for information they had requested on "women trade union leaders who are not allied with the WTUL and who are conservative and thoroughly in accord with the principles of the AFL."[134]

Reviewing the results of their efforts and the growth of the welfare work that they had observed, the report of the Women's Department to the NCF Annual Meeting, "What are Employers voluntarily doing to improve the working and living conditions" of workers, described the improvement in canneries they had visited. Canneries were of "two-fold interest because such improvements affect as directly the public health as they do the welfare of the cannery workers." They continued:

Because of the large number of married women who work in the canneries, some employers have provided nursery rooms, attendants and equipment, thus keeping the children out of the cannery proper and providing for them adequate care while the mothers are occupied in the workrooms.[135]

The Women's Committee had conducted its very own investigation of arsenals and had actually visited one, they reported. They found it clean and said that although the men had baseball and football, so far there was nothing for the women, who did have washrooms but only "hard rattan couches for relaxation." They recommended small reading rooms so the girls could lie down if they felt ill. They had previously heard of the dangerous effects on workers in arsenals of picric acid, "which so permeates the skin as to take months to secure its removal and sometimes causes nausea," and so they investigated it thoroughly. What they found out from the management, which was cooperative in this respect, "served to dispel the fear as to the menace to health." Picric acid, they learned, can cause "sore throat and distressing cough, necessitating the use of a respirator." They concluded: "But these symptoms are mere inconveniences not affecting general health. The acid serves as a tonic and has an appetizing effect."[136]

These "investigations" which the women of the NCF did were in striking contrast to the critical, extensive reports on working and living conditions which were done by social reform groups like the Women's Trade Union League, the National Consumers' League, settlement houses like Greenwich House, or the Russell Sage Foundation, which have been discussed in other chapters here.

The close connection between top-level leadership of the AFL and the NCF, despite widespread criticism of the NCF within the unions, indicates the depth of the conservatism and the kinds of influences there were on the leadership of the AFL. It is not surprising that *both* the AFL and the NCF came out against minimum wage legislation when that became an issue. The NCF's own Minimum Wage Commission conducted a lengthy inquiry into the subject using Marie Obenauer's work and their own investigation in Seattle regarding the effects of the minimum wage law there. They ultimately concluded:

> After surveying the field both in foreign countries and the U.S. our Commission was unable to arrive at any conclusion as to the desirability of minimum wage legislation . . .

> Our Commission has concluded, therefore, that for the present, it is the part of wisdom for all states, not having minimum wage laws, to watch those having such statutes before adopting similar legislation, lest undue haste may lead to the disparagement of what might otherwise prove to be a powerful force for social betterment.[137]

The amount of energy the NCF devoted to the minimum wage issue is in striking contrast to their singular lack of notice regarding other kinds of protective legislation for women, such as hours regulations, night work laws, and prohibited employment. On the minimum wage issue, however, both the NCF and the AFL leadership could agree. The NCF report included a copy of testimony before the New York Factory Investigating Commission by Hugh Frayne, general organizer for the AFL, who stated: "Organized labor of the State of New York is not asking for this law.

They have not endorsed or proposed any law, neither have they author-
ized those who are promoting it to speak for them." Activity on behalf of
minimum wage legislation came from "representatives of colleges and
social workers," and he contended, "While they have some intercourse
with the labor movement they do not speak or have authority to speak
for a law of this kind."[138]

Other information gained by the NCF's commission was that some
employers might stand to gain by minimum wage legislation, "for then
the individual proprietor [was] not placed in the position where his competition [could] underbid him," and "many employers in the Mercantile
lines" would welcome it for that reason; however, it was "very doubtful"
whether the wage earner would gain.[139]

CONCLUSION

From the foregoing discussion, it is apparent that two different
approaches were taken by employers: the NAM used the iron fist, while
the NCF preferred the velvet glove in its relations with organized labor.
The NAM was interested in smashing unionism completely, and only
when a direct frontal attack was bound to fail did it resort to less aggressive forms of labor relations. Their struggle to eliminate craft unions'
control over labor supply and to gain control over the work process (illustrated by the foundry owners) was expressed through the ideology of
individualism, which was a direct attack on the "collectivism" from which
unions drew their strength. Employers of the NAM argued that unions
discouraged "individual initiative" (like ratebusting and scabbing); they
therefore opposed unions but asserted their common interests with "industrious," "independent" workers. It was considered inevitable and natural
that some should prosper while others should not, since the "primordial
rights" of man (and woman) to labor, and the wealth which accrues to the
superior individual necessarily results in unequal distribution of goods,
and in some men employing others. But, rather than being exploitation,
this was held to be in the best interests of both workers and employers.
The "Harmonious State," to use Wolfe's term, was the ideology which
proclaimed that there was no basic conflict between capital and labor:
they were, as one employer put it, "like the two blades of the scissors."[140]

The NAM opposed any kind of labor legislation, including protective labor laws for women, but preferred to defeat this kind of legislation
quietly rather than to launch a public campaign against it. Manufacturers denied that their business practices or working conditions in their

factories were detrimental to the health of workers. They admitted no responsibility for the long-run condition of workers as a class. The most elementary sanitary provisions, ventilation, and fire prevention measures, were considered unnecessary by these employers, and they resisted attempts to set some kind of minimum standard through legislation. Alternating slack periods with intense overwork was also the norm in many trades.

The NCF, on the other hand, was not involved in opposing protective labor legislation, but neither did they support it. In areas they were interested in, such as workmen's compensation, they worked to develop principles and standards which would be acceptable to employers. They drafted their own version of acceptable legislation and successfully influenced the outcome. They worked at "conciliation" in labor disputes and at reaching settlements with unions that were favorable to the employers' interests. This process was assisted by their close collaboration with the AFL and by the antisocialist, conservative approach to labor issues which they both shared. If the NCF sought to improve working conditions in factories, it was by voluntary means, in the belief that this "welfare work" would prevent a militant labor movement from gaining ground.

In the early part of this period, then, these two sectors of capital were frequently at loggerheads with each other and pursued opposite policies with regard to organized labor. While the NAM was bringing suit against Gompers and others, the NCF was financing his defense. (There was also apparently a split among employers regarding the use of child labor.) However, the basic similarities of outlook began to reemerge as the NAM came to recognize that the newly emerging body of legislation which tentatively granted legitimacy to union activity and which provided for minimum standards of working conditions (such as for women workers) was an accommodation they could live with. (As Marx had noted of earlier manufacturers, once the laws were in effect, their objections that their business would be strangled disappeared.)

The relationship of forces within the state was undergoing a shift during this period, and the interests of workers were being represented in a limited fashion within the processes of the state itself. For example, the U.S. Commission on Industrial Relations heard testimony from socialists as well as from manufacturers despite attempts of the NCF to stop the hearings, and its final report was highly critical of employers. The commission had been formed because of concern over the industrial violence and labor unrest at the time. But it is clear that the interests of the subordinate classes were represented in a qualitatively different fashion from those of the dominant classes, as Poulantzas put it, and that the policy making of the state in this instance also revealed the intrastate contradictions and tensions. This commission ultimately produced three separate reports—one by the head of the commission, and a majority and a minority report. Little concrete legislation resulted from the commission's findings, but according to Weinstein, "the main effect of the Commission was to win the support of workers and radicals to the Wilson administration and to the idea that unions and radical intellectuals possessed real power over social policy."[141]

However, with regard to their position against protective labor legislation for women, the NAM was caught in a bind. On the one hand, they were the chief cause of the laws; it was the conditions in their factories and stores which gave rise to the laws. But they could not deny their respect for motherhood and the family; their reverence for womanhood was frequently proclaimed. They therefore had to grant that laws which were supposed to protect the "future mothers of the race" had a noble aim; but the practical consequences of the laws could always be attacked. Employers wished to preserve the family (on which reproduction of their work force depended), but also wished to employ women workers, and at the lowest possible wages for the most profitable time periods. In this case, the passage of these laws served to force individual capitalists to do what they were unable to do for themselves, that is, limit the extent to which women workers could be exploited, when this exploitation was potentially undermining the basis for the reproduction of the labor force, or when it crystallized labor militancy.

Drawn by *Nina E. Allender*

EQUAL PAY FOR EQUAL WORK.

Waitress: "But how do I get this equal work?"
Judge: "Ah, the law 'protects' you from that."
Waitress: "He is protected—not I."

Chapter Nine
Conclusion

This study has analyzed the historical forces surrounding the emergence of legislation that helped to define the position of working women; it has explored the constraints and priorities which shaped the development of that legislation and the different kinds of justifications used in its passage. The pattern for these laws was established from about 1905-1925, although its constitutionality was considered problematic throughout the period.

Liberal public opinion at the time generally thought that these laws were a desirable reform which was necessary to improve conditions for women, who were unable to improve their working conditions by themselves. It was only in the early 1920s that serious opposition to these laws was voiced by any group outside of business interests.

Protective labor legislation set up a kind of protected status for women which appeared to be responding to their special needs as working women but which did so by leaving the major premises about women's position intact. In other words, these laws did not challenge the traditional assumption that woman's place was properly, or at least primarily, in the home, but rather reinforced it.

These laws developed as an attempt to mediate the contradiction, under capitalism, between the need to reproduce the labor force (which takes place within the family and is based on the domestic labor of the wife outside the labor force) and the desire of capital to use women's

227

labor to the limits of human endurance as cheap, relatively unskilled wage labor (since the wage structure of women was based on the assumption that women are not the primary breadwinner in a family). Capital both depended upon the family for the maintenance and reproduction of its labor force and also, in its exploitation of women workers in particular, tended to destroy it. This is the significance of the social reformers' pleas for the "preservation of the family," despite their quaint, moralistic tone.

These laws reinforced the subordinate position of women in the work force while at the same time ameliorating some of the worst abuses of their working situation. During this twenty-year period, the working day went from a frequent twelve hours to one approaching an eight-hour standard, and some of the more unhealthful, arduous forms of labor were eliminated, partly in response to protective legislation. This meant a redefinition of the terms under which surplus value (profit) could take place: a shift in emphasis from prolonging the working day to its upper limits to increasing the "efficiency" of labor. Rationalization of the work process, exemplified by the precepts of scientific management, and protective labor legislation for women both contributed to this process.

The legal ideology of laissez-faire, which had but recently been developed to permit the expansion of business activity, among other things, now was used by employers against protective legislation for women workers. During this period, in direct response to conditions for women workers, as well as in a number of specific industries employing men, the nature of judicial argument and the use of precedent were changed to allow the introduction of protective labor legislation.

The impetus for passage and legitimation of this kind of legislation came from a range of social reform groups which wished to alleviate class conflict and social unrest and sought to improve the conditions of women workers as one means to that goal. Organized labor initially gave conditional support but was more enthusiastic when the legislation limited women workers' participation in skilled jobs or eliminated them as competition with men in specific crafts.

INDUSTRIAL CAPITALISM AND WOMEN'S LABOR

I have assumed throughout this work that the subordinate position of women is not biologically determined by the fact of childbearing, nor is their relegation to the home. Rather, this condition was part of a long-term historical process which occurred along with the development of class society and private ownership of property. Even before the advent of industrialization and the factory system in the United States, women had been engaged in many different occupations within the home, and then as part of the wage labor force outside the home as well. In the lower classes, women were expected to work whenever possible. Paupers worked in poorhouses, others who could, worked in the newly developing manufacturing establishments.

From the beginning of industrialization, women formed a kind of industrial reserve labor force, with a pay scale distinctly lower than men's.[1] In this country, women entered the industrial labor force in increasing numbers around the turn of this century, although they had participated in industrial work from its beginnings. However, their labor came to be seen as something which was detracting from women's functions in the home, rather than, as earlier, an addition to it. Why this newly found concern for the sanctity of the home and family?

One of the contradictions which arises in the course of capitalist relations of production is that capitalism both depends upon, and also tends to destroy, the creator of surplus value or profit, that is, the worker. This is exemplified by the struggle over the length of the working day, described by Marx.[2] Capital, left to its own devices, prolonged the workday to the maximum; the result was the real prospect of the destruction of the lives and health of the workers as a class. The Factory Acts in England were the result of workers' efforts as a class "to prevent the very workers from selling, by voluntary contract with capital, themselves and their families into slavery and death."[3]

Marx viewed protective labor legislation as a victory won by workers and other reform groups which opposed the tendency of capital to kill the goose which lays the golden egg. However, this view did not consider the question of what this legislation, directed as it was towards women and children specifically, did to the situation of women. Women worked both outside the home as wage laborers, and also within the home. Although housework is nonwaged labor, it is essential for the maintenance of the labor force. Protective labor legislation for women served to legitimate and reinforce this function by defining the chief role of women as unpaid workers in the home, while also "adjusting" their work force participation to prevent it from impinging upon their primary function in capitalist society. This legitimation was not simply a question of "stereotyping" of women or a way of discriminating against them. It was preserving the basis for capitalist production. Women's work was a necessary part of this production, within the home and outside it as well.

Outside the home, it is in the differential wage scales that the structural differences between male workers and female workers can be seen. Capitalism did not create differential wage scales between men and women. That difference existed whenever women were employed for wages, from colonial times on. The patriarchal family structure, with the man as legal and economic head and the wife and children subordinate, formed a basic part of the preindustrial age hierarchy. Female labor meant cheap labor, and to a limited extent, less physically demanding labor (although that is less clear, since both women and children worked in the English mines until prohibited by law).

Wage labor under capitalism built upon and incorporated this preindustrial gender hierarchy by defining men's wages as a family wage and women's wages as, at best, an individual wage. Reformers argued for a living wage for *men* workers so that they could support their families unaided; women were assumed to be dependent upon a man and part of some family unit as well, and therefore did not "need" the same wages men did. Although many reformers, especially the more labor-oriented Women's Trade Union League, argued that women must be paid a living wage, it would have been considered patently unrealistic to argue that women needed enough to support a family—it was drastic enough to argue that they needed to be able to support *themselves*.

But under capitalism, the wage level is not determined on the basis of "need" of the workers, and capitalists have always vehemently denied that it ought to be. On the contrary, they argued that "wages paid, however inadequate to support, inflict no injury," and are a strictly individual matter to be contracted between employer and employee, like the price of any other commodity. Therefore the connection between protective labor legislation for women and the preservation and reproduction of the labor force is also shown by the fate of minimum wage legislation for women throughout this period. The proponents' view was that the "wage bargain" must take into account not simply some kind of individual "work-worth" of the human worker, but also the production of her labor power. It would force the employer to consider the need of the workers to survive as a class—something which the employers, especially when women's wages were concerned—were unwilling to do. Reformers argued that the employer was a parasite upon the community as a whole if he paid the worker less than it took to support and reproduce the labor he used. No laws of competition forced the capitalist to pay a "living wage" to women workers, and the drive for profits and competition between capitalists (seen, for instance, in laundries and retail stores) worked against the employer who wished to do so. The only means of protecting the "progressive" employer from the cutthroat competition of his fellow capitalists, then, was for the state to intervene and delimit the sphere within which competition could take place, or, as Filene put it, "fix a limit beyond which cupidity shall not go."

Setting a bottom limit to wages meant that the pressure would be shifted from one element in the production and accumulation process to another. It encouraged technological improvements to increase the productivity of labor and the adoption of new processes and organization of work. Employers argued that "poor widows" and aged or defective workers would be cruelly thrown into the streets as a direct consequence of minimum wage legislation because it would then no longer be profitable to hire them, while more acute observers argued that allowing these ("inefficient") sectors of the working class to compete with other, more competent, workers had disastrous effects on the entire wage structure.

In fact, numerous studies of family budgets and wages of industrial workers during the period show that the income of working-class families was dangerously close to or below the subsistence level, and this included all sources of income for a family. The majority of families depended upon working children and wives or boarders for additional income, although this income was usually a smaller proportion of the family budget than the man's income, where there was one. These additional sources were essential, given the high proportion of budgets spent on food and the high percentage of families earning near or below the subsistence level. There was probably a *loss* in real wages from the end of the nineteenth century until World War I, and, relative to the increased productivity, only a minimal increase in real wages during and after the war. (Hours of work did decrease, however.)

Wages of men workers were generally insufficient to support a family, but women's wages were about half that. Where the woman worker was part of a family—either a daughter or wife—her wage was used for the maintenance of the family and did not contribute to her own independence. Single women living alone (the "girl adrift") either barely survived or required other subsidies, such as the boarding houses and dining halls sponsored by charities of the period.

The relative failure of minimum wage legislation for women throughout this period, compared with hours and no-night-work laws, can be taken as an indication that these laws were intended to "protect" women only insofar as their function in the home was threatened. Arguments that low wages contributed to ill health and encouraged immorality were therefore ineffective. In those states where minimum wage rates were instituted, they were set so low as to be no real inconvenience to employers. A low wage structure for women contributed to keeping them in the home unless absolutely necessary and insured that they could not be the sole support of a family, or, in most cases, of themselves. In this way, women were "brought into industry" on a carefully defined basis which differed structurally from that of men. It is this difference which traditional analyses—from Engels on—have ignored, and which these laws helped to "protect."

MALE-DOMINATED UNIONS AND WOMEN WORKERS

A gender-based hierarchy in the labor market literally capitalized upon a preexisting subordination of women, and meant constant pressure on the wage structure of "men's jobs" as well, since if women could be substituted for men in a job, the pay would be drastically lowered. Men workers frequently responded to this possibility by attempting either to exclude women altogether from the trade, or by confining them to separate, lower-paid jobs within it. The iron molders lobbied successfully for laws to restrict and eventually eliminate women from core rooms in foundries with little more argument than that it was "no place for a woman." Other unions relied on restrictive apprenticeship rules to eliminate women from skilled trades (such as printing).

When the question of legislation for women workers came up, male unionists and employers put aside their differences and united over the need to "protect" women out of skilled trades. Both the molders and the foundry owners helped write the restrictions on women workers in core rooms. It could easily be argued that it was not in the male unionists' best interests as workers to allow this to happen, since women were then used (as other groups were used who were allowed to remain outside the ranks of organized labor) as a reserve work force ready to undercut wages, and as potential strikebreakers. But the acceptance of a male-supremacist outlook on the part of men workers made it possible to exclude women, and American workers viewed women as intruders who were taking "their" jobs. Male workers did benefit from this exclusion in another sense, by keeping women available in the home to take care of them, which, I could speculate, was why they bemoaned the lack of homemaking skills of girls who left home to work all day. It also benefited them in the short run by eliminating women as competition for jobs. Since the craft unions of this period were conservative, exclusionary, and showed little sense of class unity, this position was consistent with their overall view of their best interests.

However, there were other forces at work which tended to undermine the control of craft unions over a given trade. Employers were concerned with technological improvements which reduced costs, and they were also concerned with maintaining control over the work force. Both these aims could be achieved by subdividing work processes and introducing machinery which replaced skilled craft labor. During the start of the period, around 1902 and after, employers went on a concerted drive to break the power of craft unions in many different trades. Employers openly stated that their aim was to destroy unions and union-based apprenticeship systems, to take control of the conditions of work, and to substitute machine processes for hand processes wherever they felt they were more "efficient." The system of scientific management provided the principles and rationale for this drive. Taylorism purported to be an impartial, "scientific" system which benefited both the worker and the employer by increasing productivity, because it would insure the most "efficient" use of labor. It was supposed to take these workplace decisions out of the realm of conflict between workers and employers and to provide a rational scientific basis for determining workers' output and wages.

For this reason, scientific management appealed to some social reformers, who saw it as a "fair" way of resolving issues between employers and workers which would ameliorate class conflict and deflect potential unrest away from revolutionary solutions. Reformers' support for the "efficiency" movement of management, and their similar support for protective legislation had in common their hope that social reforms of this type would make socialism "unnecessary." Rather than prolong the working day beyond endurance, employers would now seek to increase productivity of labor by introducing machine processes, and reorganizing existing processes along lines suggested by Taylor.[4]

Both the "efficiency" movement and protective labor legislation for women served to rationalize the work process, contributed to segmenting the work force, and furthered the process of deskilling conditions of work for the work force as a whole, despite the fact that protective labor legislation *reduced* the hours of work. This legislation helped to shift the emphasis from long hours to more "productive" ones. Its proponents claimed that a shortened workday would not result in decreased output because the work would be done more efficiently if the workers were not completely fatigued, and therefore employers did not need to worry about their profits if they shortened hours. Although some observers claimed that these laws benefited employers as well as workers, employers did not agree. They considered these laws meddlesome interferences with their businesses, as well as dangerous precedents.

THE STATE AND CLASS INTERESTS

The next issue to be considered, is why *state* action was invoked, in light of the contention here that the state acts in the overall interests of the dominant class, not against it. The passage of protective labor legislation for women was, as it turned out, a reform that worked in the interests of the dominant class. This legislation, rather than demonstrating that the state acted as a neutral arbiter, revealed a more complex process at work.

First, although employers were the chief opponents of protective legislation at both the legislative and judicial levels, and although their organizations lobbied continuously against the passage of labor legislation of all sorts, *some* employers conceded that legislation of uniform conditions (such as hours limitations) might work to their benefit. They saw that they could not unilaterally reduce the working day in one shop alone because their competitors would gain an advantage. Only if all were forced to change would this problem be overcome. These employers, evidently a small minority, recognized that an authority outside the immediate realm of production and competition between firms could solve this problem. Capitalists in the absence of this coercion were fully capable of physically destroying the worker as a consequence of their desire to cut costs and increase production. Therefore, in this instance, the state was invoked to solve a problem which arose in the course of capitalist development, although that action was counter to the immediate demands of capitalists to pursue unlimited exploitation of labor power. The relative "autonomy" of the state from the interest of individual capitalists meant that it could act in their long-run interest. Employers grudgingly came to see that these laws prohibiting "unconscionable and oppressive practices . . . protecting mothers and children" were not a serious infringement on their ability to do business. It was also true, of course, that if laws regulating an industry as a whole were beneficial to employers, it was still advantageous for any *individual* employer to seek to evade them. Enforcement of these laws was notoriously lax.

Some employers came to accept these laws, although not eagerly, for another key reason. Employers opposed labor unions and enabling legislation which provided the groundwork for union organizing. Perhaps legislative remedies for the worst industrial abuses were better than unionization. As one employer put it, "Let the state narrow the field of industrial warfare." As a matter of tactics, legislation could be preferable to leaving the issue to be resolved by open class conflict. However, when worker opposition seemed less likely, employers renewed their opposition to the laws. For example, during the war period, patriotism was used to argue in favor of maximum production, and attempts to repeal protective laws were mounted in many states.

This legislation represented an unstable compromise which materially aided the working class and which was continuously threatened by the capitalists. However, throughout this period the actions of the workers through the unions were directed less at the passage of these laws than at insuring their right to organize and strike. As this study has shown, the passage of labor laws for women workers did not come about as a consequence of any mighty show of force by labor in their favor. Nevertheless, these laws must be seen as a result of the need to consider the interests of wage labor within the state. The use of state power affects the power relation between classes, in this case to "succor the weaker party" in the wage contract. However, the subordinate class exercises its power within the arena of the state differently than the dominant class does, and struggles outside the state affect the state's policies.

One illustration of this process occurred following the Triangle Shirtwaist fire in 1911. This fire was one of the most dramatic events of the period, and it served to crystallize workers' outrage at the low priority which employers gave to their lives and safety. The fire was followed by a mass protest and a huge public funeral procession. The employers, of course, expressed regrets but admitted no responsibility. But workers were determined that these conditions be changed, and the result was . . . a government investigation.

The New York State Factory Investigating Commission met over a period of several years and heard testimony from "all sides" regarding fire regulations, as expected, but also a wide range of health and safety issues. The commission itself was composed of labor union officials, prominent social reformers, and professionals; it heard evidence from workers, employers, medical and fire safety experts, and others. Gompers argued loudly in hearing rooms with representatives of capital who contended that long hours were necessary, industrial hazards were an "assumed risk" by the worker, and industrial pollutants like sulfuric acid fumes were beneficial to workers' health. The outcome of all this was the passage of laws.

It would be hard to find a more specific response by the state to a popular movement which both responded to demands for change and also served to routinize conflict, as Miliband put it.[5] This commission met over a period of years, and by the end, employers had become more adept at giving testimony and the original burst of outrage had subsided. The commission continued to hear testimony, but the resulting legislation was minimal. In this instance, the demands by workers for change were responded to by state action, which also drew upon differences of opinion between employers and provided an arena within which changes could be carefully controlled (through legislation).

The preceding discussion has focused on the way in which the state maintained and reproduced a structure of domination which was centered in *productive* relations. This study has demonstrated how the state also contributed to the maintenance of the subordinate position of *women* through its support for a certain kind of family structure and the unpaid domestic labor of women; it has also shown that the wage structure is also based upon this family structure, regardless of whatever struggle between capital and (male) labor may be taking place. Advocates of protective labor laws for women recognized this truth. These laws were intended to allow participation of women in the paid labor force while also defining her primary function in terms of the family and *reproduction* of the "race." The state was not only a "capitalist" state, but therefore also a "patriarchal" one,

> through its support for a specific form of household: the family household dependent largely upon a male wage and upon female domestic servicing. This household system is in turn related to capitalist production in that it serves (though inadequately) for the reproduction of the working class and for the maintenance of women as a reserve army of labor, low-paid when they are in jobs and often unemployed.[6]

The state mediated the contradiction between the sphere of family and domestic unpaid labor, and the paid labor force activity of women. It also maintained the gender-based hierarchy of labor. If this compromise was in the interests of capital as whole for all the reasons indicated,it was also in the interests of male labor, at least as they saw it.

When it came to their own protection, male unionists relied on other means than legislation. The conservative AFL was very leery of protective legislation for any but women and child workers. They feared (as the employers hoped) that it would undercut worker unionism. In addition, they argued that what the legislature granted, the legislature or the courts could take away. This, of course, was a real problem. One of the means at hand by which these laws could be overturned or undermined was by court challenges to their constitutionality. The legal processes by which these laws were gradually legitimated will be considered next, as an example of the changing relationship between the law and the economic sphere.

THE LAW: IDEOLOGIES OF INDIVIDUALISM

Employers' opposition to labor unions and protective labor legislation was expressed in the courts by means of the legal doctrine of freedom of contract. This was the legal expression of the fact that each individual employer wished to be free to use his labor force to the utmost. Employers did not wish to treat their workers collectively, that is, as a class, and neither did they accept any social responsibility for workers' continuation and reproduction as a class. The legal doctrines which the capitalists as a class developed to oppose all kinds of regulation of their businesses towards the second half of the nineteenth century demonstrate this position.

Because the legal system appears as an internally consistent, formal set of rules, the relation between law and the economic forces in the society is obscured. The principles themselves appear to have a kind of independent existence. It was felt at the time that American principles of jurisprudence, including laissez-faire and freedom of contract, were the obstacles to protective labor legislation. Freedom of contract appeared to constitute a legal restraint which operated independently of the economic interests which could invoke it. Doctrines of natural rights, and the due process and equal protection clauses of the Constitution, were the legal means by which protective labor laws were struck down.

The long-standing legal precedent of usury laws (which protect the borrower as a weaker party to the contract) was held *not* to apply to inequalities of the worker's bargaining power in relation to the employer. On the contrary, the "right to work" was considered a property right which ultimately derived from God. Laissez-faire principles in the market were upheld by the court, and came to include wage labor. The social Darwinist view that inequality was natural and just was translated into legal precepts and used to declare labor legislation a violation of inalienable rights.

However, these "rights" which, it was asserted, derived from the Constitution and were based on the natural rights of man, in fact were first articulated only in the 1880s, and therefore are an example of the way in which the principles themselves were created to serve a specific end—the development of the rights of the employer over wage labor as a commodity. Laissez-faire doctrines even in the nineteenth century were never used to the detriment of business, but rather provided the legal milieu in which business activity could flourish.[7] Formal equality under freedom of contract was used to uphold and legitimate the substantively unequal bargaining power of worker and capitalist.

As protective labor legislation increasingly came to be seen as a remedy for certain problems created by industrialization, its proponents argued that there was no effective equality of bargaining power where the wage bargain was concerned, and especially where the workers were women. Since it was permissible to interfere with basic freedoms under the police power when public health, morals, or safety were at stake, these laws should be upheld on that basis, they contended. The principle of "reasonableness" then became the means by which the real world entered into the judicial process, since judges had to have some knowledge of the "facts" which led the legislature to enact the law. During this period, the courts increasingly relied on factors outside the formal legal structure to justify decisions in labor cases. This reliance limited the use of precedent, since the "facts" had to be decided in each instance. Precedent is supposed to result in impartial, predictable adjudication of a "government of laws not men." But since the court is free to choose its precedent and can use previous decisions either to uphold a given law or to show that the previous decision does not apply, precedent becomes a tool of the courts.[8]

It was by means of the Brandeis Brief that substantive economic conditions regarding the harmful effects of overwork were presented to the court and were used to uphold a ten-hour law for women workers. But other legislation affecting men (such as miners) had also been upheld; therefore protective laws were *not* validated just when women workers were involved. However, when the law in question affected women only, the court accepted the assumption that although women did work, it was not desirable and should not be allowed to impinge on her primary function in the home. Sometimes the court distinguished women from children (who were wards of the state); laws limiting women's "freedom of contract" or right to work were then struck down. Other laws were upheld on the grounds of women's special situation regarding motherhood, physical weakness, and "dependence upon men." Thus women's subordinate position in the family and the work force was being legally recognized. In addition, protective laws for women were justified on the grounds that women were the "future mothers of the race" and that hence it was in the public interest to protect them. Working women may or may not have been mothers, but it was the future of the class that was being protected.

The judicial system over the period discussed here first allowed the development of wage labor as a commodity to take place unhindered by means of the freedom-of-contract doctrines, and then allowed for the limitation of that process when other forces required the restriction of the power of the employer over wage labor. This need to limit the employer's freedom to exploit the worker was recognized in other situations besides that of women workers, as I have pointed out.

The Feminist Opposition: the Debate Continues

The only group which protested this legal definition of women's special need for protection from a truly feminist standpoint was the National Woman's Party, after the women got the vote. Before women could vote, all suffragists agreed that one of the uses to which women would put the vote, once they gained it, would be to pass legislation to benefit women and children. The vote was seen as a means of strengthening the home and women's position within it, not the opposite.

It is ironic that this group of militant suffragists, whose knowledge of working-class interests was that of an outsider looking in, sought to define women in terms that foreshadow modern feminists' demands for equal treatment before the law. They evoked only condemnation from social reformers and trade unionists, and no response at all from the vast numbers of unskilled and underpaid women workers. The small group of unionized women printers who protested against the legislation which "protected" them out of their jobs linked up with these suffragists in condemning the laws. They argued pragmatically against the effect of the laws, and also used the feminist arguments for equality that were put forth to justify the first equal rights amendment in the early 1920s.

These laws, which limited women's work force activities to "protect" her family duties, are now classified as discriminatory under federal legislation, but the debate over the best way to legally define women workers' "special situation" continues. The dilemma of how to recognize the fact that women bear children, and most often are still responsible for raising them, continues. Again, proponents of women's rights are divided on the issue: whether pregnancy and childbirth are "unique" and need no apologies when they are dealt with as such in the law, or whether they should be viewed as another condition affecting workers' lives like others, although sex-specific. Mindful of past problems which a specialized legal status caused for working women in the earlier period, current activists are trying to forge policies which will respond realistically to women's needs, while also recognizing that they are integral members of the work force—something which was never granted throughout the period which has been studied here.

Appendix:
Chronology and Types of Protective Labor Legislation for Women

HOURS LAWS

1895. Eight-hour law for factory women in Illinois struck down (Ritchie v. People 155 Ill. 98).

1900. Pennsylvania act limiting hours to twelve per day and sixty per week upheld (Commonwealth v. Beatty, 15 Pa. Super. 5).

1902. State hours laws upheld in Nebraska (Wenham v. State, 65 Neb. 394) and Washington (State v. Buchanan, 29 Wash. 602).

1908. Landmark U.S. Supreme Court decision upholding an Oregon ten-hour law affecting women in factories and laundries (Muller v. Oregon, 208 U.S. 412). The Brandeis Brief was developed here, and after this case hours limits were usually passed and upheld by the courts.

1910. Ten-hour law for women upheld in Illinois (Ritchie and Co. v. Wayman, 244 Ill. 509).

1912. New York fifty-four-hour-per-week law upheld in New York for women in factories but not canneries.

LAWS PROHIBITING NIGHT WORK FOR WOMEN

Unless night work was prohibited, hours limitations were unenforceable, since women could work any hour of the day or night with no way of determining how long they had been there. They also could work two shifts back-to-back through midnight.

1907. New York law prohibiting night work for women struck down (People v. Williams, 189 N.Y. 131). The argument used precedent only, not substantive evidence.

1915. New York law prohibiting night work for women upheld (People v. Charles Schweinler Press, 214 N.Y. 395). Successfully defended as a health measure using substantive evidence, in contrast to the earlier law, which was struck down.

1923. No-night-work law affecting women in restaurants in New York upheld by U.S. Supreme Court (Radice v. People, 264 U.S. 292).

MINIMUM WAGE LAWS

1912. First minimum wage law passed in the United States in Massachusetts; Oregon passed one in 1913.

1917. Court challenges to these laws (Simpson v. O'Hara 70 Ore. 261 [1914]), and Stettler v. O'Hara, 243 U.S. 629 [1917]). A divided court let the minimum wage laws stand.

1918. More state courts upheld minimum wage laws: Washington and Massachusetts; Texas and Washington in 1920 and 1921.

1923. Washington, D.C., minimum wage law found unconstitutional (Adkins v. Children's Hospital; Adkins v. Lyons, 261 U.S. 525). This decision evoked a storm of controversy because by 1923 protective legislation was usually upheld.

Notes

CHAPTER 1. INTRODUCTION

1.   Leo Kanowitz, *Sex Roles in Law and Society* (Albuquerque, NM: University of New Mexico Press, 1973), 309.

2.   Roslyn Feldberg, "Comparable Worth: Toward Theory and Practice in the United States," *Signs* 10, no. 21 (1984), 312,320. Also statement of Ronnie Steinberg in U.S. Commission on Civil Rights, *Comparable Worth: Issue for the 80's*, vol. 2: *Proceedings*, 56-57.

3.   Howard Hayghe, "Research Summaries," *Monthly Labor Review* (December 1984), 32.

4.   See, for example, Steve Max, "The Need for Parental Leaves," *The New York Times*, August 27, 1986, A23.

5.   Joan Smith, "The Paradox of Women's Poverty: Wage-Earning Women and Economic Transformation", *Signs: Journal of Women in Culture and Society* 10, Winter 1984:307.

6.   Judith Scott, "Keeping Women in Their Place: Exclusionary Policies and Reproduction," *Double Exposure: Women's Health Hazards on the Job and at Home* ed. Wendy Chavkin (New York: Monthly Review Press, 1984), 90.

7.   For this point, see Maureen Hatch, "Mother, Father, Worker: Men and Women and the Reproductive Risks of Work," in Chavkin, *Double Exposure*, 161-179.

8.   Florence Kelley, "Should Women be Treated Identically with Men by the Law?" *American Review* 3 (May-June 1923), 277. Note the similarity of her view with this contemporary view about pregnancy and breast feeding: "It is crucial that we overcome any aversion to describing these functions as 'unique' "; the equal treatment model "fails to focus on the effect of the very *real* sex difference of pregnancy on the relative positions of men and women in society and on the goal of assuring equality of opportunity and effect within a heterogeneous 'society of equals'." In Wendy Williams, "Equality's Riddle: Pregnancy and the Equal Treatment/Special Treatment Debate," *New York University Review of Law and Social Change* 13, no. 325 (1984-85):326.

9.   Williams, "Equality's Riddle," 327.

10.   Williams disagrees: "The enormous pressure created by the changed demography of the workforce as well as initiatives by public and private groups indicates that major change is indeed possible. To settle for special treatment now would be to sell equality short." See ibid., 380.

11.   See, for example, Eli Zaretsky, *Capitalism, the Family and Private Life* (New York: Harper, 1976), for a description of the public/private problem.

12.   Frederick Engels, *Origin of the Family, Private Property and the State,* with an introduction by Eleanor Leacock (New York: New World Paperbacks, 1972), 128.

13.   Eleanor Leacock, Introduction to *Origin of the Family, Private Property and the State,* by Frederick Engels, 41.

14.   Engels, *Origin of the Family,* 138.

15.   Leacock, Introduction to *Origin of the Family,* 40. For this debate in anthropology, see Michelle Zimbalist Rosaldo and Louise Lamphere, *Woman, Culture and Society* (Stanford, CA: Stanford University Press, 1974).

16.   Zillah Eisenstein, "Developing a Theory of Capitalist Patriarchy and Socialist Feminism," in *Capitalist Patriarchy and the Case for Socialist Feminism,* ed. Zillah Eisenstein (New York: Monthly Review Press, 1979), 28.

17.   See, for example, Shulamith Firestone, *Dialectic of Sex* (New York: Bantam, 1971), for this more global interpretation.

18.   Roisin McDonough and Rachel Harrison, "Patriarchy and Relations of Production," in *Feminism and Materialism* ed. Annette Kuhn and Ann Marie Wolpe (London: Routledge & Kegan Paul, 1978), 34-35.

19. Heidi Hartmann, "Capitalism, Patriarchy, and Job Segregation by Sex," in Eisenstein, *Capitalist Patriarchy and the Case for Socialist Feminism*, 208. Hartmann defines patriarchy as "a set of social relations which has a material base and in which there are hierarchical relatives between men, and solidarity among them, which enable them to control women. Patriarchy is thus the system of male oppression of women" (232).

20. See McDonough and Harrison, "Patriarchy and Relations of Production," 31.

21. Ellen DuBois, "The Nineteenth-Century Woman Suffrage Movement and the Analysis of Women's Oppression," in Eisenstein, *Capitalist Patriarchy and the Case for Socialist Feminism*, 149.

22. Barbara Brown et al., *Women's Rights and the Law* (New York: Praeger, 1977), 209.

23. Albie Sachs and Joan Hoff Wilson, *Sexism and the Law* Oxford, England: Martin Robertson & Co., 1978), 116.

24. See Veronica Beechey, "Women and Production: A Critical Analysis of Some Sociological Theories of Women's Work," in Kuhn and Wolpe, *Feminism and Materialism*, 167-172, for this critique.

25. David Gordon, *Theories of Poverty and Underemployment* (Lexington, MA: Heath & Co., 1972), 71, 74.

26. For a recent analysis which does focus on women, particularly in low-paid service sector jobs, see Smith, "The Paradox of Women's Poverty."

27. Edith Abbott, *Women in Industry* (New York: D. Appleton & Co., 1910), 52, quoting a manufacturer.

28. Ibid., 90. Abbott states that in 1819 at Lancaster women were 88 percent of mill operatives, in 1819 at Waltham they were 95 percent, etc.

29. For this early mill girl militance, see, for example, Mary Ryan, *Womanhood in America*, 3rd ed. (New York: Franklin Watts, 1983), 124-125.

30. For an example of an interpretation of protective labor legislation as "interest group conflict," see James Willard Hurst, *Law and the Conditions of Freedom in the Nineteenth Century United States* (Madison, WI: University of Wisconsin Press, 1956), 94-95.

31. For a good discussion of this problem, see Erik Olin Wright, *Class, Crisis and the State* (London: New Left Books, 1978), ch. 1.

32. Paul M. Sweezy, *The Theory of Capitalist Development* (New York: Monthly Review Press, 1968), 243-244.

33. The abstract equality of the "citizen" embodied in the democratic principle of "one man, one vote" gives the appearance of equality while preserving the real, substantively unequal power of the subordinate group. It therefore has a legitimating function but also may serve as a real basis for challenging that power. Wolfe calls this situation the inherent tensions between the democratic and liberal (that is, capitalist marketplace individualistic) conceptions. (Alan Wolfe, *The Limits of Legitimacy*, New York: Free Press, 1977.)

34. Nicos Poulantzas, *State, Power, Socialism* (London: New Left Books, 1978), 132. Emphasis in original throughout.

35. Ibid., 142.

36. Samuel Hays, *The Response to Industrialism, 1885-1914* (Chicago: University of Chicago Press, 1957), 79. See also Harold U. Faulkner, *The Decline of Laissez Faire, 1897-1917* (New York: Holt, Rinehart, & Winston, 1962), 256-258.

37. James Weinstein, *The Corporate Ideal in the Liberal State, 1900-1918* (Boston: Beacon Press, 1968), xv.

38. Ralph Miliband, *The State in Capitalist Society* (New York: Basic Books, 1969), 79, quoting Jean Meynaud.

39. Poulantzas, *State, Power, Socialism*, 31, 41.

40. Wright, *Class, Crisis and the State*, 163-164.

41. Ibid., 157.

42. See Theda Skocpol, "Political Response to Capitalist Crisis: Neo-Marxist Theories of the State and the Case of the New Deal," *Politics and Society* 10, no. 2 (1980):155-201, for a summary of these views. She does not discuss Poulantzas's views which are referred to here.

43. Sweezy, *Theory of Capitalist Development*, 248.

44. See Karl Marx, *Capital*, 3 vols. (Chicago: Kerr & Co., 1915), vol. 1, ch. 15, sec. 9, for his discussion of the Factory Acts.

45. Poulantzas, *State, Power, Socialism*, 133.

CHAPTER 2. THE WORK PROCESS: SCIENTIFIC MANAGEMENT,
EFFICIENCY, AND LABOR LEGISLATION FOR WOMEN

1. See Richard Edwards, *Contested Terrain* (New York: Basic Books,, 1979), ch. 6.

2. Sidney Pollard, "Factory Discipline in the Industrial Revolution," *Economic History Review* 16 (1963): 258.

3. Ibid., 267.

4. E.J. Hobsbawm, *Labouring Men* (New York: Doubleday Anchor, 1967), 409.

5. David Gordon, "Capitalist Efficiency and Socialist Efficiency," *Monthly Review* 28 (July-August 1976): 19-39.

6. U.S. Bureau of the Census, *13th Census (1910) Abstract for New York* (Washington, D.C.: Government Printing Office, 1913), 703.

7. Edith Abbott, *Women in Industry* (New York: D. Appleton & Co., 1910):258.

8. Ibid., 259.

9. Mary Van Kleeck, "Changes in Women's Work in Binderies," in *The Economic Position of Women* (New York: The Academy of Political Science, 1910), 27-28. The printing trade was one of a series of different studies she conducted on women's occupations.

10. Ibid., 36

11. Mary Van Kleeck, *Women in the Bookbinding Trade* (New York: Survey Associates, Russell Sage Foundation Publications, 1913), 45-46.

12. Ibid., 66.

13. H. Seager, Introduction to *Women in The Bookbinding Trade*, by Van Kleeck, ix.

14. Van Kleeck, *Bookbinding*, 49.

15. Ibid., 57.

16. Ibid., 87.

17. Edith Abbott, "Employment of Women in Industries: Cigar-Making—Its History and Present Tendencies," *Journal of Political Economy* 15 (January 1907):23.

18. Ibid., 24.

19. *International Socialist Review* 11 (1910), p. 694.

20. William English Walling, "The New Unionism—The Problem of the Unskilled Worker," *Annals of the American Academy of Political and Social Science* 24 (1904):310.

21. Ibid., 311.

22. Ibid., 299-300.

23. Louise D. Odencrantz, *Italian Women in Industry* (New York: Russell Sage Foundation, 1919), 41.

24. Ibid., 42.

25. Annie Marion MacLean, *Wage-Earning Women* (New York: Macmillan, 1910; reprint ed. New York: Arno Press, 1974), 33.

26. Josephine Goldmark, *Fatigue and Efficiency* (New York: Charities Publication Committee, 1912), part I, p. 58.

27. Frederick Taylor, *Principles of Scientific Management* (New York: W.W. Norton & Co., 1911; reprint ed., 1967), 119.

28. Edwards, *Contested Terrain*, 97-98. He points out that Taylorism was never completely accepted, but this is not the issue here.

29. Harry Braverman, *Labor and Monopoly Capital* (New York: Monthly Review Press, 1974), 86.

30. Hugh Aitkin, *Taylorism at Watertown Arsenal* (Cambridge, MA: Harvard University Press, 1960), 147-148.

31. Helen Marot, *American Labor Unions* (New York: H. Holt & Co., 1914), 230.

32. Ibid., 231.

33. Ibid., 233-234.

34. Ibid., 239.

35. Ibid., 236.

36. U.S. Commission on Industrial Relations, *Final Report Testimony*, vol. 1, S. Doc. 21, 64th Cong., 1915, p. 213.

37. Ibid., 215-216.

38. Ibid., 217.

39. Ibid., 217.

40. Ibid., 219.

41. Ibid., 223.

42. Ibid., 230.

43. Ibid., 232.

44. Ibid., 992.

45. Ibid., 996.

46. Milton Nadworny, *Scientific Management and the Unions, 1900-1932* (Cambridge, MA: Harvard University Press, 1955), ch. 3.

47. Sue Ainslie Clark and Edith Wyatt, *Making Both Ends Meet: The Income and Outlay of New York Working Girls* (New York: Macmillan, 1911), 249.

48. Goldmark, *Fatigue*, 194.

49. Ibid., 203.

50. Karl Marx, *(Capital*, Chicago: Kerr and Co., 1915), p. 263-264. The preceding discussion is based on his chapter "The Working Day," 256-260.

51. Goldmark, *Fatigue*, 3.

52. Ibid., 13.

53. Ibid., 38-39.

54. Ibid., 127.

55. Ibid., 142.

56. Marx, *Capital*, 327.

57. "Overwork," *Survey* 23 (1909-1910), 442.

58. Ibid., 446.

59. MacLean, *Wage-Earning Women*, 177-178.

60. Florence Kelley, *Modern Industry in Relation to the Family, Health, Education, Morality* (New York: Longmans, Green & Co., 1914), 16.

61. See, for example, Agnes de Luna, "How Night Work of Women is Menacing Maternity," *American Labor Legislation Review* 11 (March 1921):85-86.

62. U.S. Women's Bureau, *Health Problems of Women in Industry*, (Washington, D.C.: U.S. Government Printing Office, 1921), Bulletin no. 18.

63. Ibid., 5.

64. Mary Van Kleeck, "Working Hours of Women in Factories," *Charities and the Commons* 17 (October 1906):18.

65. Ibid., 20.

66. Louis Brandeis and Josephine Goldmark, *The Case Against Night Work for Women, Brief for People v. Schweinler Press* (New York: National Consumers' League, 1918), 307.

67. Ibid., 9.

68. Ibid., 11.

69. Ibid., 157.

70. Ibid., 276.

71. Ibid., 291.

CHAPTER 3. LEGAL IDEOLOGIES AND SOCIAL CHANGE:
PROTECTIVE LABOR LEGISLATION FOR WOMEN

1. See Michael Tigar and Madeleine Levy, *Law and the Rise of Capitalism* (New York: Monthly Review Press, 1977), for this general point.

2. Charles Grove Haines, *The Revival of Natural Law Concepts* (New York: Russell & Russell, 1965), 49.

3.   Ibid., 86, quoting Justice Chase in Calder v. Bull, 3 Dallas 386 (1798).

4.   Ibid., 230-231.

5.   See Francis W. Bird, "The Evolution of Due Process of Law in the Decisions of the U.S. Supreme Court," *Columbia Law Review* 13, (1913): 37. Also John R. Commons, *Legal Foundations of Capitalism* (Madison, WI: University of Wisconsin Press, 1924), 331.

6.   Haines, 111.

7.   Edward S. Corwin, "The Supreme Court and the 14th Amendment," *Michigan Law Review* 7, (1908):646.

8.   Benjamin R. Twiss, *Lawyers and the Constitution: How Laissez Faire Came to the Supreme Court* (Princeton, NJ: Princeton University Press, 1942). See chapter 2.

9.   Hugh Evander Willis, "Due Process of Law Under the U.S. Constitution," *University of Pennsylvania Law Review* 74, (1926):339, 342.

10.   Corwin, "Supreme Court," 647, quoting Slaughterhouse Cases, 16 Wall. 36. (1873).

11.   Twiss, *Lawyers and the Constitution*, 55.

12.   Ibid., 3.

13.   Ibid., 3.

14.   Ibid., 61. The case decided was San Mateo County v. Southern Pacific Railway Co., 116 U.S. 138 (1885).

15.   Munn v. Illinois, 94 U.S. 113 (1876), p. 142. See Twiss, *Lawyers and the Constitution*, 84.

16.   Twiss, *Lawyers and the Constitution*, 106. *In re* Jacobs, 98 N.Y. 98 (1885), p. 105.

17.   Ibid., 110-111.

18.   Ibid., 128. Also Roscoe Pound, "Liberty of Contract," *Yale Law Journal* 18, (1908-09):454, 455.

19.   In Twiss, *Lawyers and the Constitution*, 128, citing Godcharles v. Wigeman, 113 Pa. St. 431 (1886).

20.   In Pound, "Liberty of Contract," 471, quoting decision in Millet v. People, 117 Ill. 294, (1886.)

21.   Pound, "Liberty of Contract," 473, quoting decision in Frorer v. People, 141 Ill. 171 (1892).

22.   Pound, "Liberty of Contract," 476, citing Frorer v. People, p. 186 (n.).

23.   O.H. Myrick, "Liberty of Contract," *Central Law Journal* 61, (1905):487, quoting from State v. Goodwill, 33 W.Va. 179 (1889). See also the argument for *In re* Jacobs for use of this property.

24.   Ibid., 487, citing *In re* Tiburcio Parrott, 1 Fed. Rep. 481, 506. (1880).

25.   Twiss, *Lawyers and the Constitution*, 163.

26.   Edward S. Corwin, *Constitutional Revolution, Ltd.* (Claremont, CA: Claremont College, (1941), 85.

27.   Twiss, *Lawyers and the Constitution*, 254.

28.   Julius Stone, *Human Law and Human Justice* (Stanford, CA: Stanford University Press, 1965), 95.

29.   Max Weber, *On Law in Economy and Society* (New York: Simon & Schuster, 1954), 228-229. Affirmative action now centers on this question of unequal treatment of discriminated against substantively unequal groups; its opponents argue for "equality," i.e., formally equal treatment.

30.   A commonly mentioned source was Ernst Freund, *Police Power* (Chicago: Callaghan & Co., 1904), which defines such limitations as the state's exercise of "its compulsory power for the prevention and anticipation of wrong by narrowing common-law rights through conventional restraints and positive regulations which are not confined to the prohibition of wrongful acts. It is the latter kind of state control which constitutes the essence of the police power." (8).

31.   Haines, *The Revival*, 179 (n.), quoting Justice Hughes in Chicago, Burlington & Quincy Railway Co. v. McGuire, 219 U.S. 549, 569 (1910).

32.   Francis D. Wormuth, "The Impact of Economic Legislation Upon the Supreme Court," Journal of Public Law 6, (1957):306.

33.   See Albert M. Kales, "'Due Process'; the Inarticulate Major Premise and the Adamson Act," *Yale Law Review* 26, (1919):519.

34. John R. Commons and John B. Andrews, *Principles of Labor Legislation* (New York: Harper & Bros., 1916), 438.

35. See Wormuth, "The Impact."

36. Ernst Freund, "Constitutional Limitations and Labor Legislation," *Illinois Law Review* 4, (1910) p. 621.

37. See Holmes' dissent in Lochner v. New York, 198 U.S. 45 (1905).

38. For example, the court upheld a statute aimed specifically at Chinese hand laundries by suggesting that there was no such information placed before the Court, although Holmes mentioned it in his opinion. See Paul L. Rosen, *The Supreme Court and Social Science* (Urbana, IL: University of Illinois Press, 1972), 73.

39. Judge Learned Hand, "Due Process of Law and the Eight-hour Day," *Harvard Law Review* 21, (1908):502.

40. Commons and Andrews, *Principles*, 423-424, citing *In re* Morgan, 26 Col. 415 (1899).

41. Ibid., 424 (n. 4), citing Ritchie v. People, 115 Ill. 98 (1895), p. 113.

42. Ibid., 424-425, citing Lochner v. New York, 198 U.S. 45 (1905), p. 58.

43. Corwin, "Supreme Court," 668.

44. Dissent in Lochner v. New York, pp. 75-76, cited in Pound, "Liberty of Contract," 480-481.

45. See, for example, Edwin S. Corwin, *The Twilight of the Supreme Court* (New Haven, CT: Yale University Press, 1934), 86, Pollock note.

46. See the Brandeis Brief, Muller v. Oregon, 208 U.S. 412 (1908).

47. Dissent in Burns Baking Co. v. Bryan, 264 U.S. 504 (1924), p. 520.

48. Holden v. Hardy, 169 U.S. 366 (1898), p. 397.

49. Holden v. Hardy, p. 397. Also Henry R. Seager, "The Attitude of American Courts Toward Restrictive Labor Laws," *Political Science Quarterly* 19 (December 1904): 597, quoting Supreme Court of Tennessee, 53 S.W. (1899), p. 955; also cited by Justice Shiras in Knoxville Iron Co. v. Harbison, 183 U.S. 13 (1901), p. 20.

50.   In George Gorham Groat, *Attitude of American Courts in Labor Cases* (New York: AMS Press, 1969), citing Ritchie v. People.

51.   Commons and Andrews, *Principles*, citing People v. Williams, 189 N.Y. 131 (1907).

52.   Groat, *American Courts*, 306.

53.   Ibid., 307.

54.   Ibid., 295.

55.   Ibid., 296, citing Wenham v. State of Nebraska 65 Neb. 395, 91. N.W. 421 (1902).

56.   Ibid., 296.

57.   Ibid., 296-297, citing Judge Dunbar in State v. Buchanan, Washington, 29 Wash. 603, 70 Pac. 52 (1902).

58.   Ibid., 308, citing Ritchie v. Wayman, 244 Ill. 509, 91 N.E. 695 (1910).

59.   Rome Brown, "Oregon Minimum Wage Cases," *Minnesota Law Review* 1, (1917):486.

60.   Andrew Alexander Bruce, "The Illinois Ten-Hour Law," *Michigan Law Review* 8, (1909):1. (n., p. 19), quoting Justice Brewer's address to the New York Bar Association, 1893.

61.   Pound, "Liberty of Contract," 474.

62.   Seager, "Restrictive Labor Laws," 606 (n.).

63.   Ray A. Brown, "Due Process of Law, Police Power and the Supreme Court," *Harvard Law Review* 40, (1927):962.

64.   Seager, "Restrictive Labor Laws," 597, citing decision in Tennessee, 53 S.W., p. 955.

CHAPTER 4. MINIMUM WAGE LEGISLATION: LEGAL AND ECONOMIC ASPECTS

1.   The trades included two which employed mainly men (boot making and baking); three clothing trades which were predominantly female; and furniture making, because Chinese labor was undercutting wages in that industry.

2.   John R. Commons and John B. Andrews, *Principles of Labor Legislation* (New York and London: Harper & Bros., 1916), minimum wage chapter.

3.   Rome G. Brown, "Oregon Minimum Wage Cases," *Minnesota Law Review* 1 (1917):477-478.

4.   Ibid., 477.

5.   Ibid., 474.

6.   Ibid., 474.

7.   Ibid., 480.

8.   Ibid., 480.

9.   Ibid., 482, quoting the court in Coppage v. Kansas, 236 U.S. 1 (1914), pp. 17-20. This decision upheld the "open shop."

10.   United States Supreme Court, *Records and Briefs*, Stettler v. O'Hara, October term 1916-17, Docket #25, C.W. Fulton, brief for plaintiff in error, pp. 25-26.

11.   Ibid., 27.

12.   Ibid., 52.

13.   Ibid., 53.

14.   Ibid., 56.

15.   Ibid., 56.

16.   United States Supreme Court, *Records and Briefs*, Bunting v. Oregon, October term 1916-17, Docket #38, vol. 9, C.W. Fulton et al., counsel for plaintiff in error, p. 32.

17.   Ibid., 6.

18.   Adkins v. Children's Hospital, 284 *Fed. Rep.* 613 (1922), Van Orsdel opinion, p. 113.

19.   *Records and Briefs*, Adkins v. Children's Hospital, Ellis Brief, p. 25.

20.   Ibid., 36.

21.   Ibid., Van Orsdel opinion, appendix B, p. 111.

22. Ibid., Ellis brief, p. 5.

23. Ibid., phrase quoted, p. 9; groups cited, pp. 6-7.

24. Ibid., 10-11.

25. Ibid., 11-12.

26. Ibid., 16.

27. Adkins v. Children's Hospital, 261 U.S. 525 (1923), J. Sutherland opinion, p. 560.

28. Ibid.

29. Ibid., 546.

30. Ibid., 557-558 (L. Ed., 796).

31. Ibid., 554 (L. Ed., 796).

32. Ibid., 556 (L. Ed., 796).

33. *Equal Rights* 1 (April 21, 1923), quoting J. Sutherland, p. 76.

34. Adkins v. Children's Hospital, 261 U.S. 525 J. Holmes dissent, p. 570.

35. Adkins v. Children's Hospital, 261 U.S. 525, Taft dissent, p. 567.

36. Barbara N. Grimes, "Constitutional Law: Police Power: Minimum Wage for Women," in National Consumers' League, *The Supreme Court and Minimum Wage Legislation* (New York: New Republic, 1925), 114.

37. George Gorham Groat, "Economic Wage and Legal Wage," in National Consumers' League, *The Supreme Court and Minimum Wage Legislation*, 77.

38. Grimes, "Constitutional Law," 118-119.

39. Thomas Reed Powell, "The Constitutional Issue in Minimum Wage Legislation," *Minnesota Law Review* 2, (1917):3.

40. Louis Brandeis, "The Constitution and the Minimum Wage," *Survey* 33 (February 6, 1915):494.

41. Henry R. Seager et al., "The Theory of the Minimum Wage," *American Labor Legislation Review* 3 (February 1913):89.

42. Paul Kellogg, "Minimum Wage Symposium," *American Labor Legislation Review* 3 (February 1913).

43. Karl Marx, *Capital*, 3 vols. (Chicago: Kerr & Co., 1915), vol. 1, 263-264.

44. "The Minimum Wage Problem," *The Independent* 72 (March 14, 1912): 584. The writer was referring to a textile strike in Lawrence, Massachusetts.

45. Henry Abrahams, "Minimum Wage Symposium," *American Labor Legislation Review* 3 (February 1913):106.

46. Seager, "Theory of Minimum Wage," 88.

47. Sidney Webb, "The Economic Theory of a Legal Minimum Wage," *Journal of Political Economy* 20 (December 1912):978.

48. Ibid., 984.

49. Irene Osgood Andrews, *Minimum Wage Legislation*, reprinted from New York State Factory Investigating Commission, *Third Report* (1914), appendix iii, quoting Webb, "Economic Theory of a Legal Minimum Wage," 982.

50. Edward A. Filene, "The Minimum Wage and Efficiency," *American Economic Review* 13 (September 1923):412, 415.

51. Andrews, *Minimum Wage Legislation*, 22-23.

52. Louise Bolard More, *Wage-Earners' Budgets, A Study of Standards and Cost of Living in New York City* (New York: Holt & Co., 1907; reprint ed. New York: Arno Press, 1971), 5.

53. Ibid., 22.

54. Ibid., 23.

55.. Ibid., ch. 3.

56. Current guidelines allow one-third of the family budget for food at the poverty level, which is considered stringent. See Mollie Orshansky, "Counting the Poor: Another Look at the Poverty Profile," *Social Security Bulletin* 28 (January 1965):7,9.

57. More, *Wage-Earners' Budgets*, 69.

58. Ibid., 70.

59.   Ibid., 83, 87.

60.   Ibid., 87.

61.   Ibid., 101-102.

62.   Ibid., 136.

63.   Ibid., 137.

64.   Ibid., 138.

65.   Ibid., 217.

66.   Ibid., 150.

67.   Ibid., 47.

68.   Ibid., 88.

69.   Robert Coit Chapin, *The Standard of Living Among Workingmen's Families in New York City* (New York: Charities Publication Committee, Russell Sage Foundation, 1909), 129.

70.   Ibid., 245.

71.   Ibid., 248.

72.   Ibid., 249. Note the contrast with the Greenwich House study. The Greenwich House interviewers attempted to change families' eating habits and wives' cooking; the cooking class the interviewers had conducted prior to the study was one source for the families which were interviewed.

73.   See Martha May, "The 'Good Managers': Married Working Class Women and Family Budget studies, 1895-1915" *Labor History* 25, no. 3 (Summer 1984): 351-372, for a discussion of these studies.

74.   For example, Gwendolyn Salisbury Hughes, *Mothers in Industry* (New York: New Republic, 1925), 8-9: "These mothers are true exponents of the economic independence of women." She noted that the proportion of married women who were wage earners doubled between 1890 and 1920.

75.   Katherine S. Anthony, *Mothers Who Must Earn* (New York: Survey Associates, Russell Sage Foundation, Mid West Side Study, 1914), 15-16.

76.   Ibid., 17.

77. Ibid., 46-47.

78. Ibid., 63.

79. Ibid., 67.

80. Ibid., 93. A labor study done during 1918-19 in Philadelphia also found that at least 44 percent of the mothers worked nine or more hours per day (Hughes, *Mothers in Industry*, p. 162).

81. Anthony, *Mothers Who Must Earn*, 95.

82. Ibid., 100.

83. Ibid., 108.

84. Ibid., 128-129.

85. Ibid., 148-149; Hughes, *Mothers in Industry*, 188-189.

86. Anthony, *Mothers Who Must Earn*, 155.

87. Ibid., 199.

88. Louise C. Odencrantz, *Italian Women in Industry* (New York: Russell Sage Foundation, 1919), 18.

89. Ibid., 21.

90. Ibid., 176.

91. Ibid., 27.

92. Ibid., 38-39.

93. For an example of this view, see U.S. Industrial Commission, *Report* (Washington, D.C.: U.S. Government Printing Office, 1901), vol. 15: "It is the Italian woman, working in her close tenement, whose cheap labor has almost driven out all other nationalities from that class of work which is still mainly done in the home, namely the hand sewing on coats and trousers (369). The *Report* continued: "This practice not only has a damaging effect on the shop worker in the sewing trade, but it also affects the people engaged in the same calling as the Italian laborers" (370). (This *Report* was in favor of restricting immigration.)

94. Odencrantz, *Italian Women in Industry*, 285-286.

95.   Sue Ainslie Clark and Edith Wyatt, *Making Both Ends Meet: The Income and Outlay of New York Working Girls* (New York: Macmillan, 1911), 11.

96.   Hughes, *Mothers in Industry*, 10.

97.   Ibid., 13.

98.   New York State Factory Investigating Commission, *Preliminary Report* (Albany, NY: Argus Co. Printers, 1912), vol. 2, p. 540.

99.   Ibid., vol. 3, p. 1599.

100.   New York State Factory Investigating Commission, *Second Report* (1913), vol. 1, p. 113.

101.   Agnes de Luna, "How Night Work of Women is Menacing Maternity," *American Labor Legislation Review* 11 (1921-22):86.

102.   Hughes, *Mothers in Industry*, 17.

103.   Beatrice Webb, *The Wages of Men and Women: Should They Be Equal?* (London: Fabian Society, 1919), 7.

104.   Ibid., 45.

105.   Hughes, *Mothers in Industry*, 17.

106.   Susan M. Kingsbury, "Relation of Women to Industry," *American Sociological Society Proceedings* 15 (1920):142-143.

107.   Ibid., 157-158.

108.   Scott Nearing, "The Adequacy of American Wages," *Annals of the American Academy of Political and Social Science* 59 (1915):111-112.

109.   Ibid., 118.

110.   Ibid., 123.

111.   John R. Commons, *History of Labor in the United States*, 4 vols. (New York: Macmillan, 1935), vol. 3, p. 111.

112.   Whitney Coombs, *The Wages of Unskilled Labor in Manufacturing Industries in the United States, 1890-1924* (New York: Columbia University Press, 1926; reprint ed. New York: AMS ed., Columbia University Studies in the Social Sciences #283, 1968), 120-121.

113.   Henry Pratt Fairchild, "The Standard of Living—Up or Down?" *American Economic Review* 6 (March 1916):24. Also, I.M. Rubinow, "The Recent Trend of Real Wages," *American Economic Review* 4 (December 1914):793-817; and Erville B. Woods, "Have Wages Kept Pace with the Cost of Living?" *Annals of the American Academy of Political and Social Science* 89 (1920):146-147.

Chapter 5. The Suffragists: The Feminist Opposition

1.   For example: "The Negro has no name. He is Cuffy Douglas or Cuffy Brooks, just whose Cuffy he may chance to be. The Woman has no name. She is Mrs. Richard Roe or Mrs. John Doe, just whose Mrs. she may chance to be." (Catherine Stimpson, "'Thy Neighbor's Wife, Thy Neighbor's Servants': Women's Liberation and Black Civil Rights," in *Woman in Sexist Society*, ed. Vivian Gornick and Barbara Moran [New York: Basic Books, 1971], 627-628.)

2.   See Eleanor Flexner, *Century of Struggle* (New York: Atheneum, 1973), 144, quoting Douglass: "When women, because they are women, are dragged from their homes and hung upon lamp-posts . . . then they will have [as great] an urgency to obtain the ballot" as former slaves.

3.   Ibid., 249.

4.   Doris Stevens, *Jailed for Freedom* (New York: Boni & Liveright, Inc., 1920), 42. This is her account of the suffrage campaign.

5.   Ibid., 92.

6.   Ibid., 110.

7.   Ibid., 111.

8.   Rose Schneiderman also commented on the non-working-class composition of women who were active suffragists, and appealed to them to "understand" why the working woman was not as active as they would wish her to be in the suffrage cause. (Rose Schneiderman, *Collected Papers* [New York: Tamiment Library].)

9.   *National Suffrage News* (February 1917): 15.

10.   *Suffragist* (May 26, 1917): 3.

11.   See Maurine Greenwald, *Women, War and Work: The Impact of World War I on Women Workers in the United States* (Westport, CT: Greenwood Press, 1980).

12. *Woman Citizen* (July 19, 1919):163.

13. *Woman Citizen* (July 19, 1919):167.

14. *Woman Citizen* (June 7, 1919):8.

15. *Woman Citizen* (July 12, 1919):142.

16. *Woman Citizen* (July 12, 1919):143.

17. *Woman Citizen* (July 26, 1919):100.

18. *Woman Citizen* (October 4, 1919).

19. *Woman Citizen* (June 19, 1920):73.

20. *Woman Citizen* (April 7, 1923):13. See also *Woman Citizen* (February 10, 1923):13 for their readers' poll on housework.

21. *Headquarters News Letter* (December 15, 1915):8. Emphasis in original.

22. *Woman Citizen* (January 27, 1923):12,25.

23. *Woman Citizen* (September 8, 1923):10.

24. *Woman Citizen* (August 9, 1924):17.

25. Letter of Attorney General Herman L. Ekern to Mabel R. Putnam, 1922, in Mabel R. Putnam, *Papers* (New York: New York Public Library, Manuscript Division).

26. *Woman Citizen* (April 19, 1923).

27. *Suffragist* (February 8, 1919):4.

28. *Suffragist* (March 1, 1919):3.

29. *Suffragist* (February 15, 1919):4

30. *Suffragist* (May 24, 1919):3. See Maurine Greenwald, *Women, War and Work*, ch. 4., regarding women as streetcar conductors during World War I.

31. *Suffragist* (March 1920):20.

32. For an account of this from the other side, see Mary Anderson, with Mary N. Winslow, *Woman at Work* (Minneapolis: University of Minnesota Press, 1951), ch. 19.

33. *Equal Rights* 1 (February 24, 1923):16. It also favored equal pay for equal work.

34. *Equal Rights* 2 (May 31, 1924):124.

35. *Equal Rights* 2 (May 31, 1924):124, editorial.

36. *Equal Rights* 2 (June 7, 1924):132, editorial.

37. *Equal Rights* 2 (April 19, 1924):77-79. The argument that individuals should be considered on the basis of their ability to perform the job is the same reasoning adopted in the guidelines of Title VII of the 1964 Civil Rights Act.

38. *Equal Rights* 2 (April 26, 1924):84.

39. *Equal Rights* 2 (March 3, 1924):94.

40. *Equal Rights* 1 (October 6, 1923):268.

41. *Equal Rights* 2 (January 12, 1924):244. See also *Equal Rights* 2 (July 5, 1924) and *Equal Rights* 2 (June 14, 1924).

42. See, for example, the National Woman's Party pamphlet entitled "Night Work for Women," in National Woman's Party—Miscellaneous Papers, *Alma Lutz Collection* (Poughkeepsie, NY: Vassar College).

43. *Equal Rights* 2 (February 9, 1924):412.

44. *Equal Rights* 2 (February 9, 1924):416.

45. National Woman's Party, "Night Work for Women."

46. National Woman's Party, "Night Work for Women." See also cover cartoon of *Equal Rights* 2 (February 23, 1924), showing woman with hands on hips addressing policeman. Caption reads: "WHOSE STREETS ARE THEY?" The Law: "Streets are not safe for working women at night." Working Woman: "Well then, make 'em safe."

47. "Special Privileges for Women," *Alma Lutz Collection*, pamphlet.

48. *Equal Rights* 1 (July 21, 1923):179. Article by Lavinia Egon.

49. *Equal Rights* 1 (October 13, 1923):115. Article by Consuelo Furman.

CHAPTER 6. THE WOMEN'S TRADE UNION LEAGUE
AND PROTECTIVE LABOR LEGISLATION

1.   Gladys Boone, *The Women's Trade Union Leagues* (New York: Columbia
University Press, 1942), 18.

2.   For other studies of the WTUL, see Nancy Schrom Dye, *As Equals and As
Sisters* (Columbia, MO: University of Missouri Press, 1980); Colette Hyman, "Labor
Organizing and Female Institution-building: The Chicago Women's Trade Union
League, 1904-24," in *Women, Work and Protest*, ed. Ruth Milkman (Boston:
Routledge & Kegan Paul, 1985); and Meredith Tax, *The Rising of the Women*
(New York: Monthly Review Press, 1980), ch. 5, "Leonora O'Reilly and the Wom-
en's Trade Union League."

3.   Boone, *Women's Trade Union League*, p. 99, quoting Alice Henry in *Life and
Labor* (January 19, 1911):p. 99.

4.   New York Women's Trade Union League, *Papers* (New York: Department of
Labor Research and Statistics Division Library, World Trade Center), letter from
H. Marot to Unions, September 3, 1908.

5.   Alice Kessler-Harris, "Organizing the Unorganizable: Three Jewish Women
and Their Union," in *Class, Sex and the Woman Worker* ed. Milton Cantor and
Bruce Laurie (Westport, CT: Greenwood Press, 1977), 149. (These strikers were
mainly Jewish women who predominated in this occupation.)

6.   See Tax, *Rising of Women*, ch. 8, "The Uprising of the Thirty Thousand," for
an account of this strike.

7.   Sue Ainslie Clark and Edith Wyatt, "Working Girls' Budgets—The Shirtwaist
Makers and Their Strike," *McClures Magazine* 36 (November 1910):70-86.

8.   William Mailly, "The Working Girls' Strike," *Independent* 67 (December 23,
1909):1416-20.

9.   Wood Hutchinson, "The Hygienic Aspects of the Shirtwaist Strike," *Survey*
23 (January 22, 1910):547.

10.   Sue Ainslie Clark and Edith Wyatt, *Making Both Ends Meet* (New York:
Macmillan, 1911), 77.

11.   Ibid., 84.

12.   *American Federationist* 17 (February 1910).

13. *American Federationist* 17 (March 1910):209.

14. *American Federationist* 17 (March 1910):210.

15. This was the beginning of the "era of protocol" agreements in the garment trades, under which joint boards consisting of labor and management representatives worked out grievances with an outside arbiter available when necessary. Sometimes union representatives on such boards, for example, the Joint Board of Sanitary Control, were also members of the WTUL.

16. Hutchinson, "Hygienic Aspects," 550.

17. Mary E. Dreier, *Margaret Dreier Robins, Her Life, Letters and Work* (New York: Island Press Cooperative, 1950), 75-76. See also Mary Anderson, with Mary N. Winslow, *Women at Work* (Minneapolis: University of Minnesota Press, 1951), 23.

18. See Tax, *Rising of Women*, ch. 9, "Lawrence, 1912," for the IWW and the WTUL; also Ardis Cameron, "Bread and Roses Revisited: Women's Culture and Working-Class Activism in the Lawrence Strike of 1912," in Milkman, *Women, Work and Protest*, pp. 42-61.

19. Rose Schneiderman, *Collected Papers* (New York: Tamiment Library, box 2, folder no. 3).

20. New York Women's Trade Union League, report of secretary to meeting, April 27, 1911 (World Trade Center) papers.

21. New York Women's Trade Union League, May 29, 1919, correspondence folder no. 3.

22. New York Women's Trade Union League, letters of May 2, 1919, and May 5, 1919, correspondence folder no. 3.

23. New York Women's Trade Union League, president's report, April 29-July 22, 1915.

24. Robin Jacoby Miller, "The Woman's Trade Union League and American Feminism," *Feminist Studies* 3 (Fall 1975), p. 216, quoted by Canter and Laurie, *Class, Sex and the Woman Worker.*

25. Rose Schneiderman, with Lucy Goldthwaite, *All for One* (New York: Erikson, 1967), 121.

26. Ibid., 121-122.

27. Schneiderman, *Papers*, folder no. 10, December 16, 1913, to Suffrage School.

28. Schneiderman, *Papers*, folder no. 10, December 16, 1913.

29. Schneiderman, *Papers*, box no. 1, folder no. 2, letter from M. Fruchter, March 5, 1911.

30. *Life and Labor* 5 (September 1915). See also *Life and Labor* 5 (April 4, 1915).

31. *Life and Labor* 6 (January 1916).

32. New York Women's Trade Union League, report of secretary to Executive Board, June 22, 1909. See also report to Executive Board, April 29, 1915, and minutes of meeting, January 13, 1915.

33. New York Women's Trade Union League, vol. 9, correspondence, letter to Agnes Nestor, January 23, 1919. See also report of October 3, 1910, regarding summer work.

34. Schneiderman, *Papers*, box no. 2, folder no. 6.

35. National Women's Trade Union League, *Proceedings of 2nd Biennial Convention*, 1909:11.

36. Schneiderman, *Papers*, box no. 4, folder no. 1, *Evening Post* article dated April 24, 1920.

37. *Life and Labor* 5 (November 1915):165.

38. *Life and Labor* 5 (November 1915):169. See chapter 7 for a fuller discussion of Gompers and the AFL's position.

39. *Life and Labor* 1 (November 1911):325.

40. Schneiderman, *Papers*, New York League Annual Report 1913-1914, box no. 2, folder no. 5.

41. *Life and Labor* 9 (February 1919):30.

42. *Life and Labor* 1 (September 1911):279.

43. *Life and Labor* 1 (September 1911):280.

44. Schneiderman, *Papers*, clipping from *Evening Mail*, February 2, 1914.

45. Ibid.

46. Schneiderman, *Papers*, clipping from *Evening Mail*, March 21, 1912.

47. Ibid.

48. Ibid.

49. Elizabeth Faulkner Baker, *Protective Labor Legislation, With Special Reference to Women in the State of New York* (New York: Columbia University Press, 1925), 202.

50. See Hyman, "Labor Organizing," for the slightly different course of the Chicago league.

51. See Maurine Weiner Greenwald, *Women, War and Work* (Westport, CT: Greenwood Press, 1980), ch. 4.

52. New York Women's Trade Union League, organizer's report to league meeting, January 4, 1914.

53. *Life and Labor* 8 (December 1918):275.

54. *Life and Labor* 9 (April 1919):77.

55. New York Women's Trade Union League, 1916-18, proceedings secretary's report, April, 1918. See also correspondence from Women's Joint Legislative Conference, February 4, 1919, and reply to correspondence from Women's Joint Legislative Conference, February 4, 1919, to Grace Phelps from Secretary Swarz, February 6, 1919, for the WTUL's personal attacks on the women printers.

56. New York Women's Trade Union League, secretary's report, August 1918.

57. New York Women's Trade Union League, secretary's report, October 1918.

58. New York Women's Trade Union League, correspondence, February 11, 1919, with Assemblyman Charles Solomon.

59. New York Women's Trade Union League, letter to C. Solomon from league, February 15, 1919. The WTUL also tried to link the dissidents with manufacturers' interests, according to Dye, *As Equals and as Sisters*, 158.

60. New York Women's Trade Union League, reply to William Young, July 1, 1919.

61. New York Women's Trade Union League, letter to Miss Mary Murray, president of Brooklyn Rapid Transit Women's Equal Opportunity League, February 10, 1921.

62. New York Women's Trade Union League, open letter from M. Murray to *Woman Citizen*, n.d. WTUL asked to reply to it, February 2, 1921. For an account of this dispute, see Dye, *As Equals and as Sisters*, 149-150.

63. *Life and Labor* 8 (March 1918):58.

64. *Life and Labor* 8 (March 1918):58.

65. *Life and Labor* 8 (March 1918), "The Editors."

66. *Life and Labor* 9 (February 1919). See Greenwald, *Women, War and Work*, ch. 4, for the treatment of women conductors in different cities.

67. *Life and Labor* 9 (January 1919):15.

68. *Life and Labor* 9 (January 1919):16.

69. *Life and Labor* 7 (October 1917):59.

70. *Life and Labor* 7 (June 1917):89.

71. *Life and Labor* 8 (January 1918):15.

72. *Life and Labor* 6 (December 1916):15.

73. *Life and Labor* 7 (April 1917):68.

74. *Life and Labor* 7 (December 1917):188.

75. *Life and Labor* 8 (November 1918):240.

76. *Life and Labor* 8 (January 1918):7.

77. *Life and Labor* 9 (January 1919):4,6.

78. *Life and Labor* 9 (February 1919):36.

79. *Life and Labor* 8 (December 1918):265.

80. *Life and Labor* 8 (December 1918):266-268.

81. *Life and Labor* 8 (December 1918):272.

82. *Life and Labor* 9 (January 1919):7.

83. Boone, *Women's Trade Union Leagues*, 136.

84. For example, see the *Life and Labor* 10 (September 1920):195-198, article about the Russian Cooperative Movement, with the picture of the factory committee.

85. Baker, *Protective Labor Legislation*, 175. (See also chapter 8 for the employers' role.)

86. See also article in *American Association of Labor Legislation Review* (March 1920), with statement of League of Women Voters refuting the "anti-American" charges; also a defense of the bills by Mackenzie, who quotes Senator Davenport that the independent workers who favored workman's compensation were, on the contrary, "the greatest bulwark against radicalism that we have in America. The employing class cannot continue to appeal to them to keep their judgment safe in order to keep society safe, and then fight them at every turn in the matter of a great human need like the development of illness prevention and health insurance" (Frederick Mackenzie, "The Legislative Campaign in New York for the 'Welfare Bills,'" *American Labor Legislation Review* 10 [June 1920]:139).

87. New York Women's Trade Union League, correspondence, February 17, 1921.

88. New York Women's Trade Union League, correspondence, April 29, 1920.

89. New York Women's Trade Union League, letter from N.Y. league secretary, April 18, 1921.

90. *Life and Labor* 10 (March 1920):84, signed Yours regretfully, Marguerite Moors Marshall.

91. *Life and Labor* 10 (March 1920):84,85.

92. *Life and Labor* 10 (May 1920):152.

93. *Life and Labor* 9 (December 1919):309,310.

94. Julia Johnsen, ed., *Special Legislation for Women* (New York: H.W. Wilson Co., 1926), vol. 4, p. 62.

95. Ibid., 63.

CHAPTER 7. THE ROLE OF ORGANIZED LABOR

1. John R. Commons and John B. Andrews, *Principles of Labor Legislation* (New York: Harper & Bros., 1916), 225.

2. Sidney Webb and Beatrice Webb, *Industrial Democracy* (New York: A.M. Kelley, 1897; reprint ed. 1965), 250-251.

3. Ibid., 253-257. This is the "legitimation" problem described in chapter 1.

4. Commons and Andrews, *Principles of Labor Legislation*, 98.

5. *American Federationist* 14 (November 1907):880, 882.

6. Ibid., 882. See also, for example, the February 1908 issue.

7. *American Federationist* 15 (September 1908):736-737.

8. *American Federationist* 13 (April 1906):223. Article by Charlotte Teller.

9. *American Federationist* 13 (June 1906):383.

10. *American Federationist* 13 (February 1906):85.

11. *American Federationist* 13 (December 1906):965. For a discussion of working women's consciousness regarding marriage and work, see Sarah Eisenstein, *Give Us Bread But Give Us Roses* (London and Boston: Routledge & Kegan Paul, 1983), ch. 5.

12. *American Federationist* 13 (December 1906):966-967. Valesh was assistant editor of the *American Federationist* at the time.

13. *American Federationist* 15 (April 1908):283. "Welfare work" was the specialty of the Women's Work Committee of the National Civic Federation (NCF), but none of the labor representatives in the NCF (including Gompers and Mitchell) were members of the Welfare Committee itself.

14. *American Federationist* 14 (September 1907):679-680.

15. *American Federationist* 14 (December 1907):971.

16. *American Federationist* 16 (January 1909):58.

17. Elizabeth Marbury, "Organization the Remedy," *American Federationist* 16 (May 1909), pp. 433-434.

18. *American Federationist* 16 (May 1909):436.

19. *American Federationist* 13 (January 1906):36.

20. See Alice Kessler-Harris, "Organizing the Unorganizable: Three Jewish Women and their Union," *Class, Sex and the Woman Worker* ed. Milton Cantor and Bruce Laurie (Westport, CT: Greenwood Press, 1977), 144-165, for this view.

21. *American Federationist* 17 (March 1910):209.

22. Ibid., 210.

23. See Elizabeth Hauser, "Women Workers and the Labor Movement," *American Federationist* 17 (April 1910):305.

24. *American Federationist* 17 (August 1910). See also *Survey* 22 (1919):433-434, for J.R. Commons' similar view of the importance of women workers in the passage of the bill.

25. *American Federationist* 18 (June 1911):483, regarding WTUL organizing.

26. *American Federationist* 18 (July 1911):544.

27. *American Federationist* 20 (August 1913):626.

28. *American Federationist* 21 (January 1914):20.

29. *American Federationist* 21 (January 1914):19; (March 1914):232-233.

30. *American Federationist* 21 (July 1914):544.

31. *American Federationist* 22 (January 1915):44-45; (February 1915):114; (March 1915):167.

32. *American Federationist* 22 (March 1915):168.

33. *American Federationist* 22 (February 1915):113.

34. *American Federationist* 22 (February 1915):46.

35. *American Federationist* 22 (August 1915):577-578.

36. *American Federationist* 19 (August 1912):709.

37. *American Federationist* 22 (May 1915):333; (April 1915), p. 256.

38. *American Federationist* 22 (March 1915):200.

39. *American Federationist* 22 (July 1915):518.

40. American Federation of Labor, *Report of Proceedings of Annual Conventions*, 1916 Convention, p. 286. Speech by Warren S. Stone to convention.

41. Ibid., 365-366. Speech by W.G. Lee, president, Brotherhood of Railway Trainmen.

42. *American Federationist* 23 (March 1916):193.

43. *American Federationist* 23 (March 1916):269; (May 1916):333.

44. American Federation of Labor, 1916 Convention, p. 90.

45. American Federation of Labor, 1918 Convention, p. 61. Executive Council Report.

46. Ibid., 178. Resolution No. 77, by a woman from Battle Creek Federated Labor Council.

47. Ibid., 182. Resolution No. 92.

48. Ibid., 196-197.

49. American Federation of Labor, 1919 Convention, p. 73. Executive Council Report.

50. American Federation of Labor, 1921 Convention, pp. 122-123.

51. *American Federationist* 30 (May 1923):400-401.

52. *American Federationist* 30 (May 1923):393.

53. New York State Factory Investigating Commission, *Second Report* (1913), vol. 1, p. 260.

54. New York State Factory Investigating Commission, *Preliminary Report* (1912), vol. 3, p. 992.

55. Ibid., 1165.

56. Ibid., 1179.

57. Ibid., 1271.

58. New York State Factory Investigating Commission, *Second Report*, vol. 4, 1809-1810.

59. Ibid., vol. 1, p. 261.

60. Ibid., 262.

61. Ibid., 263.

62. Ibid., 170-171.

63. George A. Stevens, *New York Typographical Union #6* (Albany, NY: J.B. Lyon Co., 1913), under direction of John Williams, Commissioner of Labor, State of New York, p. 422.

64. Ibid., 423-424.

65. Ibid., 425-426.

66. Ibid., 428-429.

67. International Typographical Union, *Report of Officers and Proceedings* (1916), 175. See also *Typographical Journal* 48 (May 1916):848. Also, John B. Andrews and W.D.P. Bliss, *History of Women in Trade Unions*, S. Doc. 645, 61st Cong., 2nd sess., vol. x, p. 189.

68. Edith Abbott, *Women in Industry* (New York: D. Appleton & Co., 1910), 260-261.

69. Ibid., 254.

70. *Industrial Equality* 2 (January 8, 1923):2.

71. *Industrial Equality* 2 (April 16, 1923):4.

72. *Industrial Equality* 2 (May 16, 1923):2.

73. For these attacks, see *Industrial Equality* 2 (January 27, 1923):2; (February 15, 1923):1; (April 16, 1923):1; (December, 1923):3.

74. *Industrial Equality* 2 (January 8, 1923):1.

75. Ibid., 2.

76. *Industrial Equality* 2 (January 27, 1923):4 (regarding a New York eight-hour no-night-work law).

77. *Industrial Equality* 2 (January 8, 1923):3.

78. Ibid., 1.

79. *Industrial Equality* 2 (January 27, 1923):1.

80. *Industrial Equality* 2 (February 15, 1923):2.

81. *Industrial Equality* 2 (January 8, 1923):2.

82. *Industrial Equality* 2 (July 15, 1923):4; also (January 8, 1923):3.

83. *Industrial Equality* 2 (July 15, 1923):3.

84. *Typographical Journal* 67 (September 1925):428.

85. James M. Lynch, *Epochal History of the International Typographical Union* (New York, 1925), 36.

86. Associated Industries of New York State, "Albany Hearings," *Monitor* 5 (March 1919):28-29.

87. *Typographical Journal* (April 1918):408; (April 1919):369; (September 1918):294.

88. Andrews and Bliss, *History of Women in Trade Unions*, 183.

89. For example, in a report on the Silver Jubilee celebration of the Bakers' Union, the ILGWU stated, "Its membership consists of German-American and Jewish elements and this perhaps accounts for the fact that compared with more or less purely American trade unions, the Bakers' International Union is more advanced and socialistic" (*Ladies Garment Worker* [June 1911]:5).

90. Louis Levine, *The Women's Garment Workers* (New York: B.W. Huebsch, Inc., 1924), 124-126.

91. International Ladies Garment Workers' Union, *Financial Report*, 17th Convention (1924), 15. $3,900.00 donation to the *New York Call*.

92. International Ladies Garment Workers' Union, *Reports* (1914), 131.

93. International Ladies Garment Workers' Union, *Reports* (1916), 60.

94. *Ladies Garment Worker* (February 1918):30.

95. *Ladies Garment Worker* (January 1912):243.

96. *Justice* (May 17, 1919):5. Article by Juliet Stuart Poyntz.

97. See, for example, *Ladies Garment Worker* (December 1914).

98. See, for example, John H.M. Laslett, *Labor and the Left: A Study of Socialist and Radical Influences in the American Labor Movement, 1881-1924* (New York: Basic Books, 1970), 120-122. He emphasizes the fact that these unionists were Jewish socialists, "lacking a strong sense of loyalty to any one country."

99. *Ladies Garment Worker* ((November 1912); also (August 1917):1.

100. See ILGWU *Archives*, Schlesinger correspondence, folder 3 (November 20, 1918), to New York Board of Education.

101. American Federation of Labor *Report of Proceedings*, 1919 Convention, p. 143.

102. See, for example, *Justice* (March 16, 1923, January 21, 1921), etc.

103. *New York Call* (November 7, 1912, November 9, 1912), etc.

104. For example, *New York Call* (1910).

105. *Ladies Garment Worker* (March 1912):15.

106. *Ladies Garment Worker* (December 1912):14.

107. *Ladies Garment Worker* (July 1913):15.

108. *Ladies Garment Worker* (November 1915):8-9.

109. *Justice* (February 9, 1923):4.

110. Levine, *The Women's Garment Workers*, 107.

111. *Ladies Garment Worker* ((May 1913):16.

112. *Ladies Garment Worker* (June 1911):13.

113. *Ladies Garment Worker* (August 1914):22.

114. *Ladies Garment Worker* (November 1914):22.

115. *Ladies Garment Worker* (July 1915).

116. *Ladies Garment Worker* (September 1915):11.

117. *Ladies Garment Worker* (March 1916):3.

118. *Ladies Garment Worker* (October 1917):22.

119. *Ladies Garment Worker* (October 1915); also (October 1916):10.

120. *Justice* (February 1, 1919). Article by Juliet Stuart Pyntz.

121. *Justice* February 16, 1923):4.

122. *Ladies Garment Worker*: for example, see (May 1916):7; also (March 1917):20.

123. *Ladies Garment Worker* (March 1918):32-35. See also, for example, issue of September 1911 for a description of the ability of women to persevere in their struggles.

124. *Ladies Garment Worker* (April 1912):37-38.

125. *Justice* (April 6, 1923):4. Story by Sylvia Kopald.

126. *Ladies Garment Worker* (November 1917):32. Also (December 1917):30; and "On Lightheaded Woman," *Justice* (March 8, 1919):1. "What a vile slander the words are . . ."

127. *Justice* (May 25, 1923):5. See also Matilda Robbins, "What's to be Done with the Children?" *Justice* (May 18, 1923):5.

128. *Ladies Garment Worker* (October 1912):15-16. Vice-president Israel S. Feit.

129. *Ladies Garment Worker* (December 1917):30.

130. *Justice* (January 13, 1922):5.

131. *Ladies Garment Worker* (July 1917):13.

132. *Ladies Garment Worker* (February 1918):28. See also International Ladies Garment Workers' Union, *Archives*, Benjamin Schlesinger papers and correspondence, box 2, folder 5, from Emma Steghagen (WTUL), dated September 28, 1918, to Abe Baroff.

133. *Ladies Garment Worker* (August 1910):3.

134. *Ladies Garment Worker* (May 1912):13-14.

135. *Ladies Garment Worker* (November 1912):11.

136. *Ladies Garment Worker* (March 1913).

137. *Ladies Garment Worker* (January 1916):6-7. See also June 1918 for similar criticisms of Gompers.

138. *Justice* (May 31, 1919):6.

139. *New York Call* (March 24, 1923):4.

140. *Justice* (Feburary 23, 1923):10.

141. *Justice* (December 15, 1922):4.

142. See also *Justice* (April 20, 1923):8; (June 22, 1923):5.

143. *New York Call* (March 6, 1919).

144. *New York Call* (February 20, 1913).

145. *New York Call* (March 21, 1923).

146. *Justice* (for example, March 1, 1919).

CHAPTER 8. EMPLOYERS' ASSOCIATIONS

1. Eleanor Flexner, *Century of Struggle* (New York: Atheneum, 1973), 296-298.

2. Ibid., 299.

3. Ibid., 302, 301.

4. Ibid., 296.

5. See Albion Guilford Taylor, *Labor Policies of the National Association of Manufacturers* (Urbana, IL: University of Illinois Press, 1928), 13; and Robert M. Wiebe, *Businessmen and Reform: A Study of the Progressive Movement* (Chicago: Quadrangle Books, 1968), 25.

6.   Albert K. Steigerwalt, *The National Association of Manufacturers, 1895-1914* (Ann Arbor, MI: University of Michigan Press, 1964), ch. 4.

7.   Wiebe, *Businessmen and Reform*, 25-26.

8.   Steigerwalt, *The National Association of Manufacturers, 1895-1914*, 152.

9.   Steigerwalt, *The National Association of Manufacturers, 1895-1914*, 123; Wiebe, *Businessmen and Reform*, 29-30. The name of this group was changed to the National Industrial Council in 1919 to avoid its being confused with the war effort.

10.   Taylor, *Labor Policies of the National Association of Manufacturers*, 29-30.

11.   Ibid., 137-138.

12.   Ibid., 82.

13.   *American Industries* 7 (February 15, 1908):16.

14.   Isaac Marcosson, "Labor Met by Its Own Methods," *World's Work* 7 (January 1904):4311.

15.   William Franklin Willoughby, "Employers' Associations for Dealing with Labor in the U.S.," *Quarterly Journal of Economics* 20 (November 1905):112.

16.   Ibid., 149.

17.   *The Review* (May 1906):11.

18.   *The Review* (October 1907):20-21. See also (July 1907):11.

19.   *Square Deal* 2 (October 1906):32, advertisement. See also 2 (December 1906):2.

20.   National Association of Manufacturers, *Proceedings*, 8th Annual Convention (1903), 117.

21.   *Square Deal* 4 (May 1908):55.

22.   *American Industries* 4 (October 16, 1905):3.

23.   U.S. Commission on Industrial Relations, *Report*, S. Doc. 21, 64th Cong. vol. 1., p. 746.

24.   *American Industries* 7 (May 1, 1908): 28. Article by John Kirby, Jr. See also David M. Parry, "Is Organized Labor Right? The Only Question," *Bankers' Magazine* 47 (November 1903): 669.

25.   *Square Deal* 2 (September 1906):20.

26.   *The Review* (May 1908):5.

27.   *The Review* (December 1909):32.

28.   *The Review* (January 1909):6.

29.   *The Review* (January 1909):13.

30.   *The Review* (January 1909):14.

31.   *American Industries* 9 (April 15, 1909):8.

32.   Ibid., 5.

33.   National Association of Manufacturers, *Proceedings*, 8th Annual Convention, (1903):17.

34.   Ibid., 23.

35.   Ibid., C.W. Post address, 115-116.

36.   *American Industries* 7 (June 1, 1908):12.

37.   *The Review* (January 1909):4.

38.   *American Industries* 7 (May 1, 1908):28.

39.   *American Industries* 7 (August 1, 1908):6.

40.   *The Review* (January 1907):12.

41.   *The Review* (January 1907):13.

42.   *American Industries* 7 (February 15, 1908):17.

43.   Walter Gordon Merritt, *History of the League for Industrial Rights* (New York: League for Industrial Rights, 1925), 5.

44. Ibid., 12. Selig Perlman and Philip Taft, *History of Labor in the United States*, vol. 4, ed. John Commons, *Labor Movements* (New York, 1935; reprint ed. 1966), 154, credit D.E. Loewe and Chas. H. Merritt, another nonunion hat manufacturer, with forming the association in 1902.

45. Merritt, *History of the League*, 12, 13.

46. Ibid., 23.

47. Perlman and Taft, *History of Labor in the United States*, 155.

48. Merritt, *History of the League*, 29.

49. Ibid., 34.

50. Ibid., 38.

51. "David M. Parry to Organized Labor," *National Association of Manufacturers' pamphlet*, (October 24, 1903):14.

52. *Square Deal* 3 (April 1908): 85.

53. See, for example, "Splendid Factory Conditions," *Square Deal* 13 (August 1913); also May 1907, pp.8-9, wage increase noted, "granted voluntarily by employers."

54. "Factory Fact vs. Fair Play," *Square Deal* 13 (September 1913):156.

55. *Monitor* 3 (February 1917): 39.

56. National Council of Industrial Defense, *Bulletin #16*, circa 1916, no paging.

57. National Industrial Conference Board, *Employment of Young Persons in the U.S.* (New York: National Industrial Conference Board, 1919), p. 39.

58. Ibid., 40.

59. Ibid.

60. Ibid., 88-89.

61. National Association of Manufacturers, *Educational Series #18*, p. 26, also *Square Deal* 2 (December 1906):5.

62. *Square Deal* 2 (July 1907):16.

63. *Square Deal* 13 (September 1913): 143; also *American Industries* 15 (March 1915):8.

64. *The Review* (September 1909):20. Women in core rooms also were opposed by New York iron molders, as is described in chapter 7.

65. *The Review* (September 1909):22.

66. New York State Factory Investigating Commission, Preliminary Report (1912), vol. 2, pp. 501,502.

67. New York State Factory Investigating Commission, *Fourth Report* (1915), p. 2292.

68. *Monitor* 2 (November 1915):14-15.

69. *Monitor* 2 (December 1915):15-16.

70. *Monitor* 1 (June 1914).

71. *Monitor* 1 (September 1914).

72. See Taylor, *Labor Policies of the National Association of Manufacturers*, 111.

73. National Council for Industrial Defense, "Charges Against Members of the House and Lobby Activities," *House Report #113*, 63rd Cong., 2nd sess., pp. 70,71. Cited in Taylor, *Labor Policies of the National Association of Manufacturers*, 115-116; also in Kenneth G. Crawford, *The Pressure Boys* (New York: Julian Messner, Inc., 1939), 51-52.

74. Steigerwalt, *The National Association of Manufacturers, 1895-1914*, 148. It is not clear that they did not continue to influence legislation as indicated by, for example, *Law and Labor* (published monthly by the League for Industrial Rights) and the National council for Industrial Defense *Bulletins*.

75. Taylor, *Labor Policies of the National Association of Manufacturers*, 40, 42-43.

76. Steigerwalt, *The National Association of Manufacturers, 1895-1914*, 169.

77. New York State Factory Investigating Commission, *Fourth Report* (1915), vol. 5, p. 2752. See Edwards, *Contested Terrain*, 91-97. He describes this "welfare work" as a strategy used by employers to undermine worker militance.

78.   *American Industries* 14 (May 1914):14.

79.   *American Industries* 3 (November 15, 1904):2.

80.   *American Industries* 4 (April 1, 1905):7.

81.   *American Industries* 5 (August 15, 1906):4.

82.   *American Industries* 9 (June 1, 1919):13, Van Cleave's address to Annual Meeting.

83.   *Square Deal* 3 (April 1908):85-86.

84.   *Square Deal* 3 (July 1908):32. Article by Walter Drew.

85.   *American Industries* 14 (May 1914):15.

86.   *Square Deal* 13 (October 1913):235.

87.   *Square Deal* 13 (November 1913):353.

88.   *Square Deal* 13 (September 1913):192.

89.   *Square Deal* 13 (September 1913):150.

90.   *Monitor* 2 (December 1915):20.

91.   *Monitor* 6 (March 1920):9, 10.

92.   *Monitor* 1 (August 1914), no paging.

93.   *Monitor* 1 (February 1915):26.

94.   *Monitor* 1 (March 1915):1.

95.   *Monitor* 1 (April 1915):29.

96.   *Monitor* 2 (July 1915):2.

97.   *Monitor* 5 (March 1919):15.

98.   *Monitor* 5 (March 1919):16-17.

99.   *Monitor* 5 (March 1919):19.

100.   *Monitor* 5 (March 1919):18-19.

101.   *Monitor* 5 (March 1919):2-3.

102.   *Monitor* 5 (March 1919):8-9.

103.   *Monitor* 6 (June 1919):1.

104.   *Monitor* 6 (June 1919):3.

105.   *Monitor* 6 (June 1919):5. See also *Monitor* 6 (January 1920):37-38, where they quote Harriot Stanton Blatch also arguing that legal limitation tends to lower women's wages or throw them out where they are in a minority like printers.

106.   *Monitor* 6 (January 1920):39,40.

107.   *Monitor* 5 (March 1919):19.

108.   New York State League of Women Voters, "Report and Protest to the Governor . . ." *American Labor Legislation Review* (March 1920):101.

109.   *Monitor* 6 (March 1920):32-33, 36-38.

110.   Gladys Boone, *The Women's Trade Union Leagues* (New York: Columbia University Press, 1942):136.

111.   See, for example, *Law and Labor* 1 (August 1919).

112.   *Law and Labor* 2 (November 1920):250.

113.   *Law and Labor* 1 (April 1919):12.

114.   *Law and Labor* 2 (February 1920):30.

115.   *Law and Labor* 2 (February 1920):39.

116.   National Council for Industrial Defense, *Bulletin #37* (1919), no paging.

117.   *Law and Labor* 2 (August 1920); 1 (May 1919); 2 (November 1920); 5 (July 1923); etc.

118.   *Law and Labor* 1 (March 1919):9, 10.

119.   *Law and Labor* 1 (April 1919):3.

120. Philip S. Foner, *The Policies and Practices of the American Federation of Labor 1900-1909* (New York: International Publishers, 1964), 75.

121. Lewis L. Lorwin, *The American Federation of Labor: History, Policies and Prospects* (New Jersey: A.M. Kelly Publishers, 1972), 84.

122. National Civic Federation, *Papers*, box 220, letter February 13, 1907, from Easley to Gompers.

123. National Civic Federation, *Papers*, box 220, letter February 9, 1915, from Easley to Gompers.

124. National Civic Federation, *Papers*, box 220, letter November 24, 1908, from Easley to Gompers.

125. National Civic Federation, *Report of Annual Meeting* (1912), p. 182.

126. Foner, *The Policies and Practices of the American Federation of Labor 1900-1909*, 75.

127. National Civic Federation, *Papers*, box 124, Women's Department Reports, n.d.

128. National Civic Federation, *Papers*, box 124, meetings, March 6, 1908.

129. National Civic Federation, *Conference on Welfare Work* (March 6, 1904), pp. xii-xiii.

130. Ibid., 61.

131. National Civic Federation, *Report of Annual Meeting* (1912), 184.

132. National Civic Federation, *Papers*, box 123-A, general correspondence A., letter July 2, 1908, to Mrs. Martha Moore Avery from Woman's Department.

133. See, for example, National Civic Federation, *Papers*, box 123-A, letter July 2, 1908, to Mrs. S.T. Ballard; letter July 6, 1908, to Mrs. Ballard.

134. National Civic Federation, *Papers*, box 123-A, correspondence, letter July 8, 1919, from Mrs. Ralph M. Easley to Miss R. Lee Guard.

135. National Civic Federation, *Papers*, box 187, 16th Annual Meeting (1915), Report of Woman's Department, Report on canneries, insert, 10.

136. National Civic Federation, *Report of Annual Meeting* (1912), 352, 355.

137.   National Civic Federation, *Papers*, box 135-A, Minimum Wage Commission form letter, February 16, 1917.

138.   National Civic Federation, *Papers*, box 135-A, Minimum Wage Commission, Reports, etc., p. 41B.

139.   National Civic Federation, *Papers*, box 135-A, Minimum Wage Commission, Reports, etc., "Is the Minimum Wage by Law the Solution?"

140.   *American Industries* 7 (April 1, 1908):28.

141.   James Weinstein, *The Corporate Ideal in the Liberal State, 1900-1918* (Boston: Beacon Press, 1968), 213.

CHAPTER 9. CONCLUSION

1.   Mary P. Ryan, *Womanhood in America*, 3rd ed. (New York: Franklin Watts, 1983), 117-123, et al.

2.   For example, Karl Marx, *Capital*, 3 vols. (Chicago: Kerr & Co., 1915), vol. 1, p. 291.

3.   Ibid., 330.

4.   Whether or not Taylor's system was explicitly followed, the principles of rationalization which he set forth have become incorporated into the work process. "Unnecessary" motions are eliminated, supplies of materials are kept ready at hand, and so forth.

5.   Ralph Miliband. *The State in Capitalist Society* (New York: Basic Books, 1969), 80-81.

6.   Mary McIntosh, "The State and the Oppression of Women," *Feminism and Materialism* Annette Kuhn and Anne Marie Wolpe (London: Routledge & Kegan Paul, 1978), 255. The welfare system and social security also illustrate this dynamic.

7.   Arthur Selwyn Miller, *The Supreme Court and American Capitalism* (New York: Free Press, 1965), 42.

8.   Edward S. Corwin, *Constitutional Revolution, Ltd.* (Claremont, CA: Clairmont College, 1977), 31.

Bibliography

Abbott, Edith. "Employment of Women in Industries: Cigar-Making—Its History and Present Tendencies." *Journal of Political Economy* 15 (January 1907): 1-25.

_____. *Women in Industry.* New York: D. Appleton & Co., 1910.

Abrahams, Henry. "Minimum Wage Symposium." *American Labor Legislation Review* (February 1913):105-106.

The Academy of Political Science. *The Economic Position of Women.* New York: The Academy of Political Science, 1910.

Adams, Thomas Sewall, and Helen Sumner. *Labor Problems.* New York and London: Macmillan, 1905.

Addams, Jane. "Reaction of Simple Women to Trade Union Propaganda". *Survey* 36 (July 1, 1916):364-66.

Aitken, Hugh. *Taylorism at Watertown Arsenal.* Cambridge, MA: Harvard University Press, 1960.

Anderson, Mary, with Mary N. Winslow. *Woman at Work.* Minneapolis: University of Minnesota Press, 1951.

Andrews, Irene Osgood. *Minimum Wage Legislation.* Reprinted from New York State Factory Investigating Commission, 3rd. Report, appendix iii (Albany, NY: J.B. Lyon Co., 1914).

Andrews, John B., and W.D.P. Bliss. *History of Women in Trade Unions.* S. Doc. 645, 61st Cong., 2nd sess., vol. x.

Anthony, Katherine S. *Mothers Who Must Earn.* New York: Survey Associates, Russell Sage Foundation, Mid West Side Study, 1914.

Baer, Judith A. *The Chains of Protection, the Judicial Response to Women's Labor Legislation.* Westport, CT: Greenwood Press, 1978.

Baker, Elizabeth Faulkner. *Protective Labor Legislation, With Special Reference to*

Women in the State of New York. New York: Columbia University Press, 1925.

_____. "We Need More Knowledge." *Survey* 55 (February 15, 1926): 531-32.

Balbus, Isaac D. "Commodity Form and Legal Form: An Essay on the 'Relative Autonomy' of the Law." 11 *Law and Society Review*:571. (1977).

Barker, Diana Leonard, and Sheila Allen. *Dependence and Exploitation in Work and Marriage*. New York: Longman, Inc., 1976.

Benston, Margaret. "The Political Economy of Women's Liberation." *Monthly Review* 21 (September 1969):13-27.

Bernheimer, Charles. *The Shirt Waist Strike*. New York: Union Settlement, 1910.

Best, Harry. "Extent of Organization in the Women's Garment Making Industries of N.Y." *American Economic Review* 9 (December 1919): 776-92.

Beyer, Clara Mortenson. "What is Equality?" *The Nation* 116 (January 31, 1923): 116.

Bickel, Alexander M. *The Supreme Court and the Idea of Progress*. New York: Harper & Row, 1970.

Bikle, Henry Wolf. "Judicial Determination of Questions of Fact Affecting the Constitutionality of Legislative Action." 38 *Harvard Law Review*: 6 (1924).

Bird, Francis W. "The Evolution of Due Process of Law in the Decisions of the U.S. Supreme Court." 13 *Columbia Law Review*: 37 (1913).

Blatch, Harriot Stanton. "Do Women Want Protection: Wrapping Women in Cotton-Wool." *Nation* 116 (January 31, 1923):115-16.

Blatch, Harriot Stanton, and Alma Lutz. *Challenging Years: The Memoirs of Harriot Stanton Blatch*. New York: G.P. Putnam's Sons, 1940.

Boles, Janet K. *The Politics of the Equal Rights Amendment*. New York: Longman, Inc., 1979.

Bonacich, Edna. "Advanced Capitalism and Black/White Relations in the United States: a Split Labor Market Interpretation." *American Sociological Review* 41 (February 1976):34-51.

Bonnett, Clarence E. *Employers' Associations in the U.S.* New York: Macmillan, 1922.

Boone, Gladys. *The Women's Trade Union Leagues*. New York: Columbia University Press, 1942.

Bosworth, Louise M. *The Living Wage of Women Workers*. Philadelphia: The American Academy of Political and Social Science, 1911.

Brandeis, Louis. "The Constitution and the Minimum Wage." *Survey* 33 (February 6, 1915):490-94.

_____. The Living Law." 10 *Illinois Law Review*:461 (1916).

Brandeis, Louis, and Josephine Goldmark. *The Case Against Night Work for Women (Brief for People v. Schweinler Press)*. New York: National Consumers' League, 1918.

Braverman, Harry. *Labor and Monopoly Capital*. New York: Monthly Review Press, 1974.

Breckinridge, Sophonisba. "Legislative Control of Women's Work." *Journal of Political Economy* 14 (February 1906):107-09.

Bridenthal, Renate. "Dialectics of Production and Reproduction in History." *Radical America* (April 1976):3-11.

Brissenden, Paul F. *Earnings of Factory Workers 1899 to 1927*, Census Monographs X. Washington, DC: Government Printing Office, 1929.

Brown, Barbara, et al. *Women's Rights and the Law*. New York: Praeger, 1977.

Brown, Ray A. "Due Process of Law, Police Power and the Supreme Court." 40 *Harvard Law Review*: 943 (1927).

Brown, Rome G. "Oregon Minimum Wage Cases." 1 *Minnesota Law Review*: 471 (1917).

Bruce, Andrew Alexander. "The Illinois Ten-Hours Law for Women." 8 *Michigan Law Review*: 1 (1909).

————. "Statutory Regulation of the Employments of Women." 58 *Central Law Journal*:123 (1904).

Butler, Elizabeth Beardsley. *Women and the Trades, Pittsburgh 1907-1908*. New York: Charities Publication Committee, 1911.

Cahn, Edmond, ed. *Supreme Court and Supreme Law*. New York: Simon & Schuster, 1954.

Cain, Maureen. "The Main Themes of Marx's and Engels' Sociology of Law." *British Journal of Law and Society* 1 (1974):136-48.

Cairns, Huntington. *Law and the Social Sciences*. New York: Harcourt, Brace & Co., 1935.

Cantor, Milton, and Bruce Laurie. *Class, Sex and the Woman Worker*. Westport, CT: Greenwood Press, 1977.

Carroll, Mollie Ray. *Labor and Politics*. Boston: Houghton Mifflin, 1924.

Cary, John W. "Limitations of the Legislative Power in Respect to Personal Rights and Private Property." 15 *American Bar Association Reports*: 245 (1892).

Catt, Carrie Chapman, and Nettie Rogers Shuler. *Woman Suffrage and Politics*. New York: Scribner's Sons, 1923.

Chapin, Robert Coit. *The Standard of Living Among Workingmen's Families in New York City*. New York: Charities Publication Committee, Russell Sage Foundation, 1909.

Chavkin, Wendy, ed. *Double Exposure. Women's Health Hazards on the Job and at Home*. New York: Monthly Review Press, 1984.

Clark, John Bates. "The Minimum Wage." *Atlantic Monthly* 112 (September 1913):289-97.

Clark, Sue Ainslie, and Edith Wyatt. *Making Both Ends Meet: The Income and Outlay of New York Working Girls*. New York: Macmillan, 1911.

————. "Working Girls' Budgets—The Shirtwaist Makers and Their Strike." *McClure's Magazine* 36 (November 1910):70-86.

Clark, Victor S. *History of Manufactures in the United States*. 3 vols. Washington, DC: Carnegie Institution of Washington, 1929, v. 3.

Clarke, Allen. *The Effects of the Factory System in England*. London: G. Richards, 1899.

Cohen, Harry. "Minimum Wage Legislation and the Adkins Case." 2 *New York University Law Review*: 48 (1925).

Cohn, Fannia. "Meeting the Machine's Challenge." *Labor Age* 5 (1928):485.

Collective Agreement Between the Dress and Waist Manufacturers' Association and the ILGWU, Locals 10, 25, 58. April 7, 1919.

Commons, John R. *History of Labor in the United States,* 4 vols. New York: Macmillan, 1935, vol. 3.

————. "Labor Legislation." *Survey* 22 (April 17, 1909):133-35.

————. *Legal Foundations of Capitalism.* Madison, WI: University of Wisconsin Press, 1924.

Commons, John R., and John B. Andrews. *Principles of Labor Legislation.* New York, London: Harper & Bros., 1916.

Coombs, Whitney. *The Wages of Unskilled Labor in Manufacturing Industries in the United States, 1890-1924.* New York: Columbia University Press, 1926; reprint ed. New York: AMS ed., Columbia University Studies in the Social Sciences #283, 1968.

Corwin, Edward S. *Constitutional Revolution, Ltd.* Claremont, CA: Claremont College, 1941.

————. "The Supreme Court and the 14th Amendment." 7 *Michigan Law Review*: 643 (1908).

————. *The Twilight of the Supreme Court.* New Haven, CT: Yale University Press, 1934.

Crawford, Kenneth G. *The Pressure Boys.* New York: Julian Messner, Inc., 1939.

Davis, Allen F. "The Women's Trade Union League: Origins and Organization." *Labor History* 5 (1964):3-17.

Davis, Mike. "The Stop Watch and the Wooden Shoe: Scientific Management and the IWW." *Radical America* 8 (January-February 1975):69-95.

deBeauvoir, Simone. *The Second Sex.* New York: Bantam, 1953.

de Luna, Agnes. "How Night Work of Women is Menacing Maternity." *American Labor Legislation Review* 11 (March 1921):85-86.

District of Columbia. *District of Columbia Minimum Wage Cases.* New York: Steinberg Press, 1922.

Dorr, Rheta Childe. "Bully the Woman Worker." *Harper's Weekly* 51 (March 30, 1907):458-59.

Douglas, Paul H. *Real Wages in the United States 1890-1926.* Boston: Houghton Mifflin, 1930.

————. *Wages and the Family.* Chicago: University of Chicago Press, 1927.

Dreier, Mary E. *Margaret Dreier Robins, Her Life, Letters and Work.* New York: Island Press Cooperative, 1950.

Drew, Walter. "The Labor Trust's Crusade Against the Courts." *Square Deal* 2 (October 1906).

Dubofsky, Melvyn. *Industrialism and the American Worker, 1865-1920.* Arlington Heights, IL: Crowell Co., 1975.

————. *When Workers Organize. New York City in the Progressive Era.* Amherst, MA: University of Massachusetts Press, 1968.

Dye, Nancy Schrom. *As Equals and as Sisters. Feminism, the Labor Movement and the Women's Trade Union League of New York.* Columbia and London:

University of Missouri Press, 1980.

————. "Creating a Feminist Alliance: Sisterhood and Class Conflict in the New York Women's Trade Union League." *Feminist Studies* 2 (1975):24-38.

————. "Feminism or Unionism? The New York Women's Trade Union League and the Labor Movement." *Feminist Studies* 3 (Fall 1975): 112-25.

Edgeworth, F.Y. "Equal Pay to Men and Women for Equal Work." *Economic Journal* 32 (December 1922):431-57.

Edwards, Percy L. "Constitutional Interpretation and Limitation as Applied to Laws Limiting the Hours of Labor." 74 *Central Law Journal*: 228 (1912).

Edwards, Richard. *Contested Terrain. The Transformation of the Workplace in the Twentieth Century.* New York: Basic Books, 1979.

Edwards, Richard, Michael Reich, and David Gordon. *Labor Market Segmentation.* Lexington, MA: Heath, 1975.

Edwards, Richard, Michael Reich, and Thomas Weisskopf, eds. "The Economics of Racism." In *The Capitalist System.* Englewood Cliffs, NJ: Prentice-Hall, Inc., 1972.

Eisenstein, Sarah. *Give Us Bread But Give Us Roses: Working Women's Consciousness in the United States, 1890 to the First World War.* London, Boston: Routledge & Kegan Paul, 1983.

Eisenstein, Zillah R., ed. *Capitalist Patriarchy and the Case for Socialist Feminism.* New York: Monthly Review Press, 1979.

Ely, Richard. "Economic Theory and Labor Legislation." *Proceedings*, vol. 1. Madison, WI: American Association for Labor Legislation, 1907, 10-39.

Emery, James A. "Use and Abuse of Injunctions in Trade Disputes." *Annals of the American Academy of Political and Social Science* 36 (1910): 137-141.

Engels, Frederick. *The Condition of the Working Class in England.* Oxford: Blackwell, 1938.

————. *Origin of the Family, Private Property and the State.* New York: New World Paperbacks, 1972.

Esbeck, Carl H. "Employment Practices and Sex Discrimination: Judicial Extension of Beneficial Female Protective Labor Laws." 59 *Cornell Law Review*: 133 (1973).

Fairchild, Henry Pratt. "The Standard of Living—Up or Down?" *American Economic Review* 6 (March 1916):9-25.

Faulkner, Harold U. *The Decline of Laissez Faire 1897-1917.* New York: Holt, Rinehart, & Winston, 1962.

Favill, Henry B., M.D. "The Toxin of Fatigue." *Survey* 24 (September 3, 1910): 767-73.

Fawcett, Millicent. "Equal Pay for Equal Work." *Economic Journal* 28 (March 1918):1-6.

Feldberg, Roslyn. "Comparable Worth: Toward Theory and Practice in the United States." *Signs* 10, no. 21 (1984):311-28.

Filene, Edward A. "The Minimum Wage and Efficiency." *American Economic Review* 13 (September 1923):411-15.

Firestone, Shulamith. *Dialectic of Sex.* New York: Bantam, 1971.

Fitch, John A. "The Rockefeller Interests in Industry and Philanthropy." *Survey* 33 (February 6, 1915):477-80.

Flax, Jane. "Do Feminists Need Marxism?" *Quest* 3 (Summer 1976):46-58.

Flexner, Eleanor. *Century of Struggle*. New York: Atheneum, 1973.

Foner, Philip S. *The Policies and Practices of the American Federation of Labor 1900-1909*. New York: International Publishers, 1964.

Frankel, Lee H. "The Relation Between Standards of Living and Standards of Compensation." *Charities and the Commons* 17 (November 17, 1906): 304-14.

Frankfurter, Felix. *The Case for the Shorter Working Day*. New York: National Consumers' League, 1916.

————. "Hours of Labor and Realism in Constitutional Law." 29 *Harvard Law Review*: 353 (1916).

Freund, Ernst. "Can the States Cooperate for Labor Legislation?" *Survey* 22 (June 12, 1909):409-11.

————. "Constitutional Limitations and Labor Legislation." 4 *Illinois Law Review*: 609 (1910).

————. "Limitations of Hours of Labor and the Federal Supreme Court." 17 *Green Bag*:411 (1905).

————. *Police Power*. Chicago: Callaghan & Co., 1904.

Freund, Paul A. *On Law and Justice*. Cambridge, MA: Harvard University Press, 1968.

Gabel, Peter. "Intention and Structure in Contractual Conditions: Outline of a Method for Critical Legal Theory." 61 *Minnesota Law Review*: 601 (1976-77).

Garraty, John. *Labor and Capital in the Gilded Age*. Boston: Little, Brown, 1968.

Gilbreth, Frank, and Lillian Gilbreth. *Fatigue Study, The Elimination of Humanity's Greatest Unnecessary Waste. A First Step in Motion Study*. New York: Macmillan, 1919.

Ginger, Ray. *Age of Excess: The United States from 1877-1914*. New York: Macmillan, 1965.

Goldmark, Josephine. *Fatigue and Efficiency*. New York: Charities Publication Committee, 1912.

————. *Impatient Crusader*. Urbana, IL: University of Illinois Press, 1953.

————. "Some Considerations Affecting the Replacement of Men by Women Workers." U.S. Bureau of Labor Statistics, *Monthly Review* 6 (January 1918):56-64.

Gompers, Samuel. *Seventy Years of Life and Labor*. New York: Dutton, 1943.

Goodnow, Frank J. *Social Reform and the Constitution*. New York: Macmillan, 1911.

Goodyear, Caroline. "The Minimum Practicable Cost of an Adequate Standard of Living in New York City." *Charities and the Commons* 17 (November 17, 1906):315-20.

Gordon, David. "Capitalist Efficiency and Socialist Efficiency." *Monthly Review* 28 (July-August 1976): 19-39.

_____. *Theories of Poverty and Underemployment*. Lexington, MA: Heath & Co., 1971.

Gornick, Vivian, and Barbara Moran. *Woman in Sexist Society*. New York: Basic Books, 1971.

Greeley, Louise N. "The Changing Attitude of the Courts Toward Social Legislation." 5 *Illinois Law Review*: 222 (1910).

Green, Marguerite. *The National Civic Federation and the American Labor Movement 1900-1925*. Westport, CT: Greenwood Press, 1956.

Greenwald, Maurine Weiner. *Women, War and Work*. The Impact of World War I on Women Workers in the United States. Westport, CT: Greenwood Press, 1980.

Grimes, Barbara. "Constitutional Law; Police Power; Minimum Wage for Women." In National Consumers' League, *The Supreme Court and Minimum Wage Legislation*. New York: New Republic, 1925.

Groat, George Gorham. *Attitude of American Courts in Labor Cases*. New York: Columbia University Press, 1911; reprint ed. New York: AMS Press, 1969.

_____. "Economic Wage and Legal Wage." In National Consumers' League, *The Supreme Court and Minimum Wage Legislation*. New York: New Republic, 1925.

_____. "The Eight Hour Movement in New York." *Political Science Quarterly* 21 (September 1906):414-33.

_____. "Minimum Wage Symposium." *American Labor Legislation Review* 3 (February 1913):106-115.

Gutman, Herbert. *Work, Culture and Society in Industrializing America*. New York: Vintage, 1977.

Haber, Samuel. *Efficiency and Uplift: Scientific Management in the Progressive Era 1890-1920*. Chicago and London: University of Chicago Press, 1964.

Haines, Charles Grove. *The Revival of Natural Law Concepts*. Cambridge, MA: Harvard University Press, 1929; reprint ed. New York: Russell & Russell, 1965.

Hamilton, Alice. "Protection for Women Workers." *Forum* 72 (August 1924): 152-60.

Hand, Judge Learned. "Due Process of Law and the Eight-hour Day." 21 *Harvard Law Review*: 11 (1908).

Harper, Samuel A. *Illinois Ten Hour Law: Brief by Counsel for Appellant, Ritchie v. Wayman*. Illinois, December 1909.

Hatch, Maureen. "Mother, Father, Worker: Men and Women and the Reproductive Risks of Work." In *Double Exposure. Women's Health Hazards on the Job and at Home*. Ed. Wendy Chavkin. New York: Monthly Review Press, 1984, 161-179.

Hayghe, Howard. "Research Summaries." *Monthly Labor Review* (December 1984) 107:31-34.

Hays, Samuel P. *The Response to Industrialism, 1885-1914*. Chicago: University of Chicago Press, 1957.

Henry, Alice. *Women and the Labor Movement*. New York: George Doran Co., 1923.

Hobsbawm, Eric. *Labouring Men.* New York: Doubleday Anchor, 1967.

Holcombe, A. N. "The Effects of the Legal Minimum Wage for Women." *Annals of the American Academy of Political and Social Science* 69 (1917):34-41.

_____. "The Legal Minimum Wage in the U.S." *American Economic Review* 2 (1912):21-37.

Holloway, John, and Sol Picciotto, eds. *State and Capital: A Marxist Debate.* Austin, TX: University of Austin Press, 1978.

Holmes, Oliver Wendell. "Natural Law." 32 *Harvard Law Review*: 40 (1918).

Hough, Charles M. "Due Process of Law—Today." 32 *Harvard Law Review*: 218 (1918).

Hoxie, Robert. *Scientific Management and Labor.* New York: A.M. Kelley, 1918; reprint ed. 1966.

_____. "The Trade-Union Point of View." *Journal of Political Economy* 15 (June 1907):345-63.

Hughes, Gwendolyn Salisbury. *Mothers in Industry.* New York: New Republic, 1925.

Humphries, Jane. "The Working Class Family, Women's Liberation, and Class Struggle: The Case of 19th Century British History." *Review of Radical Political Economics* 9 (Fall 1977):25-41.

Hurst, James Willard. *Law and the Conditions of Freedom in the Nineteenth Century United States.* Madison, WI: University of Wisconsin Press, 1956.

Hutchinson, Wood. "The Hygienic Aspects of the Shirtwaist Strike." *Survey* 23 (January 22, 1910):541-50.

Irwin, Inez Haynes. *The Story of the Woman's Party.* New York: Harcourt, Brace & Co., 1921.

Jacoby, Robin Miller. "The Women's Trade Union League and American Feminism." *Feminist Studies* 3 (Fall 1975):126-40.

Johnsen, Julia, ed. *Special Legislation for Women.* New York: H.W. Wilson Co., 1926.

Joint Board of Cloak, Skirt, Dress & Reefer Makers' Unions. *The Left Wing in the Garment Unions.* May 1927.

Judson, Frederick. "Liberty of Contract Under the Police Power." 14 *American Bar Association Reports*:231 (1891).

Kairys, David. "Book Review of Tigar and Levy, 'Law and the Rise of Capitalism.'" 126 *University of Pennsylvania Law Review*: 930 (1978).

Kales, Albert M. "'Due Process,'; the Inarticulate Major Premise and the Adamson Act." 26 *Yale Law Journal*:519 (1917).

Kanowitz, Leo. *Sex Roles in Law and Society.* Albuquerque, NM: University of New Mexico Press, 1973.

Karson, Marc. *American Labor Unions and Politics, 1900-1918.* Carbondale, IL: Southern Illinois University Press, 1958.

Kelley, Florence. "Factory Inspection." In *Woman and the Larger Citizenship*, vol. ii. Chicago: The Civics Society, 1913-14.

_____. "Minimum Wage Laws." *Journal of Political Economy* 20 (December 1912):999-1010.

_____. *Modern Industry in Relation to the Family, Health, Education, Morality.* New York: Longmans, Green & Co., 1914.

_____. "Should Women be Treated Identically with Men by the Law?" *American Review* 3 (May-June 1923):276-84.

_____. "Status of Legislation in the U.S." *Survey* 33 (February 6, 1915):487-89.

Kellogg, Paul. "Minimum Wage Symposium." *American Labor Legislation Review* 3, #1, (February 1913):100-105.

Kessler-Harris, Alice. "Organizing the Unorganizable: Three Jewish Women and their Union." In *Class, Sex and the Woman Worker.* Ed. Milton Cantor and Bruce Laurie. Westport, CT: Greenwood Press, 1977, 144-165.

_____. *Out to Work.* Oxford: Oxford University Press, 1982.

_____. "Where Are the Organized Women Workers?" *Feminist Studies* 3 (Fall 1975):92-110.

King, Willford I. *Wealth and Income of the People of the United States.* New York: Macmillan, 1915.

Kingsbury, Susan M. "Relation of Women to Industry." *American Sociological Society Proceedings* 15 (1920):141-58.

Kirchwey, Freda. "Alice Paul Pulls the Strings." *The Nation* 112 (March 2, 1921): 332-33.

Klare, Karl E. "Judicial Deradicalization of the Wagner Act and the Origins of Modern Legal Consciousness 1937-41." 62 *Minnesota Law Review*: 265 (1978).

Kuhn, Annette, and Anne Marie Wolpe, eds. *Feminism and Materialism.* London: Routledge & Kegan Paul, 1978.

Laslett, John H.M. *Labor and the Left, A Study of Socialist and Radical Influences in the American Labor Movement, 1881-1924.* New York: Basic Books, 1970.

Lerner, Max. "The Supreme Court and American Capitalism." 42 *Yale Law Journal*:668 (1933).

Levine, Louis. *The Women's Garment Workers.* New York: B.W. Huebsch, Inc., 1924.

Lorwin, Lewis L. *The American Federation of Labor, History, Policies, and Prospects.* New Jersey: A.M. Kelley Publishers, 1933; reprint ed. 1972.

Lynch, James M. *Epochal History of the International Typographical Union.* New York, 1925.

McKelvey, Jean Trepp. *AFL Attitudes Toward Production 1900-1932.* Westport, CT: Greenwood Press, 1974.

MacKenzie, Frederick. "The Legislative Campaign in New York for the 'Welfare Bills.'" *American Labor Legislation Review* 10 (June 1920): 136-49.

MacLean, Annie Marion. *Wage-Earning Women.* New York: Macmillan, 1910; reprint ed. New York: Arno Press, 1974.

Mailly, William. "The Working Girls' Strike." *Independent* 67 (December 23, 1909):1416-20.

Marcosson, Isaac. "Labor Met by Its Own Methods." *World's Work* 7 (January 1904):4309-14.

Marglin, Stephen A. "What Do Bosses Do?" *Review of Radical Political Economics* 6 (Summer 1974):60-122.

Marot, Helen. *American Labor Unions*. New York: H. Holt & Co., 1914.

_____. "The Minimum Wage Board and the Union 'by a Trade Unionist.'" *The Unpopular Review* 4 (October 1915):397-411.

Marx, Karl. *Capital*. 3 vols. Chicago: Kerr & Co., 1915, vol. 1.

_____. *Selected Works*. New York: International Publishers, 1968.

Marx, Karl, and Frederick Engels. *The German Ideology*. Moscow, USSR: Progress Publishers, 1968.

Mason, Alpheus T. "The Case of the Overworked Laundress." In *Quarrels That Have Shaped the Constitution*. Ed. John Garraty. New York: Harper & Row, 1962.

Mason, Stephen C. "How American Manufacturers View Employment Relations." *Annals of the American Academy of Political and Social Sciences* 82 (1919):124-34.

Massachusetts (State of). *Report of Commission on Minimum Wage Boards*. Boston, MA: January, 1912.

May, Martha. "The 'Good Managers': Married Working Class Women and Family Budget Studies, 1895-1915." *Labor History* 25, no. 3 (Summer 1984): 350-72.

Mead, Margaret. *Sex and Temperament in Three Primitive Societies*. New York: Bantam, 1953.

Merritt, Walter Gordon. *Factory Solidarity or Class Solidarity?* Reprint from *Iron Age*, circa 1919.

_____. *History of the League for Industrial Rights*. New York: League for Industrial Rights, 1925.

_____. *The Open Shop and Industrial Liberty*. New York: League for Industrial Rights, 1922.

Miliband, Ralph. *The State in Capitalist Society*. New York: Basic Books, 1969.

Milkman, Ruth, ed. *Women, Work and Protest*. Boston: Routledge & Kegan Paul, 1985.

Miller, Arthur Selwyn. *The Supreme Court and American Capitalism*. New York: Free Press, 1968.

Minimum Wage for Women. Appendix to Brief Filed on Behalf of Respondents in Supreme Court of Oregon, Stettler vs. O'Hara. October, 1913.

"The Minimum Wage Problem." *The Independent* 72 (March 14, 1912):584-85.

Mitchell, Juliet. *Woman's Estate*. New York: Vintage, 1973.

Moore, Blaine Free. *The Supreme Court and Unconstitutional Legislation*. New York: Columbia University Press, 1913.

More, Louise Bolard. *Wage-Earners' Budgets, A Study of Standards and Cost of Living in New York City*. New York: Holt & Co., 1907; reprint ed. New York: Arno Press, 1971.

Murphy, Joseph P. *At What Age Should Children Enter Industry?* New York: Associated Industries of New York State, 1919.

Mussey, Henry Raymond. "Law and a Living for Women." *Survey* 61 (November 1, 1928):156-58.

Myrick, O.H. "Liberty of Contract." 61 *Central Law Journal*:483 (1905).

Nadworny, Milton. *Scientific Management and the Unions, 1900-1932.* Cambridge, MA: Harvard University Press, 1955.

Nathan, Maud. "Women Who Work and Women Who Spend." *Annals of the American Academy of Political and Social Science* 27 (1906):646-50.

National Association of Manufacturers. *National Trade Associations.* Washington, D.C.: National Association of Manufacturers, 1922.

National Consumers' League. *State Minimum Wage Laws in Practice.* New York: National Consumers' League, 1924.

_____. *The Supreme Court and Minimum Wage Legislation.* New York: New Republic, 1925.

National Industrial Conference Board. *Employment of Young Persons in the U.S.* New York: National Industrial Conference Board, 1925.

_____. *A Federation of American Industries for the Study of Industrial Problems, Improvement of Industrial Relations, Promotion of Industrial Prosperity.* New York: National Industrial Conference Board, 1919.

_____. *The Five Day Week in Manufacturing Industries.* New York: National Industrial Conference Board, 1929.

_____. *Hours of Work as Related to Output and Health of Workers—Boot and Shoe Industry.* Research Report #7. New York: National Industrial Conference Board, 1918.

_____. *Hours of Work as Related to Output and Health of Workers—Cotton Manufacturing.* Research Report #4. New York: National Industrial Conference Board, 1918.

_____. *Hours of Work as Related to Output and Health of Workers—Wool Manufacturing.* Research Report #12. New York: National Industrial Conference Board, 1918.

_____. *Legal Restrictions on Hours of Work In the U.S.* Research Report #68. New York: National Industrial Conference Board, 1924.

_____. *Rest Periods for Industrial Workers.* Research Report #13. New York: National Industrial Conference Board, 1919.

_____. *Unwarranted Conclusions Regarding the Eight-hour and Ten-hour Workday.* Special Report #14. New York: National Industrial Conference Board, 1920.

_____. *Wartime Employment of Women in the Metal Trades.* Research Report #8. New York: National Industrial Conference Board, 1918.

Nearing, Scott. "The Adequacy of American Wages." *Annals of the American Academy of Political and Social Science* 59 (1915):111-24.

Nesbitt, James L. "Due Process of Law and Opinion." 26 *Columbia Law Review*: 22 (1926).

New York State Department of Labor Bulletin #30, vol. 8. Albany, NY: J.B. Lyon Co., 1906.

New York State Department of Labor Bulletin #31. Albany, NY: J.B. Lyon Co., 1906.

New York State Factory Investigating Commission. *Reports.* Albany, NY: Argus Co. Printers, 1912-15.

New York State League of Women Voters. "Report and Protest to the Governor
. . ." *American Labor Legislation Review* 10 (March 1920): 81-104.

Oakley, Ann. *Woman's Work: The Housewife, Past and Present.* New York: Vintage, 1976.

Odencrantz, Louise C. *Italian Women in Industry.* New York: Russell Sage Foundation, 1919.

O'Hagan, Anne. "'Protecting' Women Out of Their Jobs." *Touchstone* 5 (August 1919):400-405, 424.

O'Laughlin, John C. "'The Invisible Government' Under Searchlight." *Review of Reviews* 48 (1913):334-38.

Orshansky, Mollie. "Counting the Poor: Another Look at the Poverty Profile." *Social Security Bulletin* 28 (January 1965):3-29.

"Overwork." *Survey* 23 (1909-1910):442-46.

Palmer, Bryan. "Class, Conception and Conflict: the Thrust for Efficiency, Managerial Views of Labor and the Working Class Rebellion, 1903-1922." *Review of Radical Political Economics* 7 (Summer 1975): 31-49.

Parry, David M. "Is Organized Labor Right? The Only Question." *Bankers' Magazine* 67 (November 1903):668-72.

Paterson, Robert Gildersleeve. *Wage Payment Legislation in the United States.* Bulletin of the U.S. Bureau of Labor Statistics, whole no. 229. Washington, D.C.: Government Printing Office, 1917.

Peck, Mary Gray. *Carrie Chapman Catt.* New York: H.W. Wilson Co., 1944.

"Perils of the Minimum Wage." *Century Magazine* 84 (1912):311-13.

Perkins, Frances. "Do Women in Industry Need Special Protection? Yes." *Survey* 55 (February 15, 1926):529-31.

Perlman, Selig. *A Theory of the Labor Movement.* New York: A.M. Kelley, 1928; reprint ed. 1949.

Perlman, Selig, and Philip Taft. *History of Labor in the United States;* vol. 4: *Labor Movements.* John Commons, gen. ed. New York: 1935; reprint ed. 1966.

Phelps, Linda. "Patriarchy and Capitalism." *Quest* 2 (Fall 1975):34-48.

Pike, Violet. *New World Lessons for Old World Peoples.* New York: Women's Trade Union League for Education Committee, 1912.

Polanyi, Karl. *The Great Transformation.* Boston: Beacon Press, 1957.

Pollard, Sidney. "Factory Discipline in the Industrial Revolution." *Economic History Review* 16 (1963):254-71.

Pollock, Sir Frederick. "New York Labour Law and the 14th Amendment." 21 *Law Quarterly Review*:211.

Pope, Jesse Eliphalet. *The Clothing Industry in New York.* Columbia, MO: University of Missouri Press, 1905.

Poulantzas, Nicos. "The Capitalist State: A Reply to Miliband and Laclau." *New Left Review* 95 (January-February 1976):63-83.

_____. *State, Power, Socialism.* London: New Left Books, 1978.

Pound, Roscoe. "Enforcement of Law." 20 *Green Bag*:401 (1908).

_____. "Liberty of Contract." 18 *Yale Law Journal*:454 (1908-09).

_____. "The Need of a Sociological Jurisprudence." 19 *Green Bag*:607 (1907).

Powell, Thomas Reed. "The Constitutional Issue in Minimum Wage Legislation." 2 *Minnesota Law Review*: 1 (1917).

Quick, Paddy. "The Class Nature of Women's Oppression." *Review of Radical Political Economics* 9 (Fall 1977):42-53.

Rawls, John. *A Theory of Justice*. Cambridge, MA: Harvard University Press, 1971.

Reed, Evelyn. *Problems of Women's Liberation*. New York: Pathfinder Press, 1970.

Reeder, Robert P. "Constitutionalism and Extra-Constitutional Restraints." 61 *University of Pennsylvania Law Review*: 441 (1912-13).

Reiter, Rayna. *Toward an Anthropology of Women*. New York: Monthly Review Press, 1975.

Report on Condition of Woman and Child Wage Earners in the United States. 19 vols. Washington, D.C.: U.S. Government Printing Office, 1911.

Richardson, Dorothy. "The Difficulties and Dangers Confronting the Working Woman." *Annals of American Academy of Political and Social Science* 27 (1906):624-26.

Robins, Margaret Dreier. "Review of *The Long Day*." *Charities and the Commons* 17 (October 1906-April 1907):484-85.

_____. "Trade Unionism for Women." In *Woman and the Larger Citizenship*, vol. 11. Chicago: The Civics Society, 1913-14.

Rosaldo, Michelle Zimbalist, and Louise Lamphere. *Woman, Culture and Society*. Stanford, CA: Stanford University Press, 1974.

Rosen, Paul L. *The Supreme Court and Social Science*. Urbana, IL: University of Illinois Press, 1972.

Rowbotham, Sheila. *Woman's Consciousness, Man's World*. Harmondsworth, England: Penguin, 1973.

Rubinow, I.M. "The Recent Trend of Real Wages." *American Economic Review* 4 (December 1914):793-817.

Russell, Phillips. "Wage Minimummery." *International Socialist Review* 13 (August 1912):155-56.

Ryan, John A. "The Task of Minimum Wage Boards in Minnesota." *Survey* 33 (November 14, 1914):171-72.

Ryan, Mary P. *Womanhood in America*. 3rd ed. New York: Franklin Watts 1983.

Sachs, Albie, and Joan Hoff Wilson. *Sexism and the Law*. Oxford, England: Martin Robertson & Co., 1978.

Saposs, David J. *Left Wing Unionism. A Study of Radical Policies and Tactics*. New York: International Publishers, 1926.

Schneiderman, Rose, with Lucy Goldthwaithe. *All for One*. New York: Erikson, 1967.

Schur, Edwin M. *Law and Society, a Sociological View*. New York: Random House, 1968.

Scott, Judith. "Keeping Women in Their Place: Exclusionary Policies and Reproduction." In *Double Exposure*. Ed. Wendy Chavkin. New York: Monthly Review Press, 1984, 180-95.

Seager, Henry R. "The Attitude of American Courts Towards Restrictive Labor Laws." *Political Science Quarterly* 19 (December 1904):589-611.

————. *Labor and Other Economic Essays*. Edited by Charles Gulick, Jr., and introduced by Wesley Mitchell. New York: Harper & Row, 1931; reprint ed. Freeport, NY: Essay Reprint Series, Books for Libraries Press, 1968.

Seager, Henry R., et al. "The Theory of the Minimum Wage." *American Labor Legislation Review* 3 (February 1913):81-91.

Seidman, Joel. *The Needle Trades*. New York, Toronto: Farrar & Rinehart, Inc., 1942.

Shattuck, Charles E. "The True Meaning of the Term 'Liberty' in Those Clauses in the Federal and State Constitutions which Protect 'Life, Liberty, and Property'." 4 *Harvard Law Review*:365 (1891).

Skocpol, Theda. "Political Response to Capitalist Crisis: Neo-Marxist Theories of the State and the Case of the New Deal." *Politics and Society* 10, no. 2 (1980): 155-201.

Smith, Joan. "The Paradox of Women's Poverty: Wage-Earning Women and Economic Transformation", *Signs: Journal of Women in Culture and Society* 10, Winter 1984: 291-310.

"The Spirit of Women Wage-Earners." *Survey* 34 (June 19, 1915):262-63.

Steigerwalt, Albert K. *The National Association of Manufacturers, 1895-1914*. Ann Arbor, MI: University of Michigan Press, 1964.

Stein, Leon, ed. *Out of the Sweatshop*. New York: Quadrangle Books, 1977.

Stevens, Doris. *Jailed for Freedom*. New York: Boni & Liveright, Inc., 1920.

————. "Suffrage Does Not Give Equality. *Forum* 72 (August 1924): 145-52.

Stevens, George A. *New York Typographical Union #6*. Under direction of John Williams, Commissioner of Labor, State of New York. Albany, NY: J.B. Lyon Co., State Printers, 1913.

Stokes, Rose H. Phelps. "The Condition of Working Women, from the Working Woman's Viewpoint." *Annals of the American Academy of Political and Social Science* 27 (1906):627-37.

Stone, Julius. *Human Law and Human Justice*. Stanford, CA: Stanford University Press, 1965.

Streightoff, Frank Hatch. *The Distribution of Incomes in the United States*. New York: Columbia University Press, 1912.

————. *The Standard of Living Among the Industrial People of America*. Boston and New York: Houghton Mifflin Co., 1911.

Sumner, Helen. *Equal Suffrage*. New York: Harper & Bros., 1909.

Sweezy, Paul M. *The Theory of Capitalist Development*. New York: Monthly Review Press, 1968.

Taft, Philip. *The A.F. of L. in the Time of Gompers*. New York: Harper & Row, 1957; reprint ed. Octagon Books, 1970.

————. *Labor Politics American Style: The California State Federation of Labor*. Cambridge, MA: Harvard University Press, 1968.

Tarrow, Sidney G. "Lochner v. N.Y.: A Political Analysis." *Labor History* 5 (Fall 1964):277-312.

Tax, Meredith. *The Rising of the Women.* New York: Monthly Review Press, 1980.

Taylor, Albion Guilford. *Labor Policies of the National Association of Manufacturers.* Urbana, IL: University of Illinois Press, 1928.

Taylor, Frederick. *Principles of Scientific Management.* New York: W.W. Norton & Co., 1967.

Taylor, Graham. "Industrial Survey of the Month." *Survey* 23 (1909-10): 205.

Technology, the Labor Process and the Working Class. New York: Monthly Review Press, July-August 1976.

Tigar, Michael, and Madeleine Levy. *Law and the Rise of Capitalism.* New York: Monthly Review Press, 1977.

Trubeck, David M. "Complexity and Contradiction in the Legal Order: Balbus and the Challenge of Critical Thought About Law." 11 *Law and Society Review*:529 (1977).

_____. "Max Weber on Law and the Rise of Capitalism." 3 *Wisconsin Law Review*: 720 (1972).

Tucker, Frank. "The Social Significance of the Standard of Living." *Charities and the Commons* 17 (November 17, 1906):299-303.

Tushnet, Mark V. "Perspectives on the Development of American Law: A Critical Review of Friedman's 'A History of American Law.'" 1 *Wisconsin Law Review* 81 (1977).

Twiss, Benjamin R. *Lawyers and the Constitution—How Laissez Faire Came to the Supreme Court.* Princeton, NJ: Princeton University Press, 1942.

U.S. Bureau of the Census. *13th Census (1910), Abstract for New York.* Washington, D.C.: U.S. Government Printing Office, 1913.

U.S. Commission on Civil Rights. *Comparable Worth: Issue for the 80's.* A Consultation of the U.S. Commission on Civil Rights, 2 vols. (June 6-7, 1984).

U.S. Commission on Industrial Relations. *Final Report, Testimony.* S. Doc. 21, 64th Cong., 1915.

U.S. Department of Labor, Women's Bureau. *Bulletins.* nos. 2-47. Washington, D.C.: U.S. Government Printing Office, 1918-25.

U.S. Industrial Commission. *Report.* Vol. 5. Washington, D.C.: U.S. Government Printing Office, 1900.

_____. *Report.* Vol. 15. Washington, D.C.: U.S. Government Printing Office, 1901.

Van Kleeck, Mary. "Changes in Women's Work in Binderies." In *The Economic Position of Women.* New York: The Academy of Political Science, 1910, 27-39.

_____. *Women in the Bookbinding Trade.* New York: Survey Associates, Russell Sage Foundation Publications, 1913.

_____. "Working Hours of Women in Factories." *Charities and the Commons* 17 (October 1906):13-21.

Vogel, Lise. "Questions on the Woman Question." *Monthly Review* 31 (June 1979):39-59.

Waggamon, Mary. "National Women's Trade Union League of America." *Monthly Labor Review* 8 (April 1919):237-45.

Wald, Lillian D. "Organization Amongst Working Women." *Annals of the American Academy of Political and Social Science* 27 (1906):638-45.

Walling, William English. "The New Unionism—The Problem of the Unskilled Worker." *Annals of the American Academy of Political and Social Science* 24 (1904):296-315.

Warren, Charles. "The Progressiveness of the U.S. Supreme Court." 13 *Columbia Law Review*: 294 (1913).

Washington (State of). *Report of the Industrial Welfare Commission of the State of Washington.* Prepared by Caroline J. Gleason. Olympia, WA: Frank M. Lamborn, Public Printer, 1914.

Webb, Beatrice. *The Wages of Men and Women: Should They Be Equal?* London: Fabian Society, 1919.

Webb, Sidney. "The Economic Theory of a Legal Minimum Wage." *Journal of Political Economy* 20 (December 1912):973-998.

Webb, Sidney, and Beatrice Webb. *Industrial Democracy.* New York: A.M. Kelley, 1897; reprint ed. 1965.

Weber, Max. *On Law in Economy and Society.* New York: Simon & Schuster, 1954.

Weinstein, James. *The Corporate Ideal in the Liberal State, 1900-1918.* Boston: Beacon Press, 1968.

Wiebe, Robert H. *Businessmen and Reform: A Study of the Progressive Movement.* Chicago: Quadrangle Books, 1968.

Willett, Mabel Hurd. *The Employment of Women in the Clothing Trade;* vol. 16 of *Studies in History.* Economics and Public Law Series. New York: Columbia University Press, 1902.

Williams, Wendy. "Equality's Riddle: Pregnancy and the Equal Treatment/Special Treatment Debate" 13 *New York University Review of Law and Social Change*:325 (1984-85).

Willoughby, William Franklin. "Employers' Associations for Dealing with Labor in the United States" *Quarterly Journal of Economics* 20 (November 1905): 110-50.

Wolfe, Alan. *The Limits of Legitimacy.* New York: Free Press, 1977.

Wolfson, Theresa. *The Woman Worker and the Trade Unions.* New York: International Publishers, 1926.

Wolman, Leo. "Economic Justification of the Legal Minimum Wage." *American Labor Legislation Review* 14 (1924):226-33.

Woman Suffrage: Arguments and Results. New York: National American Woman Suffrage Association, 1910.

"A Woman's Work for Women Workers." *Literary Digest* 46 (January 18, 1913): 137.

Woodard, Calvin. "Reality and Social Reform: The Transition from Laissez-Faire to the Welfare State." 72 *Yale Law Journal*: 286 (1962).

Woods, Erville B. "Have Wages Kept Pace with the Cost of Living?" *Annals of the American Academy of Political and Social Science* 89 (1920): 135-47.

Woods, Robert, and Albert Kennedy, eds., for National Federation of Settlements.

Young Working Girls. Forward by Jane Addams. Boston, New York: Houghton Mifflin Co., 1913.

Woolworth, James M. "The Development of the Law of Contracts." 19 *American Bar Association Reports*:287 (1896).

Wormuth, Francis D. "The Impact of Economic Legislation Upon the Supreme Court." 6 *Journal of Public Law*: 296 (1957).

Wright, Erik Olin. *Class, Crisis and the State.* London: New Left Books, 1978.

Wright, Philip G. "The Contest in Congress Between Organized Labor and Organized Business." *Quarterly Journal of Economics* 29 (February 1915):235-61.

Yellowitz, Irwin. *Labor and the Progressive Movement in New York State, 1897-1916.* Ithaca, NY: Cornell University Press, 1965.

————. *The Position of the Worker in American Society, 1865-1896.* Englewood Cliffs, NJ: Prentice-Hall, 1969.

Yudelson, Sophie. "Woman's Place in Industry and Labor Organizations." *Annals of the American Academy of Political and Social Science* 24 (1904): 343-53.

Zaretsky, Eli. *Capitalism, the Family and Personal Life.* New York: Harper, 1976.

Ziskind, David. "The Use of Economic Data in Labor Cases." 6 *University of Chicago Law Review*: 607 (1938-39).

JOURNALS, PROCEEDINGS, MANUSCRIPT COLLECTIONS

American Anti-Boycott Association. Miscellaneous pamphlets, including "Supreme Court Gives Death Blow to Boycott." (Vassar collection, Poughkeepsie, NY).

American Federationist. 1900-1925. Journal of the American Federation of Labor.

American Federation of Labor. *Report of Proceedings.* 1905-25.

American Industries. 1904-18. Official journal of the National Association of Manufacturers.

American Labor Legislation Review. 1907-25. Published by American Association for Labor Legislation.

Catt, Carrie Chapman. *Papers.* New York: New York Public Library, Manuscript Division.

Cohn, Fannia. *Papers.* New York: New York Public Library, Manuscript Division.

Equal Rights. 1923-24. Journal of the National Woman's Party.

Headquarters News Letter. 1915-17. Journal of the National-American Woman Suffrage Organization.

Industrial Equality. 1923-24. Journal of the Women's Equal Opportunity League.

The Industrial Outlook. 1914-16. A Business Review published by the national Retail Dry Goods Association.

International Bookbinder. 1903-21. Journal of the International Brotherhood of Bookbinders.

International Ladies Garment Workers' Union. *Archives.* New York: Benjamin Schlesinger papers and correspondence.

————. *Reports and Proceedings.* 1912-25.

International Socialist Review. 1910-11.

International Typographical Union. *Report of Officers and Proceedings.* 1911-16.

Justice. 1919-25. Official organ of the International Ladies Garment Workers' Union.

Ladies Garment Worker. February 1910-19. Official journal of the Ladies Garment Workers' Union (later became *Justice*).

Law and Labor. 1919-23. Published by the League for Industrial Rights.

Life and Labor. 1911-21. Journal of the Women's Trade Union League.

Monitor. June 1914-23. Published by Associated Industries of New York State.

National-American Woman Suffrage Association. *Proceedings.* 1909-19.

National Association of Manufacturers. Educational Literature Series, assorted pamphlets. Vassar College Library, Poughkeepsie, NY.

National Civic Federation. *Papers and Proceedings.* New York: New York Public Library Annex.

National Consumers' League. *Executive Committee Minutes.* Cornell School of Industrial and Labor Relations, Ithaca, New York.

National Council for Industrial Defense. *Bulletins.* 1912-21.

National Suffrage News. 1917. Published by the National-American Woman Suffrage Association.

National Woman's Party. *Alma Lutz Collection,* miscellaneous papers. Vassar College Library, Poughkeepsie, NY.

New York Call. 1909-23. New York: Tamiment Library and New York Public Library annex.

New York Women's Trade Union League. *Papers.* New York: Department of Labor Research and Statistics Division Library, World Trade Center.

The Protectionist. 1915-17. A Monthly Magazine of Political Science, published by the Home Market Club, Boston, MA.

Putnam, Mabel R. *Papers.* New York: New York Public Library, Manuscript Division.

The Review. 1906-10. Journal of the National Founders' Association and National Metal Trades Association.

Schneiderman, Rose. *Collected Papers.* New York: Tamiment Library.

Square Deal. 1906-14. Organ of the Citizen's Industrial Association of America.

The Suffragist. 1913-20. Journal of the National Woman's Party.

Typographical Journal. 1910-23. Journal of the International Typographical Union.

Woman Citizen. 1917-25. Journal of the National-American Women's Suffrage Association.

"Working Women." Miscellaneous pamphlets, including women printers' attacks on eight-hour law. Vassar College Library, Poughkeepsie, NY.

U.S. SUPREME COURT RECORDS AND BRIEFS

Adkins v. Children's Hospital, Oct. term 1922, Docket #795.

Bunting v. Oregon, Oct. term 1916-17, Docket #38, vol. 9.

Muller v. Oregon, Oct. term 1907, Docket #107.

Stettler v. O'Hara, Oct. term 1916-17, Docket #25, #26.

Cases Cited

Adair v. U.S., 208 U.S. 161, 28 Sup. Ct. 277 (1908), *146.*

Adkins v. Children's Hospital; Adkins v. Lyons, 261 U.S. 525 (1923), *71, 242.*

Bunting v. Oregon, 243 U.S. 426, 37 Sup. Ct. 435 (1917), *55, 70.*

Burns Baking Co. v. Bryan, 264 U.S. 504 (1924), *253 (fn).*

Calder v. Bull, 3 Dallas 386 (1798), *251 (fn).*

Chicago, Burlington & Quincy Railway Co. v. McGuire, 219 U.S. 549 (1910); 31 Sup. Ct. 259 (1911), *252 (fn).*

Coppage v. Kansas, 236 U.S. 1 (1914), *255 (fn).*

Frorer v. People, 141 Ill. 171; 31 N.E. 395 (1892), *252 (fn).*

Godcharles v. Wigeman, 113 Pa. St. 431 (1886), *251 (fn).*

Holden v. Hardy, 169 U.S. 366, 18 Sup. Ct. 383 (1898), *55.*

In re Jacobs, 98 N.Y. 98 (1885), *52.*

Lochner v. New York, 198 U.S. 45, 25 Sup. Ct. 539 (1905), *53, 73, 55, 59.*

Millet v. People, 117 Ill. 294; 7 N.E. 631 (1886), *252 (fn).*

Muller v. Oregon, 208 U.S. 412, 28 Sup. Ct. 324 (1908), *20, 32, 34, 55, 58, 145, 146, 177, 197, 205, 241.*

Munn v. Illinois, 94 U.S. 113 (1876), *251 (fn).*

People v. Chas. Schweinler Press, 214 N.Y. 395, 108 N.E. 641 (1915), *38, 66, 242.*

People v. Williams, 189 N.Y. 131, 91 N.E. 778 (1907), *54, 66, 242.*

Radice v. People, 264 U.S. 292 (1923), *242.*

Ritchie v. People, 155 Ill. 98, 40 N.E. 454 (1895), *53, 66, 241.*

Ritchie v. Wayman, 244 Ill. 509, 91 N.E. 695 (1910), *66, 241.*

San Mateo County v. Southern Pacific Railway Co., 116 U.S. 138 (1885), *251 (fn).*

Simpson v. O'Hara, 70 Ore. 261 (1914), *242.*

Slaughterhouse Cases, 16 Wall. 36 (1873), *47.*

State v. Buchanan, 29 Wash. 603, 70 Pac. 52 (1902), *241.*

State v. Goodwill, 33 W. Va. 179, 10 S.E. 285 (1889), *252 (fn).*

Stettler v. O'Hara, 69 Ore. 519, 243 U.S. 629 (1917), *55, 59, 68, 242.*

In Re Tiburcio Parrott, 1 Fed. Rep. 481 (1880), *252 (fn).*

Wenham v. State of Nebraska, 65 Neb. 395, 91 N.W. 421 (1902), *241.*

Index